How to Study History

How to Study History

NORMAN F. CANTOR

New York University

RICHARD I. SCHNEIDER

York University

Harlan Davidson, Inc.
Wheeling, Illinois 60090-6000

Copyright © 1967
Harlan Davidson, Inc.

Library of Congress Cataloging-in-Publication Data

Cantor, Norman F.
        How to study history.

        Includes bibliographies and index.

        1. History—Study and teaching. I. Schneider, Richard I.
II. Title.
D16.2.C32   1986   907   86-47531
ISBN 0-88295-709-0 (pbk.)

Manufactured in the United States of America
01 00 99 98 97 96 21 22 23 CM

Preface

We have set down in this book the basic rules and principles of historical study that a student should bear in mind as he enters upon his first college history course. In our experience as college teachers of history, we have found that students need to be informed on the nature and methods of history as a distinct intellectual discipline, and we have tried to communicate this information in as direct and practical a way as possible. We have not only set before the college student the standards of excellence he should strive to attain in historical study; we have attempted to show him, step by step, how he can reach these goals. We have presented the methods and principles that appear to have the widest consensus among academic historians, and we have sought to avoid extreme and idiosyncratic opinions.

We recommend that all of this book be assigned as reading in the first week of a college history course, particularly the survey course in the history of Western Civilization or Modern Europe. Alternatively, the student can read Chapters 1-6 the first week and Chapters 7-13 a month later. Chapters 1-6 contain the information the student will need immediately upon beginning historical study; the remaining chapters provide a guide to work the student will encounter a little later in the term. The beginning freshman in a survey course can be allowed to omit the second and third parts of Chapter 7; but if he is not required to read these sections, he should turn to them at the end of the term when he is ready for more advanced work in history.

We would like to thank the following people for their generous assistance: Miss Kathleen Bolster for typing the final draft of the manuscript and for some valuable suggestions on matters of pedagogy; Mrs. Barbara Ivan Schneider and Mr. C. William Westfall of Amherst College for advice and help with the iconographical discussion that appears at the end of Chapter 4; and our good friends Rev. Bernard McGinn, Professor Davis Bitton of the University of Utah, Professor David Kunzle of the University of California, Santa Barbara, and Mr. Michael S. Werthman, for critical reading of various drafts of the manuscript and for valuable suggestions that have been incorporated into the book, and Miss Anita Levine and Mr. John Mancantelli for assistance with the proofreading.

The authors are grateful to the critical readers selected by the publisher, namely Professor Stanley Payne of UCLA, Professor Nathanael Greene of Wesleyan University, and Professor Mark Hirsch of Bronx Community College for their cogent and incisive comments and suggestions, which led us to revise and improve several of the chapters of this book.

Acknowledgment must be made to John Wiley and Sons, Inc., for allowing us to use a few lines from an article published by one of the authors in the 1965 issue of *The World of Wiley*.

We wish to make clear that we alone are responsible for the statements in this book. Any error either in fact or inference, or deficiency in coverage or organization, is entirely our responsibility and in no way reflects on the many generous people who have read the manuscript and have given us their indispensable advice.

N.F.C.

R.I.S.

Contents

Prologue

The Owl of Minerva takes flight when the shadows of night are
falling.   G. W. F. HEGEL, *Philosophy of Right*

History is wholly a reasoned knowledge of what is transient and
concrete. . . . The historian's picture of his subject, whether that
subject be a sequence of events or a past state of things, appears
as a web of imaginative construction stretched between certain
fixed points provided by the statements of his authorities.
                                    R. G. COLLINGWOOD, *The Idea of History*

The understanding of other persons and life-expressions is built
on our own experience and our understanding of it, and on the
continuous interplay of experience and understanding.
                     WILHELM DILTHEY, *The Understanding of Other Persons
                                              and Their Life Expressions*

Historical explanation, too, aims at showing that the event in
question was not "a matter of chance" but was to be expected in
view of certain antecedent or simultaneous conditions. The expectation referred to is not prophecy or divination, but rational
scientific anticipation which rests on the assumption of general
laws.
                         CARL G. HEMPEL, *The Function of General Laws
                                                       in History*

This is the reason why the Past has such magical power. The beauty of its motionless and silent pictures is like the enchanted purity of late autumn, when the leaves, though one breath would make them fall, still glow against the sky in golden glory. The Past does not change or strive: . . . what was eager and grasping, what was petty and transitory, has faded away, the things that were beautiful and eternal shine out of it like stars in the night. Its beauty, to a soul not worthy of it, is unendurable; but to a soul which has conquered Fate it is the key of religion.

BERTRAND RUSSELL, A Free Man's Worship

I said the world is absurd, but I was too hasty. The world itself is not reasonable, that is all that can be said. But what is absurd is the confrontation of this irrational and the wild longing for clarity whose call echoes in the human heart. The absurd depends as much on man as on the world. . . . The absurd is born of this confrontation between the human need and the unreasonable silence of the world. This must not be forgotten.

ALBERT CAMUS, The Myth of Sisyphus and Other Essays

How to Study History

1 / A Commitment to Excellence

WHY STUDY HISTORY?

Every year in the United States and Canada about half a million college and university students are enrolled in history courses. About 80 percent of this vast number are freshmen or sophomores taking an introductory course in European or American history, while the remaining 20 percent are upperclassmen and graduate students taking more specialized courses. In the latter part of the twentieth century the study of history is accorded a special place in the academic curriculum, and the great majority of schools require their students to take at least a survey course, regardless of their ultimate field of specialization.

The study of history assumes such basic importance in the college curriculum because it is considered to be indispensable background for all other forms of knowledge, not only in the humanities but also in the social and physical sciences. The freshman survey course in European history particularly serves this function of providing a cultural, social, and political context for every other intellectual discipline and branch of knowledge. The humanities student needs history to understand the development of literature, art, music, and philosophy. Without some knowledge of the conditions of government and society in late-sixteenth-

1

century England, at least half of what Shakespeare is saying becomes incomprehensible; and without an understanding of the social and intellectual forces at work during the era of the French Revolution, we would fail to comprehend the ideas and temperament that inspired Beethoven's symphonies.

The student of the social sciences must also be well schooled in historical background, for he will gain much of his understanding of social change by examining the history of past societies. For example, the English economy of the late eighteenth century is the model and prototype of all subsequent industrialization in underdeveloped societies. Historians have noticed a common pattern in all the great revolutions in European history; they have observed for example that revolutions occur not when the masses are most severely exploited and depressed, but rather when social and economic conditions are beginning to improve, so that the great upheavals can be called "revolutions of rising expectations." Students of current social movements should be aware that in all successful revolutions in the past there has been a steady drift toward the left and a tendency for more radical and extreme leaders to replace the initial moderate ones. These obvious examples illustrate the way in which history is the prime laboratory of the social sciences.

Novice students in the physical sciences may need to know very little about the history of science, but more advanced students will have to have a firm grasp of the main trends in the history of scientific thought, which in turn is conditioned by the broad pattern of intellectual and cultural history. The history of science teaches that scientific theories have been influenced by the general intellectual assumptions that prevail in the era in which they were formulated and that a shift in these assumptions has usually signaled a reformulation of scientific doctrine. The historically minded scientist knows that no theory about the physical and biological world is sacrosanct. History shows that all scientific doctrines are intellectual paradigms, that is, conceptual models designed to explain the nature of the world in terms of current patterns of higher thought.

The most general reason for the study of history is that it provides background for all other subjects and disciplines. But there are other important reasons why college students should study history. First of all, if history is correctly taught and studied, it allows for a new level of self-discovery and a new degree of empathy with other people. Everyone has a social as well as a personal self. We are all part of all that we have met and all that we have inherited from our families and communities. Historical study allows the student to perceive how the world of today came into existence and how the texture of experience that distinguishes his particular family and community was built up by a complex combination of forces and events over many decades and perhaps centuries. Historical study allows the student to understand why he is the way he is as an American, a Canadian, a Northerner, an Anglo-Saxon, an Italian, a Jew, a Roman Catholic, etc., and also allows him to understand the historical process which has conditioned other people whom he encounters. *History is therefore a road to self-knowledge and a means of understanding the attitudes and motives of people of disparate backgrounds.*

Last but certainly not least, *history is worth studying because it is a creative act.* It not only allows for but demands serious application and industry, the exercise of a creative imagination, and high qualities of literary exposition. Historical study informs and inspires, and at the same time it is an outlet for the creative urge exhibited by people of high intelligence and deep feeling. Excellence in historical study requires the critical insight and disciplined methods of the scientist and, at the same time, the fine sensitivity to both the drama of human life and the nuances of prose style that distinguish the novelist and playwright.

Because historical knowledge is so useful in higher education, most American and Canadian college students are required to take a survey course in either the development of Western civilization or modern European history. And in our competitive society, the pressures of university life demand that students do well in these survey courses and receive good grades. We may view with nostalgia those Hollywood movies of the 1930's that depict universities as merely the setting for continuous rounds of childish fun and games. But this charmingly idiotic and irresponsible college world, if it ever existed, is very far from the university of today in which courses are a serious business indeed. Nowadays standards are high, professors are demanding, academic probation threatens potential failures, the cruel rigors of graduate-school admission tests loom menacingly before upperclassmen, and graduate students face the prospect of exhaustive comprehensive examinations.

It is an unfortunate fact that many students in American and Canadian universities—not only freshmen in survey courses but even history majors—never adequately learn sound and well-proven methods of studying and writing history. They remain in a state of doubt and confusion concerning what is required of them in historical studies. They do not clearly understand what an historical problem is; they do not know how to analyze and synthesize the excellent books they read nor how to write critical book reviews and essays. What usually happens in the history survey courses is that students learn how to study history by a painful and wasteful method of trial and error—painful and wasteful both for the instructor and the student. By the end of the academic year perhaps 75 percent of the students in the introductory history courses are doing at least adequate work, but a quarter never have a clue as to what historical study is all about, even if they cram enough names and dates into their bewildered minds to get a passing grade. Even among the more fortunate majority, more than half are defective in their approach to historical study in one way or another; and this defect, more often than not, is perpetuated right through four years of college and even into graduate school. In the larger graduate schools of history in the country there are many distinguished scholars who refuse to conduct M.A. seminars, that is, seminars for the entering graduate students, because they find that most of these students do not really know how to write an historical essay. The authors of this guide book have taught, between them, in ten universities in the United States and Canada, big and small, public and private, within and without the Ivy League, east and west; and they have found the situation roughly the same everywhere.

This book tries to improve significantly upon this distressing situation by informing the student as he begins college historical studies, particularly if he is taking one of the usual survey courses, what will be required of him and how to meet those requirements. We believe that this can be done in a straightforward, frank, and practical way. We firmly believe that history is not an occult mystery, nor even an especially difficult subject requiring an unusual cast of mind, such as physics, linguistics, logic, higher mathematics, or music. It *is* very hard to be a first-rate professional historian, because this involves an extremely rare combination of great learning, great rhetorical skill, and great humanity. But it is relatively easy to be a successful undergraduate and even a first-year graduate student of history in an American university. We believe that any college student with a comprehensive secondary education and average intelligence can do highly satisfactory work in history up to and including the M.A. level.

The history student, whether at the novice or the advanced level, who knows what is expected of him and knows how to fulfill these expectations will have a good attitude toward his work. The study of history is for him not a difficult and unpalatable chore but rather a wonderful opportunity, the means to social emancipation and intellectual maturity. He will realize that it is a privilege to study history and thereby to have the world of the past and the meaning of the present, with all their fascinating richness and complexity, opened up to him by the achievements of modern scholarship. He will understand why serious historical inquiry is sometimes prohibited by political authority and why instead students are required to accept the ruling group's propaganda myths about the past and present. *In a free society it is the right of university students to commit themselves to excellence in historical study* and to pursue unhindered by the state a full inquiry into the actual course of social, intellectual, and political change. This historical inquiry is almost as valuable for students of literature, art, philosophy, and the social and behavioral sciences as it is for the history major.

The purpose of this book is to assist undergraduates in their commitment to excellence in historical study and to supplement the all-important classroom work with a practical guide toward the attainment of this excellence. Reserving the more theoretical and intellectual aspects of historical study for the latter part of the book, we have tried to explain in as direct and practical a way as possible the specific techniques, assumptions, and rules that will make the history student's work enjoyable and rewarding. We urge the student to read this book carefully at one sitting and then a day or two later to pick it up and read it again, after which he should get to work and follow the methods recommended here. Occasionally during the term, especially when exams, book reviews, and essays are due, a quick perusal of the relevant sections will be useful. We think that this book will help instructors to teach their students the guidelines of historical study. We are certain that this book will make the freshman's lot a happier one; it should also be useful to history majors and even to the occasional gray-beard graduate student.

We intend that the student should find historical study not a dreadful, confusing ordeal, but a delightful and exciting intellectual experience; that in comprehending the development of Western civilization, he should be awakened to a deeper understanding of both himself and society; that excellence in historical study should be claimed by the student as a right that opens the door to an endless world of discovery and meaning.

PREREQUISITES FOR STUDYING HISTORY

History does not require intensive preliminary training in related fields, as physics requires advanced mathematical knowledge. Nevertheless it is necessary to set out at the beginning some basic requirements for historical study that must not be neglected. *An effective start in the study of history, at whatever level it is pursued, requires an open mind.* The student must always be ready to reconsider the historical methods and concepts with which he is familiar and be ready to adopt a new way of thinking. College freshmen in survey courses particularly need to be urged to anticipate a fundamental reshaping of their historical insights and attitudes. While it is true that history nowadays is coming to be well taught in secondary schools, in a great many high schools what passes for history is still merely a jejune miscellany of names and dates. The freshman is going to find that at the college level, chronology is merely the outer skeleton of historical study and that even total recall of every name and date in the textbook is very far from the kind of critical and imaginative thinking he will be required to undertake.

All American college freshmen will have had a high school survey course in United States history; consequently the college survey course in American history may appear at first sight to be largely a repetition of what has already been encountered. But the novice college student will be surprised to discover that even if the same textbook is used as in his senior year in high school, the level of conceptualization for the most part, and of insight into complex problems of historical change, is now much higher. Early in the term the freshman will learn that repetition of the well-known outline facts of American history is not adequate and that a much higher level of thought and communication is demanded of him. The great majority of college freshmen are likely to have had a much weaker preparation in European history. They must therefore be prepared to encounter a whole new set of concepts and methods in the Western civilization survey. Among these challenges, perhaps the most difficult for the beginning college student will be the explication of primary sources, which involves critical techniques he is not likely to have encountered in secondary school.

The history major and the graduate student must also be ready for new ways of thinking. Upper-class work in history will require much longer papers than are usually assigned to freshmen, and this involves the new experience of organizing and writing a sustained work of historical exposition. The history major will also face the challenge of reading several conflicting interpretations of one theme or era and of developing the critical tools to discriminate among these alternative views. Graduate students are going to encounter novel bibliographical and linguistic problems; and they are likely to find that their teachers demand of them, when dealing with any particular problem, an exhaustive knowledge and rigorous precision that are usually overlooked even in advanced undergraduate work.

At any level of historical study the successful student will be the one who is not going to be trapped within the confines of familiar concepts and techniques. He must be prepared for the intellectual aspiration and experimentation that make possible conceptual growth and entry upon a new level of thinking. The greatest obstacle to learning history is the student's reluctance to try an unfamiliar approach or to examine a new kind of problem. This self-defeating inhibition precludes the student from ever finding out that he is capable of original and superior work.

Students at all levels, from freshmen through graduate students, commonly attempt to avoid the challenge of a new way of historical thinking by taking refuge in humility. This failure of nerve takes the form of statements like "Who am I to criticize N's book? He is a famous historian, and I'm just a beginner." "How can I make any sense out of a collection of eighteenth-century documents? I have only a general outline knowledge of the period." If this specious modesty were to prevail, history would be a terrible bore because the student would only commit the professor's lectures and the textbook to rote memory and regurgitate them on exams. You will find this kind of humility to be worse than useless. In fact, if you let such an attitude govern your approach to historical study, you will never learn to think in an original and creative way, and the quality of your work will never rise above the lowest level of mediocrity.

Aside from its destructive effects, this defensive humility is false and unacceptable on two grounds. In the first place history is unique among social and political disciplines in that it has no particular jargon or mysterious mathematical method. All the methodological principles of the historian are derived from common sense and are as much within the intellectual capacity of a freshman at a junior college as of a professor at Oxford. The student must complement the teacher's illumination of the leading themes and problems with a *will to learn,* a desire to apply himself seriously to the examination of written material and to the analysis of ideas. A freshman cannot be given a treatise on physics by Einstein or Heisenberg and be expected to give a sensible critical evaluation of it; in order to evaluate the treatise, the student would need intensely specialized training and unusual mathematical ability. But any student in his first week of college study could, if he applied himself and thought a little bit, make some sensible comments about why Edward Gibbon's *Decline and Fall of the Roman Empire* or Arthur M. Schlesinger Jr.'s *Age of Jackson* are good or bad history books, or to what extent these works exhibit strong and weak qualities.

The second reason defensive humility is unacceptable and cannot relieve the novice student of the responsibility to undertake analysis, synthesis, and judgment on historical problems is that he is already an historian. Carl Becker, a noted American historian of a generation ago, published a book entitled *Everyman His Own Historian.* Whether or not every man is his own historian, he is at least *an* historian. Every man has a sense of history, a vision of the past, and a set of assumptions about the nature of society and the dynamics of social change. You are an historian of your own times when you read a newspaper and make a judgment favorable or unfavorable about an event that has been described. You are also an historian when you think about the events of your own life and analyze your personal relationship to your physical and social environment, making judgments about your community, family, university, and the viability of your ambitions and private goals.

All of these evaluations are of the same nature as the ones you will make in your academic historical work. The major difference is that academic historical study will be much broader in scope and will be carried out with information that is not so emotionally immediate, in the sense that your life and aspirations do not immediately depend on your decisions about the significance of this long-range historical information. In academic historical study the student will follow a more systematic, less subjective method of evaluating his information. But the student need never despair of his ability to be an historian if he has any capacity at all for making judgments about the world and of sensibly reflecting on his own experience.

The student should not lose his nerve when confronting either historians or historical information. If his intellect has allowed him to make an integrated and coherent view of the world out of the variety of his personal experiences, it can allow him to create a systematic and plausible view of the past out of the collective experience of mankind.

Not only is there a *parallel* between making sense out of your personal experience and making sense out of the collective experience of mankind, but the latter kind of judgment is also heavily *dependent* upon the former. As we examine the traces that the men of a bygone era have left behind them in the form of written records, we have to make use of extrapolated facets of our own experience to recreate in our imagination their thoughts and actions. History is about men and how they act in society. The qualities of contemporary humanity and the dimensions of current society are inevitably the starting point (although by no means the final point) for thinking about the functioning of past human society, whether in 1900 A.D. or 1900 B.C. Other things being equal, *the best historian will be the one with the most varied and sophisticated personal experience of human conduct and social change.*

The novice student of history if he is to mature into a good historian must therefore do two things. *First* he must continually broaden his experience of the world through personal involvement and through study. This is what is meant by such phrases as "growing up" and "humane studies." *Second* the student has to take advantage of what has already been thought and said about the common experience of mankind, about the history of human society and civilization. *He has to learn the particular and distinctive ways historians think, the kinds of information they deal with, and their special method for working with such information.* These are the aims of the academic study of history.

You may eventually come to regard traditional historical methods and interpretations as one-sided, limited, dull, imperfect, or even false. You may someday become a great historian who takes academic history along new paths of discovery. No false humility, but also no juvenile arrogance: before you attempt a revolution in historical thinking, you have to master the prevailing techniques and theories. This will involve hard work, mental discipline, and strenuous intellectual effort, as well as the exercise of a creative imagination.

In addition to the attitudes we have discussed, the study of history at the college level presupposes certain equipment and study habits. History majors and graduate students will have been told to employ these fundamentals—although they will sometimes, at their peril, neglect one or another of them—but most freshmen are unfamiliar with these prerequisites, and therefore it is worthwhile to emphasize them here.

The serious and successful student of history, while he is engaged in the business of learning, whether in the classroom, library, or an instructor's office, should always have with him suitable writing material. It may seem absurdly obvious to tell the history student to carry with him at all times a pen and some kind of note paper so that he can write down the titles of books or ideas and problems he discovers. But strange as it may seem, one of the most common failings of history students, even at the graduate level, is a failure to carry these simple writing materials when they are going to a conference with their instructor. It seems ironic, but from personal experience we know it is true, that the same student who complains vociferously about the inaccessibility of his "jet set" professor will turn up at the professor's office without any writing material. A famous historian at Columbia University was known to cut short any conference with a student who did not come prepared with pen and paper—and rightly so.

Undergraduates are assiduous note-takers. They need, however, to be reminded that they should find a safe, dry place to preserve their notes, preferably a locked filing cabinet. Another reminder for the undergraduate history student is that in many universities all formal work submitted in history courses, with the exception of exams written in the classroom, must be submitted in typescript. Your instructor will tell you early in the term whether he expects your papers to be in typescript. Then if you cannot type and do not have the time to learn, you should make arrangements with one or two professional typists on whose services you will be able to rely when you need them.

Aside from writing materials, the necessary equipment of the history student consists of books. *As soon as you obtain the course syllabus with its list of required books, go out and buy them.* It is characteristic of a failing student in a history course not to get around to buying textbooks until well on in the term or just before the final exam or never at all. Even if the required books for the course are available in the college library, you should nevertheless secure your own copy because you will want to facilitate your study by underlining and making marginal notes. Purchase the textbooks as early as possible in the term, and spend a few hours looking through them, noting in general their contents and organization. History majors, who are likely to have very heavy assignments in the way of papers and essays, are advised to get reading lists at the beginning of the summer vacation for the courses they will take during the coming year, and to read several of the assigned works at their leisure.

In order to facilitate study and note-taking, it is recommended that you purchase your course books in new or at least clean copies. You will inevitably be distracted, confused, and annoyed if you try to master a book that already contains someone else's markings and comments.

It is likely that you also will be given a list of supplementary books, mostly paperbacks, for optional purchase. You will have the choice of either buying copies or using the library copies. If you can at all afford it, purchase copies of the supplementary books for yourself because it will be difficult to obtain these works at the library reserve desk during the exam period, and also because you can make notes in your own copies that will make your reviewing much easier.

In addition to the required course books, the serious and successful student always has at his disposal some indispensable reference works: (1) Webster's *New Collegiate Dictionary*, which should be consulted while writing a paper for the spelling or meaning of any word that seems doubtful to you. (2) H. W. Fowler's *A Dictionary of Modern English Usage*, Bergen and Cornelia Evans' *A Dictionary of Contemporary American Usage*,

and one of the many good handbooks that are available* to provide enlightenment on any point of grammar or word usage that
strikes you as problematical or awkward. (3) William L. Langer's
Encyclopedia of World History to check any date that seems
questionable and (4) a reliable historical atlas of that part of the
world whose history you are currently studying. For European
history the best student atlas is R. R. Palmer, ed., *Atlas of World
History.*

In a later chapter we will show in detail how the college
library can become one of the history student's major pieces of
equipment. For the moment it is enough to emphasize that in
addition to building up a small working library of his own, the
student will have to make extensive use of his college library. One
of the very first things you must do is familiarize yourself with
the library on your campus, particularly the library reserve system
for books assigned in courses and the card catalogue files for
other works. In nearly all colleges freshmen are given a quick
tour of the library. Go back to the library after the initial guided
tour, wander around and ask questions until the library becomes
part of your equipment for serious work. Insist on your rights as
a student to make as full use of the library as the rules allow. Find
out about the privilege (in some institutions limited only to upperclassmen) of borrowing a book through the mail from another
college library if yours does not have it. You will very likely have
to do this if you ever come to work on an extensive research paper.
This system is called Inter-Library Loan, and all college libraries
have access to it. Also if you come across a book you would like to
read that is not in your college library, ask your instructor to have
the library order it. On every campus each professor has the right
to have the library order books varying in number per year from

---

* Among the best handbooks are Sheridan Baker, *The Complete Stylist;*
John C. Hodges, *The Harbrace College Handbook;* James M. McCrimmon,
Writing with a Purpose; Porter G. Perrin, *Writer's Guide and Index to Eng-
lish;* and William W. Watt, *An American Rhetoric.*

two or three dozen to several thousand, depending on the wealth of the institution. Many professors are too busy with teaching or research to fill up their library allotment, and they will be glad to order a book that you bring to their attention.

Every student will develop distinct study habits that are best suited to his own personality, but there are certain general principles of work procedure you will have to follow if you are going to be a successful history student. In a peculiar way it is more difficult to develop good work habits as a student of history than as a student of physics or chemistry. In the sciences you will be doing much of your work in the controlled environment of a laboratory. Aside from the requirement of attending classes, each history student is left to go to hell in his own way. You can save yourself a lot of frustration and the agony of learning how to study by trial and error if you decide at the outset to observe these rules:

1. Find a place conducive to study. If you need quiet for your work, find a quiet place, which on a college campus is most likely to be the library. If you need a background of Beethoven or the Beatles to inspire your work, find the appropriate place.

2. If during your history study you find that you have read the same line five times you will know that something is wrong, either with your place of study or with yourself. You cannot study history effectively when you are dazed, drowsy, or dopey. History study is not aimless turning of pages; it requires the full application of your intellectual resources. Artificial stimulants are no substitute for sleep.

3. There will be occasions when conferences with one or more fellow students in a course will be valuable and stimulating. But as a general rule, avoid group study, which involves either the exploitation of the conscientious student by lazy ones or the futile sharing of ignorance.

4. If the assigned required reading in a course leaves doubts and confusions in your mind, you may be greatly helped by read-

ing an alternative treatment of the same problem or subject listed among the supplementary books.

5. Cramming for exams and last-minute writing of papers produce only intellectual indigestion and poor grades. Learning history is a cumulative process. Even the brightest student has to work at history in a step-by-step way, which is outlined for you by the reading assignments. Assume that at the very least, *for every hour in the history classroom you will spend three hours working on your own*. Get started immediately the first day of the term, and proceed in a methodical manner, completing your assignments week by week. There is no other way to benefit from a history course.

6. Under no circumstances should you make use of "trots," "ponies," course outlines, or mimeographed lecture notes prepared by commercial agencies, fraternities, or student entrepreneurs. There is no short cut to learning history. You must attend and comprehend the lectures and do all the required reading. Relying upon speciously attractive short-cut summaries is equivalent to putting your health in the hands of a medical quack.

For many students this advice on equipment and study habits will appear trivial, and even the discussion of the right attitude with which to begin work in history will seem superfluous. But from our experience, the majority of students fail to observe one or another of these prerequisites, and this hampers their work along the way. Take pains to get started right, and you will be ready to take advantage of the magnificent intellectual opportunity provided by the study of history.

2 / A Matter of Definition

If a student were to travel around the country and attend the lectures of the forty or fifty most eminent historians in American universities, he would discover that these scholars do not define the nature of their subject in precisely the same way. From these lectures it would be possible to extrapolate three closely related but nevertheless distinct definitions: (1) History is the study of what men have done and said and thought in the past. (2) History is biography, that is, a work of the creative imagination in which the author attempts to recreate the life and thoughts of particular men who actually lived at a certain time. (3) History is the study of man in his social aspects both past and present.

All approaches to history and all historical schools of the twentieth century fall under one or another of these definitions. The first definition is the broadest, and those historians who do indeed try to give us a general account of what men have done and thought and said in the past constitute what is called the narrative school of history. But many historians feel this general narrative approach is too superficial and does not select sufficiently from among a variety of human actions those qualities that are the most important. So the first definition, when reconsidered in terms of the view that history is the account of the most *important* things that men have done and said and thought in the past breaks down into several schools. The political-institutional historians tell us that it is what men have done and said and thought in government and law that is the most significant. The school of intellectual history, or history of ideas, regards the development of higher thought and feeling (philosophy, art, literature, science) as the central concern of the historian. The economic historians focus on the ways in which men have made a living and have controlled their physical environment and see these as the key to human thought and action. The cultural historian is one who examines the development of ideas in the totality of a social, political, and economic situation. He is very much of a generalist in his approach, save that he makes the movement of thought and feeling the prime focus of his narrative.

The second definition regards history as the biography of important men and women. But this definition, too, is conducive to two schools: those who think we can explain motivation of men and women in the past in terms of modern psychological theory, and those who think we cannot psychoanalyze the dead and have to understand men in the past largely in terms of the theories of motivation and personality that prevailed during the era in which they lived.

The third definition identifies history with sociology and regards the past as a kind of laboratory for observing forms of social change that have relevance to current problems. This school is not interested in particular individuals but only in large groups or communities. Yet the sociological school is also divided within itself. There are those historians who believe that the Marxist doctrine of dialectical materialism explains social change, and there are those who have a different social paradigm. There are those who think that each society is ultimately peculiar and distinct, and there are those comparative sociological historians who see recurrent patterns running through all or at least several societies.

When our inquiring student becomes aware of the markedly different schools of historical thought, of the varying interests and attitudes among historians, he will see that the only universally acceptable definition of history has to be that *history is what the historian does.* And what the historian does is to obtain information about the past and then to make judgments about the significance, meaning, importance, and relevance of these bits of information. It is because historians make judgments about the information they have that they disagree on the definition of history. They make judgments in terms of principles of causation that explain how one event or person or group or institution or anything in the past affects any other thing. These historical judgments involve assumptions about what is important and real in human affairs and about what is ephemeral and unreal.

The most important principle that the novice student of history must learn is that the business of an historian is to make judgments and to establish causal relationships between facts; he must place them in some significant pattern and order and not simply be a reporter. It is true that forty or fifty years ago it was quite widely believed that history was merely a record of the past, a journal about what happened, and that the historian's responsibility was merely to collect the data ("The facts, and only the facts!") of the past for present readers. But in the last three or four decades historians have come to feel that this view of history is both inadequate and false. It is inadequate because it can only inform the reader about the mere facts of what has happened; it cannot in any way tell him the importance or the meaning of these facts. Such history tends to become merely anecdotal; it offers a disjointed recording of masses of facts and is dull and confusing to read. This older view of history, we have come to see, is also false because it is based on a naive belief that the historian can dispassionately separate himself from the events he is describing and can be "unbiased." Modern psychology and philos-

ophy have taught us that every historian comes to his material
with a previous set of assumptions about what is important and
what is not. The historian cannot tell us every fact of what happened in the past; he *invariably* selects from a great number of
events and facts the ones that he thinks are important. We now
know that the historian's mind is the dynamic creative force that
molds an historical picture out of a mass of disorganized and insignificant data. Far from bewailing the historian's "bias" and
"prejudice," we have come to realize that it is the entry of the
historian's mind into the remains of the past that creates significant relationships and establishes an ordered historical world that
seems true, beautiful, and relevant to us.

Far from prohibiting the historian from making judgments,
we now say that *the historian has an obligation to make judgments.* He seeks to demonstrate in his writing not merely the *what*
of the past but also the answer to the two fundamental questions
how and *why.* The historian sets out to tell us the how and why
of an individual life, or of an institution, a community, a state, a
culture, an economy, and a society. How did they function? Why
were they the way they were? How and why did they succeed or
fail, become better or worse? These are the fundamental questions in history.

In the light of this definition of the nature of history, the historian at any level, whether he is a student in his first college
history course or a senior professor, has a threefold obligation:
(1) He must constantly attempt to improve upon the set of assumptions that he uses to make judgments about what is important and real in human life. He must constantly endeavor through
study, reflection, and maturing experience to advance from naive,
irrational bias, which we call prejudice, to sophisticated understanding of the nature of the human mind and society, which we
call wisdom. (2) He must ever increase his knowledge, both
quantitatively and qualitatively, both in amount and variety, of
the data or facts of the past, the *what* of history. (3) He must

apply his assumptions on the significant aspects of human life so as to make judgments and establish relationships between particular facts, and he must create a systematic order out of the chaos of events to understand the *how* and *why* of history.

It is on the first and last points that the undergraduate student of history is most often deficient. He is willing enough to memorize the facts given him in the textbook, but he is reluctant to make judgments and establish relationships. When he does so, his assumptions are too often ignorant and crude.

You now know that mere facts are not adequate. You know also that you must develop intelligent and well-informed assumptions about human behavior and culture, that you must apply these assumptions in a creative and imaginative way so as to elucidate the how and why of historical change. This is the historian's craft, and it is your business to learn the tools of the craft and to apply them.

3 / The Materials of History

Whether the historian is a freshman starting his survey course or a professional in the ranks preparing his fourteenth scholarly article, he must be aware of the distinct varieties of historical sources and the particular kinds of information to be obtained from them. The basic types of sources are signified by the terms *primary* and *secondary*. The kinds of information found in historical sources are designated by the terms *fact, inference,* and *opinion.*

The starting point for all historical work is the recognition of the different uses of primary and secondary sources; fortunately, the two kinds of sources are very easy to distinguish in practical terms. *A primary source is a work that was written at a time that is contemporary or nearly contemporary with the period or subject being studied.* Thus the letters of Bismarck are a primary source for the study of German diplomatic and political development in the later nineteenth century, and *The Prince* of Machiavelli is a primary source either for the study of early sixteenth-century Italian politics or for Renaissance political theory. A certain amount of judgment is involved in deciding just what degree of contemporaneity is needed to make a source truly primary for a subject. Thus Aristotle's *Politics* could suitably be used as a primary source for a study of ancient Greek political thought, but an historian interested in examining the details of practical political life in fifth-century Athens would have to decide whether the *Politics*, written about a century after the events contemporary with this subject, could be used as an accurate primary source. For the most part, primary sources for any subject can be readily identified; however, understanding such sources, and eliciting meaning from them, as we shall show, is another, far more difficult matter.

Secondary sources can similarly be identified in terms of their time relationship to the subject being studied; *a secondary work for a subject is one that discusses the subject but is written after the time contemporary with it.* Thus L. B. Namier's studies of eighteenth-century parliaments in England, published in the 1920's and 1930's, are secondary sources for the subject of eighteenth-century English government, and David Douglas' biography of William the Conqueror, published in 1965, is a secondary source for any study of eleventh-century England. All secondary sources will be based on primary sources, and most will include reports of information derived from primary sources. But the judgments and values to be found in a secondary source must always be understood as after the fact and cannot be equated with the points of view and information to be found in primary sources.

One further example should make this distinction completely clear. A given source is primary or secondary solely in accordance with its time relationship to the subject being studied. Because of this, a single work may be a secondary source for one subject and a primary source for a different subject. For instance, the famous history of the Reformation by Leopold von Ranke, written in the 1840's, is an important *secondary* source for any study of the Reformation; but the same book is a *primary* source for a study of nineteenth-century German thought because Ranke's work reflects dominant trends in contemporary German philosophy of history.

A more theoretical definition of primary and secondary sources can be given. *Primary sources are the basic material that provide the raw data and information for the historian. Secondary sources are the works that contain the explications of, and judg-ments on, this primary material.* The same distinction between primary and secondary sources exists in the methodology of the social and behavioral sciences. The records of interviews made during the Great Blackout of 1965 with people in New York City would be a primary source; a study of the social significance of the variety of responses to the Blackout made by a sociologist after careful analysis of the interview material would be a sec-ondary source. An example can also be given from literary studies. The letters of the poet John Keats are a primary source for his life and thought; Aileen Ward's *John Keats: The Making of a Poet* is a secondary source. To return to straight historical study, the records of the English treasury in the reign of King John of Eng-land are a primary source for this period of English history; Sid-ney Painter's *The Reign of King John* is a secondary source.

So far, it has been easy to distinguish types of sources as pri-mary and secondary. But the question still remains: what is the *use* of different types of sources for the historian? To answer this question, it is necessary to grasp the general distinction between statements of fact, statements of opinion, and statements that are inferences. *A fact is a statement that is commonly accepted as true, in and of itself, and needs no other information to make it true.* A scientist would consider the existence of substances such as carbon and oxygen a fact, or would call measured observations such as thermometer readings facts.

That the Battle of Hastings was fought in 1066 is an historical fact; so too is the statement that the population of England greatly increased between 1750 and 1850. *Whatever is commonly ac-cepted information among historians is "factual."* While there is a hard substratum of basic data that is accepted as inevitably true, there is also a "gray area" of historical facts—statements that are accepted as true by many or even most historians but regarded as vulnerable or only partly true by others. Without at this time raising very difficult problems about the philosophy of history, we may conclude that "facts" in history are not entirely objective things. The historian does not simply accumulate facts as if they were so many pebbles on a beach. To a greater or less degree (the philosophy of history is uncertain on this point), *the historian's mind creates facts by making judgments on evidence.* Commonly accepted judgments on specific matters are "facts." To put it another way, *facts are the established data of history, the foundation stones for further thinking about history, the knowledge that can be accepted as already established.*

An inference is the kind of statement that in strict science is called an hypothesis; it is a conclusion or judgment stating relationships between facts and is derived from a logical consideration of a group of facts. The scientist of our earlier paragraph could infer from observing carbon and oxygen combine over and over again in the ratio of 1:2 certain points about the respective combining properties of carbon and oxygen; and if his reasoning were sound, he could expect his inferred conclusions to prove true in all cases in which carbon and oxygen combine.

The historian lacks the strict, quantitative logic of the scientist; therefore, his conclusions or judgments are necessarily subjective and imaginative to a great extent. *If historical facts are commonly accepted judgments on evidence, historical inferences are more complex, cumulative judgments on the relationship between facts. As commonly accepted truths, facts are the fixed points of historical thinking; inferences are the bridges built by the historian's mind to relate these fixed points in a network of meaning.*

Given two dozen facts, no two historians will see all the possible relationships between these facts in precisely the same way. But two, or even several, historians, attempting to discover relationships between the same set of facts, will for the most part establish an almost identical pattern of meaning. By the exercise of the methods of historical reasoning, which we will delineate in the following chapters, a number of historians will make a large number of the same inferential judgments on a given set of facts, although they are not likely to come to absolute agreement on every possible relationship between the facts. As long as an historian is methodical and fact-oriented in his inferences, his judgment will be plausible and respectable, even if it is not universally accepted; and no one will accuse him of "distorting" the significance or meaning of the facts.

The latter can happen only when the historian has been opinionated; *opinions are personal and individual conclusions, identical in kind to inferences but without any support or grounding in fact.* As a rule, opinions found in historical writing are either personal prejudices of the authors or historical clichés that everyone assumes to be true just because they have been often repeated. For example, that the Renaissance was characterized by "a renewed interest in the individuality of man" is an opinion unless supporting examples are brought in as facts and inferences to substantiate the claim.

Our point can be emphasized most clearly by an example from strict logic. If the following data are given:

Time, A.M.	*Temp., Deg.*
9	80
10	90
11	90
12	80

and the following statement is made:

Between 9 and 10 A.M. the temperature rose; from 10 until 11 the temperature remained steady; and from 11 to 12 the temperature fell.

then it is clear that the data are factual, while the statement is *not* a fact but is, rather, an inference. The factual statements remain true and unchanged even with the addition of further facts, but the inference is only as valid as the degree to which the information on which it is based is valid and complete; further facts may very well make the inference untrue. If we later discover that at 10:30 the temperature rose to 95°, the four original facts remain unchanged and are nonetheless true, but the middle term of the inference is false and needs revision. *An inference is only true to the extent to which the facts on which it is based are true, and to the extent to which it takes account of all known facts; and an inference is always a personal judgment about facts.* Especially in history writing, the more narrow the base of facts included in any inference, the less likely the possibility that the inference will have a valid general application; if an historical theory is based solely on economic data, the chance that the theory will validly explain some development in religious history or even in political history is small.

We have spent so much time with this point because the commonest source of error in history writing is to confuse the facts with inferences and to take inferences as facts; not only beginners but the most seasoned professional writers are subject to this error, which leads to the commonplace acceptance of many theories as true and factual, an acceptance that stifles original investigation into facts and inhibits new theories about the subject.

In science, which has a strictly logical language and method of reasoning, theoretical statements are commonly accepted and cited as if they were facts. Even in science, the process of re-examining and re-evaluating theories operates just as it does in history, but scientific theories are so logically based that any major change in a theory is slow in coming; indeed, when a theory is finally replaced altogether after a long period of usefulness, the change frequently causes such a radical break with tradition that it is referred to as a "scientific revolution." The Copernican conception of the universe was not more "true" than the Ptolemaic one, but rather a more useful hypothesis that replaced an older hypothesis. We are so accustomed, however, to regarding scientific hypotheses as being true as facts that we think of Copernicus as "right" and Ptolemy as "wrong." Replacement of one theory by another happens much more frequently in history than in the sciences; hence the process is less dramatic and seems less like "truth" replacing "error." The two processes are nevertheless much alike.

In history, which quite in contrast to science uses an ordinary everyday language, hypotheses and inferences must be *continually* re-examined because they are so open to the prejudices and slants created by personal connotations and informal usage. There is a common habit in everyday speaking of prefacing an opinion with the phrase "It's a fact that. . . ." "It's a fact that the Dodgers are the best baseball team this year" is an opinionated statement with only a probability of being inferentially sound. The phrase "It's a fact" adds rhetorical support and strength to the opinion that follows it; but for a discipline such as history, which depends on proof rather than on opinion, this kind of rhetoric can turn into a dangerous source of conviction founded on an absence of thought. Thus, students would be very well advised from the very start of their historical studies (1) always to recognize what in their own thinking is inference rather than true fact, and to be honest with themselves about constantly re-evaluating their own inferences; and (2) to be very careful in their reading to differentiate inferences from facts, especially when the inference is not identified as such by the author.

Let us be clear that we are *not* saying that facts are good and that inferences are bad and should be avoided. A presentation that is merely factual is nothing but a list and contributes very little to understanding. *Understanding is achieved at the level at which the relationships between facts can be explained; thus understanding, while based on facts, is almost entirely inferential.* But this means that understanding must always be seen as temporary, as the best explanation that present wisdom and information will allow. You should always feel that the next day's effort might lead to a wholly new theory or at least to a revised understanding that will be superior to the old one.

Indeed, it is in this critical attitude exactly that the very life of history resides, because the active, intellectual, searching quality that characterizes the best history writing, the striving for ideas that is the mark of the greatest historians, always is the result of an attempt to re-examine older ideas, to seek new meaning in old (and new) facts, to achieve a new hypothesis and a further understanding that will be a partial contribution to the long-range growth and development and change in historical understanding. The process will never cease, nor should it; the whole notion of an absolutely "definitive" history of any subject is completely contrary to the recognition that the aim of historical investigation is *understanding*, and that understanding is inferential.

It is a gross misunderstanding of history to think of it as a "scientific" (that is, simple fact-gathering) way of thinking. Even those scholars who, around the end of the nineteenth century and the beginning of the twentieth century, strongly asserted that history was an exact science were exerting their individual sense of judgment and of values in making historical explanations. J. B. Bury, a learned Cambridge scholar, claimed that "history is a science, no less and no more." Given this view on Bury's part, we are not surprised to find the following judgment in his book on *The Ancient Greek Historians:*

Without entering upon a minute criticism of the method of Hellanicus, it is enough to say that, mistaking the character of mythical traditions, he erected an ingenious edifice on foundations which had no solidity. The most perfect genealogies could not even approximately determine absolute dates; and the genealogies were full of inconsistencies which had to be overcome by arbitrary interpolations and manipulations. Moreover, quite recent events, which had not been recorded at the time, might present almost insuperable difficulties to a chronographer. One case, which we can control, will illustrate how dangerous the procedure of Hellanicus was. . . . His whole chronology of the thirty-five years after the Persian war was arbitrary; and it illustrates how in the absence of records precise chronology is hopeless. The instance of error which I have given suggests another observation. There were numerous stones at Athens, officially inscribed and precisely dated, from which, if they were all preserved, a modern student would probably construct without difficulty and with absolute certainty an exact chronicle of Athenian history in the fifth century. But it never occurred to Hellanicus to look for them, and in this he was only like most other Greek historians. The Greeks used such records when they came across them, but as a rule they did not seek them out systematically.[1]

Because of his pseudoscientific view of the nature of all history, Bury doubtless regarded such a passage as a very objective interpretation of ancient Greek historical thought. And yet the passage is shot through with judgments that clearly reflect Bury's values rather than those the Greeks might have held. He chides Hellanicus for being "unmethodical," "arbitrary," and "unsystematic" and hence of using a "dangerous procedure." But systematic and factual procedure did not become a positive value in historical research until the nineteenth century, and Bury is chiding Hellanicus for not writing the history that Bury himself would have written had he lived in fifth-century Athens. A more profound view would recognize that while Hellanicus in his age doubtless sought to write as "true" a history as Bury in his own age, the values that constituted "truth" in history were then altogether different. Hellanicus reveals that a sense of precise chronology was not a meaningful value for ancient Greek history writers since Hellanicus is "inaccurate" even about dates of events contemporary with himself. Bury's judgment, then, is totally inferential and is based on his own personal values, but it is this judgment that he presents as an objective and valid criticism of the ancients. Bury said that he would "not wrong these early historians if we describe them as credulous and uncritical."[2] But it is Bury himself who is truly uncritical by failing to see that he has taken his own inferential values as absolute and applicable to any his-

[1] J. B. Bury, *The Ancient Greek Historians* (London: Macmillan and Co., Ltd., 1909), pp. 30–31.
[2] *Ibid.*, p. 25.

torical examination. In other words, he is using his inferences as if they were facts, and his judgment has been led astray as a result.

Inference and fact must be kept distinguished in one's mind in order that inferences may be freely and constantly re-examined. It is a fact that Napoleon I was crowned "emperor" in Paris in 1804; but what Napoleon thought his position as "emperor" signified can never be a fact—it will always be a matter of historical inference. Inevitably, this inference will be based on facts, such as statements by Napoleon himself; but ultimately any statement about the meaning or significance of Napoleon's coronation will have to be inferences by a modern historian, and such inferences will form the original part, the *idea* or interpretation in the modern historian's study of Napoleon.

Even when using primary sources to obtain facts, the historian must do some hard thinking. The student must not only know the texts of his primary sources, but must be able to evaluate their accuracy or validity; he must analyze or, as historians say, "question" his sources. Possibly the information that the primary sources present is inaccurate in modern terms because of a difference in the prevailing point of view about fact in the period of the primary source (as in the example of Hellanicus cited earlier) or because of inaccurate methods of observing factual data in earlier periods. Or again, the information in a primary source may be slanted because of bias or opinion on the part of the writer who created the primary source. If we turn again to our example of temperature readings, we can now see that before accepting the data given, the history student should ask a few questions: (1) In the era in which this data was collected, did thermometers give the same kind of reading or scale that exists today? (2) Was the reporting of temperatures accurate in that era? (3) Did the person who reported these temperatures possibly have some reason for giving a false or misleading report of the temperature because of his personal belief about what temperature *should* be?

Let us take another example from a document that is a well-known primary source for historians studying the early Middle

Ages, the *History of the Goths* by the sixth-century writer Jordanes. Describing an encounter between the Visigoths and the Roman Emperor Theodosius, Jordanes writes:

When the Emperor Theodosius [Emperor in the East] afterwards recovered and learned that the Emperor Gratian [Emperor in the West] had made a compact between the Goths and the Romans, as he had himself desired, he was very well-pleased and gave his assent. He gave gifts to King Athanaric [of the Visigoths], who had succeeded Fritigern, made an alliance with him and in the most gracious manner invited him to visit him in Constantinople. Athanaric very gladly consented and as he entered the royal city exclaimed in wonder, "Lo, now I see what I have often heard of with unbelieving ears," meaning the great and famous city. Turning his eyes hither and thither, he marvelled as he beheld the situation of the city, the coming and going of the ships, the splendid walls, and the people of divers nations gathered like a flood of waters streaming from different regions into one basin.[3]

From this passage can be derived the view that there was a pact between Theodosius and the Visigoths, and that King Athanaric visited Constantinople: so much is fact. But suppose that we seek to use the passage as a source to answer the questions, "What was the precise nature of the relationship between Goths and Byzantines? What did the Goths think of the Empire when they came into direct contact with it?" Here a naive use of the passage in question would lead us to assert at once that "Theodosius fully appreciated the dangers of the Gothic problem, and he pursued unremittingly a policy of conciliation and friendship," as a modern historian in fact concluded; while the Goths, in their turn, were completely overawed by the majesty and grandeur of the Empire, freely acknowledging the superior greatness of the Byzantines. But here, the student who recognizes that primary-source data cannot be taken at face value, as absolutely factual evidence, should be able to see that in reading the report of Jordanes he is encountering the opinion of a Christian apologist for the Empire,

---

[3] Jordanes, *The Gothic History of Jordanes*, tr. C. C. Mierow (Princeton: Princeton University Press, 1915), p. 91.

who, although he himself was a Goth, seeks in his history to give glory to the Goths by having them take on the mantle of ancient Rome. Thus Theodosius emerges as a great and noble figure in this source because he restored greatness to the Empire and because he was a Christian ruler who was strong in his opposition to the enemies of the Church. Therefore Jordanes naturally attributes to him *traditional* Roman qualities of great emperors, such as a desire for a peaceful world order. It is not possible to learn from the passage whether *in fact* Theodosius truly desired a compact between Goths and Romans; but Jordanes feels that as a model Roman emperor this is what Theodosius *should* have desired. Similarly, the passage does not tell us what the Goths *in fact* felt upon their first encounter with Constantinople, but rather what Jordanes feels they *should* have felt because of the traditional greatness of the Roman Empire. These observations can be checked and confirmed by reference to other passages in Jordanes.

A general and vitally important principle is now clear. *Primary sources are not only sources of data or fact; they also contain opinions or value judgments, and the historian who seeks to use the primary source as evidence must be aware of the opinionated nature of all primary evidence and must evaluate it.* Primary sources cannot simply be used at face value, but must be explained and analyzed in terms of validity, accuracy, and point of view. This means that the historian must use his own inferences even in determining what is factual material, and no factual material can have any meaning in an historical study if it remains unexamined and unexplained.

Nothing about a primary source can be taken for granted; indeed, even the existence of the source itself is a problem to be examined (Why was it created? What end did it seem to serve in its own era? Is it authentic or a forgery?). Perhaps the clearest, albeit the most extreme, way to state this principle is to say that in a primary source, the only aspect that is factual is the physical existence of the source itself, e.g., the words of the text in a written source or the visual appearance of a painting. But what this existence means, what the source signifies as evidence for the history of a period, is already a matter of inference and judgment on the part of the modern historian. In the example from Jordanes, it is certainly a fact that Jordanes *says* that Theodosius "desired a compact between Goths and Romans," but whether or not it is indeed true that Theodosius had such a desire is something that the modern historian who uses Jordanes as a source must decide for himself by critical evaluation and well-informed judgment and the use, if they are available, of other primary sources for this problem.

While primary sources contain opinions and judgments, these are somewhat different in their nature from the opinions and judgments made by later historians. Primary opinions at the least represent views that were current during the period being studied, while secondary opinions are inevitably after the fact and inescapably reflect the changes in values that have occurred between the period being studied and the historian's own age. This is the point implied when we said that it is a fact that Jordanes thought *something* about Theodosius; such an observation can help a modern historian gain some perspective on the values that typify the era he is studying and thus may help him to develop his conception of that era. The existence of primary opinion, then, is to be noted by the history student as a warning against naive prima facie acceptance of primary sources as depositories of fact. But at the same time, recognition of such primary opinion may be of the greatest help to the student who attempts to present a valid picture of the ideas and culture of a previous age. Primary opinions should not be ignored by historians or dismissed as "old-fashioned prejudices" but should be carefully analyzed in the intellectual context of the period under study.

While secondary sources frequently do offer the historian a great deal of factual material, because they report data from primary sources, the secondary source should not be chiefly used for its factual contents. Ultimately, any historian who seeks to achieve a serious analysis of a previous era will want to know the primary sources from that era directly, and not at second hand; and knowing that historians' points of view always color their reporting of "facts," he would mistrust any such report taken only from a secondary source. Students preparing papers, who tend to take all of their supporting evidence from secondary sources, or even worse, from textbooks, would do well to keep this principle in mind.

The most important use that can be made of secondary sources is to read them for the points of view they present, for their inferences. To use a term current among professional historians, students should read secondary sources "historiographically." The inferential relationships drawn between facts by historians are conditioned by their assumptions about cause and effect in history. To the extent that two historians will have different conceptions of significant causes, they will see a different pattern of relationships between facts. *Historiography is the study of historians' assumptions and values about men and society that condition their inferential judgments. To separate fact from inference, to assess the validity of inferences, to derive meaning from secondary sources, the student has to think about history and read historical works historiographically.*

In this way, the student planning to write on a given subject will find his mind and imagination stimulated by the encounter with other points of view about the subject. He will realize that his explanation of the facts relevant to his subject does not exist in a vacuum but must serve as a challenge or a complement to other learned interpretations and views on corollary subjects that the student has not examined directly for himself. The historian whose main emphasis is on political struggles in the Reformation era will welcome a careful discussion of sixteenth-century theological controversies as a supplement to his understanding of dynamic forces during the period, although before using such a study, the historian would first carefully determine whether its conclusions seemed logical and whether it gave a thorough sample of the available primary sources. But in either case, whether the secondary source is being examined as another point of view on the historian's main subject or whether the source is being used as a treatment of a corollary supporting topic, it is the inferences, the interpretive ideas, of the secondary source that hold the chief interest for the historian.

This being so, some cautioning statements about the use of secondary sources must be made emphatically to prevent naive acceptance of such sources as repositories of untrammeled truth. The first is the warning, already brought up in earlier discussion, that very frequently secondary inferences will be presented as if they were factual; inferential statements and factual data will appear side by side in the course of a narrative, and it is for the student who uses the source to determine which statements are inferences by the author and hence open to question. The following passage describing an important early nineteenth-century German historian makes a number of judgments that are never identified as such:

Though Böhmer never wrote narrative history, his views were in no way concealed. He was equally convinced that lack of religion was the greatest evil of his time and that Protestantism was unable to reconstruct society on a Christian basis. He yearned for a reunited, visible Church. Brentano said of his friend, "He is more Catholic than I." The Reformation, he declared, was the greatest misfortune of the German nation, and he never forgave it for subjecting the Church to the State. The Church was the noblest and most magnificent product of history. In the conflict of Empire and Papacy he was on the side of the latter. "I cannot bear the contemptuous judgments of venerable institutions, the belittling of the Church and its blessed activity." He left money for historical work to be carried on "in a Roman Catholic sense." In his last illness he declared "I have always regarded the Church as the Mother to whom we owe the best we possess. May it regain its lost power over men's minds." He was a child of the Middle Ages born out of due time, an orphan in a strange world. . . . Böhmer was one of the most original personalities among nineteenth-century historians. His judgments of men and institutions were biased, his technique was radically imperfect, and the "Regesta" [a work which Böhmer edited] had to be edited afresh by a team of specialists; but he ranks with Stein and Pertz among the heroes of the *Monumenta* [Germaniae Historica].[4]

A student who knows that historians make judgments should be able to recognize the assumptions underlying the inferences in this passage. Gooch's view of Böhmer assumes that nineteenth-century German historical writing at its best was "scientific," impartial, highly technical, and not religious and subjective in slant. This inference has much to recommend it, but a different assumption would lead to the view that Böhmer was highly *typical* of his era because he represents the Romantic, sentimental, Catholic, and subjective attitude to the Middle Ages. Thus the Romantic tendency, which Gooch feels to be a detriment in Böhmer's work, can be seen as the quality that exactly identifies Böhmer as a typical thinker of his own time.

The student in reading Gooch's interpretation must be aware that it *is* interpretation, or inference, and must ask whether different assumptions, leading to quite different conclusions, can be applied to determine the significance of the facts. Nothing frustrates and bores a teacher more than to read a student's paper in which the conclusions of secondary works are presented unsupported and unexamined as if they were unquestionable facts. *You do not prove anything by simply quoting another historian's conclusions.* You have to reconsider the weight of the evidence, the process of reasoning, and the underlying assumptions of the writer. History has no absolute authority; the inferences drawn by an eminent and famous historian are not *ipso facto* more valid than those drawn by a college freshman.

You must be especially careful about historical opinions that are so commonplace that they have been accepted as inviolable

[4] G. P. Gooch, *History and Historians in the 19th Century* (Boston: Beacon Press, 1959), p. 66.

truth and inevitable assumption. The more fashionable and cliché-ridden an historical judgment, the more traditional a general inference, the more you must be on your guard. Such clichés influence all dependent judgments on a particular era and inhibit a fundamental reconsideration of basic trends and movements. As an example, almost every book written about ancient Greek history takes it for granted that the fifth century B.C. was the "Golden Age" of Athenian culture; and this operating principle predetermines interpretations of Greek drama, art, and higher thought prior to and after the fifth century. But if we were to assume that the earlier Homeric or later Hellenistic ages, while different in quality, were equally "golden" in a cultural sense, we would have a very different assumption on which to make judgments about the cultural history of Greece; and fifth-century Athenian culture would be viewed in a different perspective.

These cautions do not detract from what has been said earlier about the importance and necessity of the historian's inferential judgments. The facts only give us the A, B, C, D, E, etc.—the building blocks of history. The inferences establish the relationship between these particular facts and provide the structure of history. The inferences relate A to B and E to C and D to A and E to B, etc., establishing a vast complex network of causality. *The greater the number of inferential lines we can draw between the particular facts, the better the history we will write.*

4 / How to Use
Primary Sources

What kinds of primary-source material are available to students of history? The variety is almost infinite. One might say that history is an explanation of everything that has happened, and so, in a sense, everything is grist for the historian's mill. The student of seventeenth-century culture, for example, should ideally know the sources for Puritanism, Baroque music, and calculus as well as he knows the Petition of Right of 1628. This is a principle we hope every serious student will keep firmly fixed in his mind as he develops his study habits; too often historical work has confined itself to the domains of politics, economics, sociology, and biography, overlooking other aspects of culture as "not part of the discipline."

The kinds of primary sources usually encountered can be grouped into categories that reveal the nature and circumstances of their creation. *Some kinds of material are the result of immediate, everyday concerns; while others are carefully designed, sometimes with posterity even more in mind than a contemporary audience.* In the first of these categories—*documents of an immediate nature*—one finds the records of active people in everyday situations, preserved in the form of memoranda, bills, deeds, charters, records of parliaments and congresses, newspaper reports, pamphlets and broadsides, popular verse and graffiti, "snap-shots" (rather than posed photographs), and the like.

In the second category, *theoretical treatises,* the contents always reflect sober and careful planning, design and careful build-up of argument. Whatever the subject—be it political thought, economic planning, law, theology, cosmology, biological ideas, aesthetics—it is expected that the concern of the writer is for values that are deeper, more far-reaching, more "eternal" than is the case with evidence of an immediate nature. Immediate documents may certainly *reflect* deep-seated values and careful planning (as, for instance, Cavour's diplomatic correspondence shows his plans and his dreams for Italy), but the whole explicit purpose of a theoretical treatise is to develop and clarify some fundamental value the author considers to be true.

The same distinction in circumstance of creation and intended audience exists in reference to two further categories of primary sources. Both of these categories involve *narrative* accounts by contemporaries of the events and ideas described in the source. Sometimes such accounts were carefully planned, formal in nature, and often intended for a public audience, while in other cases they were incidental, spontaneous, and intended only for private use. The former category, the *contemporary formal account,* includes chronicles, annals, histories, autobiographies, contemporary character sketches, and the like. The latter category, *contemporary incidental accounts,* includes letters, eyewitness sketches and notes, private journals and diaries, and other such records.

Statistical data is evidence of a peculiar kind; it is not directly a text or record left from a past age, but is rather extrapolated from such texts and records. Because of this, students should be very cautious in dealing with statistics; while they can look quite factual, the methods of gathering them may affect the sense they convey. The example of the temperatures in the last chapter and the questions that we raised about using such data may serve as a reminder here. The information provided by statistics is inferential rather than factual. You must guard against the ever-present modern temptation to regard statistics as absolutely true and irrefutable facts.

Finally, among the most ignored categories of primary sources are those from the fields of *literature* and *nonverbal materials*. In order to avoid useless terminological disputes, we will let the student recognize by his own good common sense what kind of materials belong in the domain of literature. Literary materials are invaluable for offering insight into tastes, temperaments, styles, and ideas of an age, as long as the literary work is interpreted with historical perspective rather than in terms of modern ahistorical criticism. Nonverbal materials include some that scholars have traditionally recognized as legitimate sources, e.g., the evidence offered by coins and by archeology, but historians should give more attention to some kinds of nonverbal artifacts that many recent writers have altogether neglected, especially painting, sculpture, architecture, and music.

In dealing with primary sources, there are several basic rules and considerations you must observe. First of all, the student must be sure he is prepared fully to understand a primary source, i.e., that he is able to know what its words mean and can grasp the context of references to which the source alludes either explicitly or by implication. This point is by no means as obvious as it might seem. Any record that comes to a student from an age earlier than his own speaks to him in a language very different from his own, even though he might think that he is a native speaker of the tongue. Even English of the nineteenth century had a vocabulary, and especially a pattern of connotations, that sometimes differs drastically from midtwentieth-century English; and the student who plans to read Victorian documents needs a philological awareness of these differences. The problem is complicated further when the source is more remote in time; Shakespeare's English is much closer to Chaucer's than to our own, and yet too often we persist in reading Elizabethan literature as if it were written in contemporary terms.

This philological need becomes even more acute if the language of the primary source is one not native to the historian, and we would certainly claim that any advanced study of history is impossible without a fairly good knowledge of the language of the primary sources. Remember, this does not mean merely an understanding of the modern equivalent of the language of the source, but a philological grasp of the language as contemporary with the sources being studied. One who wishes to understand the Renaissance in Italy must know and understand the connotations of fifteenth-century Italian.

Understanding *explicit* allusions made by primary sources means that if a source mentions some contemporary figure, place, or event the modern student should know enough of the historical context of the age to be able to identify such references. *Do not read history blindly.* If you come across an allusion you do not understand, take pains to look it up.

Implicit understanding of the sources means that the student should always try to read primary sources in the light of values contemporary with the source itself. In this way he will considerably further his insight into the significance of the sources. This is perhaps especially true when reading incidental and immediate documents, where the values are very frequently only implied, not clearly stated. It is equally important to keep this point in mind when dealing with the opinions present in primary sources. To understand the importance of some primary opinion, the modern historian must *not* simply relate such values to his own modern ones, or even teleologically to values of a succeeding age (is Machiavelli's *The Prince* important because its ideas supposedly anticipate modern totalitarianism?). He should rather try to relate primary opinions to the whole of their contemporary context, in order to gain a just appreciation of the role of the primary source in its own age.

In this regard the beginning student would do well to consider the following warning by an eminent historian of literature:

Our judgments of value are characteristically dependent on attitudes peculiar to our own place and time. If we universalize these attitudes, as though they were Platonic realities, and assume that they have a validity for all time, we turn history into a mirror which is of significance to us only insofar as we may perceive in it what appear to be foreshadowings of ourselves arising from reconstructions of the evidence based on our own values. And when this happens, history, although it may seem to flatter us with the consoling message "Thou art the fairest of all," becomes merely an instrument for the cultivation of our own prejudices. We learn nothing from it that we could not learn from the world around us.[1]

Lord Acton, a great nineteenth-century liberal Catholic scholar, took a somewhat different stand: he warned that it is the historian's first duty "not to debase the moral currency." By this he meant that the historian must always point out what is good and what is evil in the actions of men in the past. But in order to do this justly, we must first establish what they actually did; and we must also have an understanding of what the men of a particular era in the past considered to be right and wrong. Therefore, in reading primary sources we have to consider the conduct and opinions of the people described for us in the light of *their* society, their system of values, *not our own*. We must constantly be on the lookout for statements in primary sources that indicate a particular society's system of values. We may *ultimately* decide that the values themselves are no good and that the whole society and culture were morally corrupt. It is possible that we will come to this conclusion; but more often we will perceive that there is much to be said both for and against a system of values that

[1] D. W. Robertson, Jr., *A Preface to Chaucer* (Princeton, N.J.: Princeton University Press, 1962), p. 3.

happens to be rather different from our own, especially when this system of values pertains to a society that is alien to our own form of social and political organization.

To put the same argument in more abstract terms: *when we read primary sources, we have to be, at least for the moment, to some degree moral relativists rather than moral absolutists.* We have to consider the ideals and actions as they are portrayed for us in the source material relative to the values of the society involved, even though in making judgments later, we may decide that we are justified in condemning them. To read primary sources with an inflexibly present-day scheme of moral values is to close one's eyes to a possibility of coming to appreciate the values and achievements of the society and people we are studying. We would in the latter case be prejudging what our sources have to tell us and not questioning them at all.

A common sign of the failure of a modern writer to adopt historically relative values is the use of simple chronological terms as critical value judgments. Rejecting a pattern of twelfth-century thought because it is "medieval" or favoring the revolutionaries of 1848 because they are "forward-looking" represents the impoverishment of the historical imagination. If you do not read the primary sources with an open mind and an intention to get inside the minds of the writers and look at things the way *they* saw them, you are wasting your time. History is a humane discipline because it presents for us the wonderful complexity and variety of human aspirations, faith and hope. The truly liberal historian approaches the study of his source material with the conviction that there may have been another era, another society, whose ideals and mode of life were as good as or even better than his own.

Turning to a more mundane, but no less important, rule for the use of primary sources, *you have to read the entire text of the particular source, whether it is five lines or five hundred pages in length.* You cannot evaluate the significance of a source and judge what information it is imparting without considering the work as a whole. Jumping to a conclusion from study of only part of the source while pretending to derive your thesis from the whole text makes you susceptible to gross error and convicts you of intellectual dishonesty. Everyone is familiar with the way a statement taken out of context can be given a significance and meaning never intended by its author. Reading only part of the source can make you a victim of this kind of distortion. This can be avoided by taking an entire text into consideration; then the relative weight of different passages is clear, and the relationship between one point and the next can be seen.

Very often undergraduates will study primary sources in anthologized collections. These have only selections from a variety of sources and not the entire texts. In this case the student should assume that the editor of the collection of source material has exercised good judgment and intellectual honesty in selecting passages that typically convey the theme of the whole work, and that nothing has been distorted by lifting material out of context. Given the need to survey long periods and the high cost of copies of complete texts, these anthologies are indispensable to the study of history at the college level. You should read each selection as if it were a complete, self-contained text and elicit the meaning and significance of the entire pre-edited selection.

It is salutary, however, for both teachers and students to remember that studying anthologized selections of primary sources is ultimately no substitute for examining these sources in their original, full-length versions. At least history majors and graduate students, as far as possible, should make use of the original complete texts when doing research for essays and papers.

Of course no one can read *all* sources at full length; when one refers to a secondary book that has a quotation from some manuscript otherwise unpublished, he is allowing the author of the secondary source to excerpt passages and is dependent on the judgment of that author about what is important in the primary source. The real danger is that students are more and more influenced to accept excerpts as enough, to feel that knowing excerpts is equivalent to knowing whole texts; if such an attitude really develops, then the handing on of clichés of evidence, in which the same passage is cited again and again, will flourish like a weed. The only possibility for absolute accuracy in interpreting a primary source is to read the entire source, and students are urged to do so as much as possible.

The use of primary sources by students of ancient and medieval history on the one side and by modern historians on the other will be somewhat different in method because of the very great difference in quantity of available records. For ancient history and for medieval history down to about 1300 A.D. there is actually a dearth of source material. The ravages of time and atrocious neglect in the keeping of records before the nineteenth century have resulted in the survival to us of only a portion of the records of life during those early centuries. Even some literary works have disappeared. If not freshmen, at least advanced college students can actually exhaust available sources on a great many of the problems of ancient and medieval history, provided they can read the languages in which they were written.

Beginning in the late thirteenth century governments at all levels began to use more written records than before; there was a sharp increase in literacy, and a much greater proportion of the written records has survived. When the nineteenth century is reached, the mass of material that is available (considering only printed works and leaving aside manuscripts preserved in archives) for use as primary sources is overwhelming. The novice student can readily confirm this fact by going to his college library and taking a quick look at the enormous volumes of nineteenth-century newspapers and legislative records.

The student of ancient and medieval history, therefore, has to begin his work by asking the question: What materials have survived? Do we have the primary sources to answer the questions I am asking? The student of modern history, at least for the period after 1800, can assume that the primary sources do exist (although not necessarily conveniently accessible) to answer any questions he may want to put to the sources. The modern student has to begin his research by asking: Where in the vast records of modern history can I find the fullest and most reliable information on the problem I am investigating?

Although the ancient and medieval historian on the one hand and the modern historian on the other approach their sources differently, in both instances they proceed in a disciplined and organized way. Research in primary sources does not mean idly picking up the first text that attracts one's eye. Rather it involves establishing the sources that are available or that can best answer the problem, and putting a series of well-defined questions to the material so as to elicit the information needed to illuminate the problem under investigation.

A PRACTICAL EXERCISE IN THE EXPLICATION OF PRIMARY SOURCES

The questioning of primary sources in order to extrapolate historical evidence from the material is an art and discipline in which the student can only become expert through long practice. The method of explication is best taught in the classroom, but it is possible to set down some general rules and commonly used questions that will be applicable to a great many, although certainly by no means all, of the primary sources you will encounter in your work.

In general, *the eliciting of significance from primary sources follows a fourfold technique, whatever the length and character of the source:*

1. Bring to your analysis of the source texts as full a knowledge of the period as possible and a *tentative* hypothesis, or at least expectation, on the significance of the passage you are going to study.

2. Keeping your hypothesis in suspension, read the text carefully from beginning to end until a pattern of meaning and significance appears.

3. Compare your original hypothesis with the pattern of significance that has arisen from your close reading of the text. If the pattern in no way confirms the tentative hypothesis, you should abandon the latter entirely. On the other hand if the hypothesis and pattern overlap to a degree but do not coincide in other respects, you should consider whether the pattern you have perceived is totally or just partly a valid interpretation of the significance and meaning of the text. You may need to read the whole text again, or several times, in order to test the full validity of your new interpretation.

4. Use the general pattern of meaning that you have established as the key to interpreting every detail in the source. Go over the text paragraph by paragraph and sentence by sentence, and work out all the implications of the general interpretation. Every idea and reference in the text must be related in some way to the general pattern of significance that you have perceived.

In this way you will arrive at a general interpretation of the source that integrates every detailed statement in the text into a meaningful thesis.

It will be helpful to the student to bear in mind a number of commonly perceived patterns that historians find in different kinds of primary sources. One or another of this common stock of patterns is frequently employed as the key motif or general interpretation that imparts a coherent and integrated unity of historical significance to the detailed parts of a particular text. In order to make these source patterns or motifs easily comprehensible, it is best to list them with one or two examples in each case.

I. FORMAL TREATISES

Commonly perceived patterns or significant motifs that are used to interpret formal treatises are "means versus ends," "the author's unresolved inner conflicts," "underlying assumptions," "the implications of rhetoric," "doctrine as psychological biography," and "doctrine as intellectual biography."

a. Means versus Ends

EXAMPLE: This pattern of meaning, or motif, is commonly used to interpret Machiavelli's *The Prince*, written at the beginning of the sixteenth century. In this work the Florentine statesman Niccolò Machiavelli delineates the apparently amoral principles of power politics that he saw at work in the courts of northern Italy and in the French monarchy and that became synonymous with his name. But was Machiavelli a "Machiavellian"? Was he advocating a new kind of statecraft based entirely on the self-interested demands of power and oblivious to moral principles? No, it can be argued, this is a false view of *The Prince*, because in the concluding part of his treatise the Florentine writer shows himself to be a fervent Italian nationalist. He is writing at a time when the Italian city-states are becoming subservient to the French and Hapsburg monarchies, and what he wants is that "some individual might be appointed by God for her [Italy's] redemption." He thinks that the time is "propitious in Italy for a new prince, . . . a prudent and capable man to introduce a new system that would do honor to himself and good to the mass of the people."[1] The meaning of *The Prince*, therefore, is that Machiavelli envisages a national redeemer, a man of justice and honor who will save Italy from civil war and invasion; and in order to do this, the prince must be "prudent and capable," i.e., he must be able to use the harsh power-politics methods of other rulers of the period. Machiavelli, then, is a great idealist who is yet aware of the hard realities of current politics and therefore advocates harsh means in order to gain noble ends.

There are other possible interpretations of *The Prince*, of course, but the means-versus-ends motif gives a pattern of meaning to the whole work and is highly plausible.

---

[1] Niccolò Machiavelli, *The Prince*, tr. Luigi Ricci, rev. E. Vincent, in Machiavelli, *The Prince and the Discourses*, ed. Max Lerner (New York: Modern Library, Inc., 1950), pp. 94–95.

b. Unresolved Inner Conflicts

EXAMPLE: It has become a rather tiresome cliché for historians to find unresolved inner conflicts in the author's mind reflected in a formal treatise. Nevertheless there are treatises where such a conflict can be genuinely perceived and can be used to provide general significance for the entire work. An obvious example of the applicability of this kind of interpretation is John Stuart Mill's *Utilitarianism,* published in 1861. As a professed disciple of the philosophical radical Jeremy Bentham, Mill begins by setting up a standard of ethics entirely in accord with Bentham's intensely individualistic moral philosophy. In fact, Mill's formulation of ethical criteria is virtually a quotation from Bentham:

The creed which accepts, as the foundation of morals, Utility, or the Greatest-Happiness Principle, holds that actions are right in proportion as they tend to promote happiness, wrong as they tend to produce the reverse of happiness. By happiness is intended pleasure and the absence of pain; by unhappiness, pain and the privation of pleasure.[2]

But later on in his treatise Mill distinguishes between the happiness of different kinds of people and greatly modifies Bentham's atomistic principle of utility by favoring the proposition "better a human being dissatisfied than a pig satisfied, better a Socrates dissatisfied than a fool satisfied." He strongly denies that "the difference between the Just and the Expedient [is] a merely imaginary distinction." Mill concludes "that justice is a more sacred thing than policy. . . . Justice is a name for certain classes of moral rules."[3] It is apparent that Mill is caught in a conflict between two quite different theories of ethics, one a genuinely utilitarian theory and the other a doctrine of hierarchy of values, which resembles the moral philosophy of Plato.

[2] John Stuart Mill, *Utilitarianism,* in *The Philosophy of John Stuart Mill,* ed. Marshall Cohen (New York: The Modern Library, Inc., 1961), p. 330.
[3] *Ibid.,* p. 391.

Once this view is established the historian can use it in a variety of ways. He can speculate about how Mill got into this intellectual conundrum. (For example, he wanted to remain loyal to Bentham on the one hand, but his education had introduced him to a very different philosophical tradition; he tried to integrate and synthesize these two philosophies but was unable to do so.) Taking note of the additional fact that Mill was the leading theorist of mid-Victorian liberalism, the historian can use *Utilitarianism* as symptomatic of a fundamental tension or contradiction within the liberal mind. On the one side, mid-Victorian liberalism was heavily inspired by the individualism and pragmatism of Bentham's Enlightenment philosophy; but on the other side, it was powerfully molded by the absolutist ethics upheld by the English Nonconformist conscience. There are of course several other ways of interpreting Mill's treatise, such as a biographical approach. The inner-conflict motif, while a little obvious, is nevertheless a viable explication; and it is particularly convincing because it fits in with the general pattern of mid-Victorian liberal thought.

c. Underlying Assumptions

EXAMPLES: Occasionally you will encounter a formal treatise in which the author makes a passing remark whose tone is sharply at variance with the ostensible theme of the work. This passing remark can be used to elicit the author's underlying assumptions, and implicit rather than explicit doctrine. The whole work can then be examined in terms of the implicit assumptions and be interpreted in a way that relates the explicit theory to the underlying doctrine. An example of this motif would be an interpretation of Walter Bagehot's *The English Constitution,* a treatise that illustrates midnineteenth-century liberal views on the institutions of the English government. In the introduction to the second edition of his treatise, which was added after the passing of the Reform Bill of 1867, Bagehot offers the characteristically liberal doctrine that the House of Commons should be given great superiority over the House of Lords.[4] This explicit argument would seem to make Bagehot a strong democrat. Bagehot also discusses the possible implications of the recent parliamentary legislation that greatly extended the suffrage in England. In the course of this discussion he lets fall a remark that would startle and outrage a midtwentieth-century liberal:

As a theoretical writer I can venture to say, what no elected member of Parliament, Conservative or Liberal, can venture to say, that I am exceedingly afraid of the ignorant multitude of the new constituencies.[5]

This passing remark places an entirely different perspective on the whole treatise and reveals Bagehot's strongly middle-class commitment and his profound fear of extensive democracy. This underlying assumption would have to take a central place in the general interpretation of *The English Constitution,* and the work would have to be viewed as indicating the deep division between liberal doctrine and democratic ideology in midnineteenth-century England.

Another treatise (which is also a government document) whose interpretation depends heavily upon the underlying-assumptions motif is the famous *Report* on Canadian and Imperial government published by Lord Durham in 1839. This work is commonly viewed as the embodiment of the new ideals of liberal empire that led to self-government for Canada and other European-settled colonies and to the modern British Commonwealth. This view is substantially true, but it is important to note the comment that Durham makes when he comes to deal with the French population in Lower Canada (Quebec):

I entertain no doubts as to the national character which must be given to Lower Canada; it must be that of the British Empire, that of the

[4] Walter Bagehot, *The English Constitution,* rev. ed. (Boston: Little, Brown & Co., 1873), pp. 20–21.
[5] *Ibid.,* p. 23.

majority of the population of British America, that of the great race which must, in the lapse of no long period of time, be predominant over the whole North American continent.[6]

This statement is loaded with a racist philosophy and a belief in the manifest destiny of the British race to rule the whole North American continent. In interpreting Lord Durham's report, we would have to emphasize this underlying assumption. The general interpretation would be that while Durham takes a liberal view on some aspects of colonial self-government, he is at the same time devoted to a racist and expansionist doctrine that is commonly associated with the so-called "new imperialism" of the late nineteenth century rather than with the liberal imperialism of the 1830's and 1840's. By emphasizing this implicit motif in the Durham report, the historian would have evidence to support a claim that the sharp distinction often drawn between Durham's liberal imperialism and the later new imperialism is not altogether tenable and that the two brands of imperialism have very much in common.

d. The Implications of Rhetoric

EXAMPLE: An interpretive motif can be established by concentrating on the quality of the author's rhetoric. Emotionally charged words can be shown to form an ideological pattern, and then the whole treatise can be interpreted in terms of this ideology. Working out the implications of rhetoric is especially useful if the treatise does not take a straightforward, didactic form. The significant theme of a pamphlet addressed to a wide audience on some current problem, or what purports to be an historical account but is actually a polemical work, can be extrapolated by concentration on the author's choice of words.

An example of the latter case would be a rhetorical examina-

[6] Carl Stephenson and F. G. Marcham, eds. *Sources of English Constitutional History* (New York: Harper & Brothers, 1937), p. 778.

tion of *The Origins of Prussianism,* a pseudohistorical polemic by Heinrich von Treitschke, the midnineteenth-century apologist for Prussia and advocate of a Big Germany. Treitschke is ostensibly giving an account of the medieval Teutonic knights:

> What portion of the past continues to live as history in the soul of this people? . . . There is hardly even an outline sketch to convey to the mind of a South German boy an intimation of the most stupendous and fruitful occurrence of the later Middle Ages—the northward and eastward rush of the German spirit and the formidable activities of our people as conqueror, teacher, discipliner of its neighbors. . . .
>
> What thrills us inhabitants of petty German particularist States . . . is the profound doctrine of the supreme value of the State, and of civic subordination to the purposes of State, which the Teutonic Knights perhaps proclaimed more loudly and clearly than do any other voices speaking to us from the German past.[7]

The historical value of Treitschke's work is very small if we wish to understand the outlook of the medieval Teutonic knights. The use of his work is in the form of a primary source for the ideology of the new militant German nationalism. Although a south German rather than a Prussian himself, Treitschke had completely absorbed the mystical statist philosophy that was used to justify Prussia's advance to hegemony in Germany. "Soul of this people," "German spirit," "petty German particularist States," "supreme value of the State," "civic subordination to the purposes of State"—here is the rhetoric of the new German ideology that Treitschke is metaphorically expounding in the form of a glorification of the Teutonic Order.

e. Doctrine as Psychological Biography

EXAMPLE: A formal treatise can be interpreted so as to provide evidence for the author's biography. This is a controversial

[7] Heinrich von Treitschke, *The Origins of Prussianism,* tr. E. and C. Paul (London: George Allen & Unwin Ltd., 1942), pp. 17–18, 21.

method, and it tends to presuppose a Freudian psychoanalytic view of personality. But if this psychological assumption can be made, the historian can then interpret statements in a treatise in such a way as to show a coincidence with the author's biography and to reflect his subconscious feelings. Susceptible to this treatment of doctrine as psychological biography is the following statement from Adolf Hitler's *Mein Kampf:*

It suffices to state here that from my earliest youth I came to a conviction which never deserted me, but on the contrary, grew stronger and stronger: that the protection of the German race presumed the destruction of Austria, and further, that national feeling is in no way identical with dynastic patriotism. . . . Even then I had drawn the necessary deductions from this realization: an intense love for my native German-Austrian country and a bitter hatred against the "Austrian" state.[8]

A Freudian treatment of Hitler's remarks could run as follows: the passage is shot through with hatred for Austria whose destruction is desired, and this hatred is tied in with Hitler's youth, Austria is identified with the unhappiness of Hitler's early life, and the destruction of Austria is the way of satisfying deep-seated feelings of remorse and guilt derived from some event in his early childhood. Austria could also be seen as identifying with Hitler's father, presumably a harsh and cruel man for whom the adult Hitler has only a bitter hatred. The German race on the other hand, or a united German-Austrian country, represents Hitler's mother, for whom he has an intense love. In this way the extract from *Mein Kampf* can be given meaning in terms of psychological biography. It should be noted that this kind of psychoanalytical interpretation is still eschewed by the majority of scholars, but it is becoming more acceptable in academic circles.

[8] Adolf Hitler, *Mein Kampf,* ed. John Chamberlain *et al.* (New York: Reynal and Hitchcock, 1939), pp. 21–23.

f. Doctrine as Intellectual Biography

EXAMPLE: The use of doctrine as evidence for psychological biography is controversial; the interpretation of theoretical and polemical statements as source material for intellectual biography is a very common and academically orthodox way to elicit a pattern of meaning from a treatise. Intellectual biography concerns itself with the life of an important thinker and tries to show the steps by which he arrived at his novel doctrine. One way of doing this is to go back to the theorist's early work, before he published the treatise that made his reputation, and to find in the early work reflections of his struggles to formulate and refine his great idea. The most exciting intellectual biography is one that shows the famous thinker making a revolutionary discovery in the heat of conflict over some immediate and practical issue. As an example of this kind of interpretation of a primary source we can examine *The Economic Consequences of the Peace* by John Maynard Keynes, who was later to become the most influential economic theorist of the twentieth century. Keynes' book, which was published in 1920, can be characterized as a formal treatise in economic theory and also as a document of an immediate nature because its chief aim is polemical, and it was written in response to a very particular problem: the lack of economic vision—in Keynes' view—on the part of the authors of the peace settlement at the end of the First World War.

Keynes' work is susceptible to a variety of interpretations, but one that is entirely viable is treatment of it as evidence for his intellectual biography. *The Economic Consequences of the Peace* can be given significance by emphasizing the ideas in it that anticipate later major Keynesian contributions to economic theory. Keynes' idea of "macroeconomics," i.e., that a national economy has to be considered as a whole, in terms of "aggregates" such as wages, rates of interest, and demand, rather than in terms of individual economic units, is plainly evident when he attempts to estimate Germany's potential to pay reparations.[9] A constant theme in *The Economic Consequences of the Peace* is the characteristic Keynesian idea that government, because of its tremendous power over supply and demand, productivity and utilization of resources, must play a major role in regulating economic activity:

Unless, therefore, the present Allies are prepared to encourage the importation of German products, a substantial increase in total volume can only be effected by the wholesale swamping of neutral markets. . . .

. . . If the Allies were to "nurse" the trade and industry of Germany for a period of five or ten years, supplying her with large loans, and with ample shipping, food, and raw materials during the period, building up markets for her, and deliberately applying all their resources and goodwill to making her the greatest industrial nation in Europe, if not in the world, a substantially larger sum could probably be extracted thereafter [in reparations].[10]

Elsewhere in the work Keynes reveals his great fear of inflation and his abhorrence of money manipulation and the debasing of the currency:

The inflationism of the currency systems of Europe has proceeded to extraordinary length. The various belligerent governments, unable, or too timid or too shortsighted to secure from loans or taxes the resources they required, have printed notes for the balance. . . . The presumption of a spurious value for the currency, by the force of law expressed in the regulation of prices, contains in itself, however, the seeds of final economic decay, and soon dries up the sources of ultimate supply.[11]

The Economic Consequences of the Peace can be used to reveal a milestone in Keynes' development as an economic theorist

[9] See for example the analysis of Germany's potential for annual payments in terms of productivity, exports, and imports and "the aggregate wealth-producing capacity of the country": John Maynard Keynes, *The Economic Consequences of the Peace* (New York: Harcourt, Brace and Company, Inc., 1920), pp. 187–88.

[10] *Ibid.*, pp. 196, 203.

[11] *Ibid.*, pp. 238–40.

It can be interpreted to substantiate the claim that in 1919 Keynes had already outlined the major aspects of his theory that would make him famous and influential in the 1930's. It also could be used to give substance to the view that Keynes' experience as an economic advisor to the British delegation at the peace conference forced him to clarify and refine his thinking and take a public stand on important issues of the day. Very frequently the early works of an important theorist in any field can be analyzed in a similar manner.

II. CONTEMPORARY FORMAL HISTORY

The historical accounts of a movement or series of events written by contemporaries to these events require a special kind of explication. A modern historian can derive factual information from contemporary formal history, but if at all possible he should only do so when the data are confirmed by other kinds of sources. This caution is necessary because the contemporary historian has molded his portrayal of the events by his own assumptions on the nature of causality, personality, social structure, etc. These assumptions are, however, of great importance to the historian of ideas. *The prime use of a contemporary formal history is its revelation of the pattern of ideas and judgments about the nature of historical change that prevails in the era in which the work was written.* At least until the eighteenth century, and even to a certain degree thereafter, all events described by an historian were made to conform to an image of reality that governed all social thought. Historians did not argue from the particular to the general; rather they made particular events and people conform to the traditional types or patterns. This is why historians of ideas examine all formal history written before the eighteenth century, and even more recent works, in order to establish what is called the author's *typology*. A great twentieth-century historian of literature, Eric Auerbach, in his truly seminal work *Mimesis,* has discussed the development of the image of reality in Western thought by making extensive use of historians' typologies.

EXAMPLES: The central role of typology in contemporary formal history and the need for the student to make typological analysis of this kind of primary source can be demonstrated from the works of three historians who wrote, respectively, in the fourth century, the seventeenth century, and the nineteenth century.

The biography of the fourth-century Roman Emperor Constantine the Great was written by the emperor's friend, the Church historian Eusebius. This writer was in a position to know in great detail the circumstances of Constantine's life. But what comes through in *The Life of Constantine* is mostly Eusebius' typology, which is the Christian doctrine of the central role of divine providence in determining the course of history:

And God Himself, Whom Constantine worshipped, has confirmed this truth by the clearest manifestations of His will, being present to aid him at the commencement, during the course, and at the end of his reign, and holding him up to the human race as an instructive example of godliness. Accordingly, by the manifold blessings He has conferred on him, He has distinguished him alone of all the sovereigns of whom we have ever heard as at once a mighty luminary and most clear-voiced herald of genuine piety.[12]

In *The History of the Rebellion and Civil Wars* of midseventeenth-century England by the contemporary writer and statesman, Lord Clarendon, the providential theme is still prominent. But this traditional typology is now combined with two corollaries derived from the thought-world of early seventeenth-century Christian humanism. These additional patterns governing Clarendon's judgments are a strong sense of social hierarchy and

[12] Eusebius, *The Life of Constantine,* tr. E. C. Richardson, in *A Select Library of Nicene and Post-Nicene Fathers of the Christian Church,* 2nd ser., Vol. I: *Works of Eusebius* (New York: Charles Scribner's Sons, 1904), Bk. I, Ch. IV, p. 482.

order, and a belief in the retribution that awaits pride and arrogance:

And then, though the hand and judgment of God will be very visible, in the infatuating a people (as ripe and prepared for destruction) into all the perverse actions of folly and madness, making the weak to contribute to the designs of the wicked, and suffering even those, by degrees, out of the conscience of their guilt, to grow more wicked than they intended to be . . . whilst the poor people, under the pretence of zeal to religion, law, liberty, and parliaments (words of precious esteem in their just significance) are furiously hurried into actions introducing atheism and dissolving all the elements of Christian religion; cancelling all obligations, and destroying all foundations of law and liberty; and rendering, not only the privileges, but very being of parliaments desperate and impossible: I say, though the immediate finger and wrath of God must be acknowledged in these perplexities and distractions; yet he who shall diligently observe . . . will find all this bulk of misery to have proceeded, and to have been brought upon us, from the same natural causes and means, which have usually attended kingdoms, swoln with long plenty, pride, and excess, towards some signal mortifications, and castigation of Heaven.[13]

The Christian typologies that dominated all historical writing since the fourth century began to dissolve under the impact of the secular Enlightenment doctrine in the eighteenth century. But contemporary formal history in the nineteenth and twentieth centuries must also be explicated in terms of controlling typological forms. Religious typology was replaced for the most part by new secular typologies. As an example we may take Karl Marx's account of the Paris Commune of 1871. Marx's narrative of these dramatic events is largely an exercise in the typology of dialectical materialism. Marx is so convinced by the reality of his historiographical categories that he makes reference to particular events merely to illustrate the universal patterns he sees in social change:

[13] Clarendon, *Selections from The History of the Rebellion and Civil Wars,* etc., G. Huehns (New York: Oxford University Press, Inc., 1955), pp. 1–2.

The gigantic broom of the French Revolution of the eighteenth century swept away all these relics of bygone . . . hindrances to the superstructure of the modern state edifice raised under the First Empire, itself the offspring of the coalition wars of old semi-feudal Europe against modern France. During the subsequent *regimes* the government, placed under parliamentary control,—that is, under the direct control of the propertied classes—became not only a hotbed of huge national debts and crushing taxes, with its irresistible allurements of place, pelf, and patronage, it became not only the bone of contention between the rival factions and adventurers of the ruling classes; but its political character changed simultaneously with the economic changes of society. At the same pace at which the progress of modern industry developed, widened, intensified the class antagonism between capital and labour, the state power assumed more and more the character of the national power of capital over labour, of a public force organized for social enslavement, of an engine of class despotism. . . .The direct antithesis to the Empire was the Commune. The cry of "social republic" with which the revolution of February was ushered in by the Paris proletariat did but express a vague aspiration after a republic that was not only to supersede the monarchical form of class rule, but class rule itself. The Commune was the positive form of that Republic.[14]

As a primary source for the history of the Paris Commune, Marx's account is of little or no significance. As a primary source for the Marxist philosophy of history, his statement is extremely valuable.

Marx's history of the Paris Commune appears in his speech to a meeting of the International Working Men's Association. Contemporary formal history need not be presented in conventional literary form; it can appear as a speech to a meeting or convention. Similarly, since the eighteenth century, contemporary formal history is often encountered in newspapers and magazines. In order to establish the reliability and significance of these journalistic accounts, you have to perceive the underlying typological assumptions that shaped the author's selection of material and his

[14] Karl Marx, *Address to the General Council of the International Working Men's Association on the Civil War in France, 1871,* in K. Marx and F. Engels, *Selected Works* (Moscow: Foreign Languages Publishing House, 1962), Vol. I, pp. 516–19.

judgments. Typologies appear in any other kind of source that makes statements presupposing a view of social reality and historical change, such as policy statements by governments, formal treatises in political theory, and descriptions of current events in private letters. To elicit meaning from contemporary accounts, you have to consider the author's criteria of meaning.

III. PUBLIC RECORDS

Thus far in this practical exercise in the explication of primary sources we have been concerned with material that is formal in nature—works that are the product of long reflection and carefully contrived exposition. These kinds of primary sources are especially valuable to historians of ideas; and, if anything, intellectual historians have relied too exclusively on formal kinds of source material, so that what they give us is a history of higher thought and consciously expounded doctrine. *The other prime category of primary sources—contemporary documents of an immediate nature—comprises the greater part of the material used by political, economic, and social historians.*

In a document of immediate nature the literal or explicit context confronts the historian with all the complexity, confusion, fragmentary quality of minute-to-minute everyday life and an absence of clear-cut organization and well-defined theme. This category of sources imparts a feeling that "you are there." When properly analyzed, such source material gives the historian his knowledge of the course of events and the operation of institutions. Implicit in documents of immediate nature are also, however, values and world views; but these ideas are not obvious and have to be subtly and judiciously extrapolated from the sources.

Because of the contrived and conscious nature of treatises and contemporary histories, the student will be on his guard against accepting any statements at face value in these formal sources. He will look for implicit assumptions, hidden conflicts, and ulterior motives; and we have listed several of the questions that may be put to the sources in order to elicit this underlying significance. But you also have to be careful in dealing with documents of an immediate nature; you must avoid the temptation to engage in a simple literal-minded acceptance of the statements in this kind of material. Here, too, you must consider the values and assumptions of the author, what impression he was trying to convey, and the particular circumstances in which the document was written. You must also constantly bear in mind that a document of immediate nature written for a particular purpose can, if intelligently analyzed, be made to illuminate issues and events with which the author is not immediately concerned. To use a phrase popular among French historians, documents of an immediate nature must not only be questioned, they have to be "tortured" in order to yield their full meaning.

Among documents of an immediate nature, the ones that are most extensively used and valued by twentieth-century scholars are those generally termed *public records*. These are the spontaneous, day-to-day records of public organizations, whether national states, provincial governments, municipalities, or business corporations. *Public records are the documents in which man's continual struggle for power, wealth, and order is recorded.* They are of supreme value to the historian because so much of human history is concerned with the struggle for power, wealth, and order, and also because these documents were written not to advertise an ideology or to impress posterity (as is the case with treatises and contemporary formal history), but to move the wheels of government and business. *The more spontaneous and unselfconscious a document is, the more valuable is it likely to be to the institutional historian.* He can see in these documents the actual functioning of administration, law, business, and social structure; and in explicating them, the historian is able to penetrate behind the screen erected by the state's propaganda and the intellectuals' wishful thinking. Modern historical scholarship is commonly said to have begun when the midnineteenth-century German historian Leopold von Ranke made use of Venetian ambassadors' reports to establish a functional view of sixteenth-century diplomacy and power politics.

Public records fall into five main categories: (1) records of government and of business operation and administration; (2) records of legislative debates; (3) judicial cases and decisions; (4) statutes, laws, and proclamations; and (5) public letters, that is, letters written by statesmen, politicians, and business executives in their public capacity.

At a conservative estimate 80 percent of our knowledge of the development of political, social, and economic institutions in the history of Western civilization is derived from these kinds of public records. Some critics have questioned this overwhelming reliance on public records and have claimed that this dependence on governmental documents tends to make us look at the past largely through the eyes of the ruling groups and the dominant classes. It would indeed be salutary to make extensive use of private letters and journals in order to test the validity of the patterns of law, administration, economics, and social organization we derive from public records. In recent decades historians have tried to follow this method, sometimes with startling results. But public records have the advantage over private letters of being enormous in volume and relatively full and consistent in providing information. Furthermore they are well-preserved and easily accessible in national, provincial, and municipal archives. Private papers, on the other hand, especially of ordinary people, have rarely been preserved for eras before the eighteenth century. But even when they are extant and the historian wants to use them to illuminate the functioning of institutions, he finds them fragmentary, often badly preserved, and if open to historical research, sometimes preserved in inconvenient places. *Therefore, whether we like it or not, we shall have to derive much the greater part of our knowledge of political, economic, and social history from public records;*

*and any student of history at whatever level must be familiar with
the leading questions to be used in analyzing this kind of material.*

Usually undergraduates have access to public documentary
evidence only in the form of carefully edited volumes of selections.
This precludes asking some questions that can only be answered
when the historian has in front of him the bulk of the original
records. Nevertheless even the novice student of history can undertake the fruitful and intelligent analysis of public records and
work out for himself the functioning of institutions and the pattern of ideas these kind of sources provide. Most undergraduates
initially find public records, in comparison with formal sources,
to be formidable, forbidding, and obscure. *You must, of course,
have a firm command of the general history of the period from
which the public document stems.* Government officials admin-
istering a province and lawyers pleading a case will naturally
assume that the people they are addressing are familiar with the
general structure of contemporary institutions. Therefore, before
you begin your study of a document, you, too, must make yourself familiar with the context of its provenance and comprehend
the institutional nexus of the particular society. Your textbooks,
collateral reading in other secondary sources, and the course lectures will provide this. Assuming that you have this background,
you can then proceed to explicate the source; and you will be
surprised to discover how fully you can enter into the public and
social life of the era and even derive from your textual study
original insights into the functioning of institutions and the values
that conditioned political and judicial decision-making.

As was the case with sources of a formal nature, there are
some commonly employed questions that you should bear in mind
and prepare to use as analytic tools when you explicate government and business documents.

*You will succeed in fully explicating the meaning of the five
categories of public records if you examine them for four kinds
of information: (1) the functioning of institutions, that is, the*

method and degree of achievement of power, wealth, and social order and welfare; (2) the aims and policy of the government or corporation, whether explicitly stated or implied; (3) underlying assumptions and values that suggest the political and social theory held by the author(s) of the document; (4) indices of current social change with which the government or corporation has to contend. As you study any administrative, legislative, judicial, or business document, you will be able to explicate its full historical significance if you apply this quadruple topical analysis.

EXAMPLES: The first document to be subjected to fourfold topical analysis is an extract from an English administrative record of the year 1130, the "Pipe Roll" of the thirty-first year of King Henry I's reign. This is the earliest surviving record of the Exchequer, the accounting division of the English treasury:

(1) Geoffrey de Clinton renders account of 44s. 8d. blanch from the old farm. He has paid it into the treasury. And he is quit.

(2) The earl of Warwick renders account of £72. 16s. 8d. and two war-horses for pleas concerning stags. . . .

(3) Ralph Halselin renders account of 200m. of silver and 1m. of gold for the relief of his father's land. . . .

(4) Essex. . . . And the same (Richard Fitz-Gilbert) owes 200m. of silver for the help that the king gave him in connection with his debt to the Jews. . . .

(5) Norfolk. . . . Benjamin renders account of £4. 5s. that he may keep the pleas that belong to the king's crown.

(6) Lincolnshire. . . . Lucy, countess of Chester, renders account of £266. 13s. 4d. for the land of her father. In the treasury £166. 13s. 6d. And she owes £100; also 500m. of silver that she need not take a husband inside five years.

(7) Durham. . . . And the same Geoffrey renders account of the old farm of the bishopric for the previous year. . . . And the same Geoffrey renders account of the new farm of the bishopric. . . .[15]

Institutions: This document is rich in institutional information: (1) shows a sheriff from one of the counties paying into the

[15] Stephenson and Marcham, *Sources of English Constitutional History,* pp. 49–53.

treasury the ordinary taxation income or "farm" of his county. The coins are assayed to make sure they are white (blanch) and not black, that is, debased money. (3) and (6) show the enormous income that came to the Exchequer from the incidence of feudal taxation—relief (an inheritance tax)—and from royal wardship over dependent heirs—in this case, an unmarried daughter—of the king's feudal vassals. (7) reveals royal control of the Church and the use of the Church's lands for royal incomes. (2) and (5) illuminate aspects of the king's relations with the feudal aristocracy. (2) shows a great earl paying for the privilege of hunting in one of the vast royal forests, and (5) shows that lords are still allowed to have private feudal courts but that this privilege must now be purchased from the king. (4) illustrates the way in which the Jews were special dependents of the royal treasury and how the royal government played off the king's vassals against their Jewish creditors, so that a lord who wished to default on his debts to a Jewish moneylender had to pay heavily for royal approval.

Policy: The Pipe Roll selection demonstrates that it is the general policy of this government to make use of feudal institutions to increase the king's wealth and power. Institutions on the Continent that tended toward localism and disorder are being used by Henry I to create a centralized and extremely ordered regime. *Values and theories:* Running through the whole document is the assumption that all members of the feudal hierarchy should be subject in every important matter to "the king's crown" —not just to the king, but to his crown, that is, to the king as an impersonal public authority. Implicit in this statement is a revolution in political thought, the advance from the early medieval ideal of personal kingship toward the modern ideal of the public authority of the state. *Social change:* Finally the selection from the Pipe Roll indicates certain trends in social history—the emergence of trained bureaucrats who engage in rational decision-making and public planning, the transformation of the old warrior nobility into a landed aristocracy, and the central importance of land and family relations in the life of the lordly class. The student of economic history will note (after translation into equivalent modern buying power has been made) the vast sums of money available to the aristocracy for paying taxes, indicating great landed prosperity. He will also note the almost exclusive use of the silver specie rather than produce and barter for payment of taxes, proving the availability of a steady supply of silver for royal coinage.

The second example to be subjected to the fourfold topical analysis is a document from the reign of King Henry VIII of England that falls under the category of statutes and laws. It is The Order for the Council of the North, drafted by the King and his Privy Council and proclaimed by King Henry VIII in 1545:

(1) His majesty, much desiring the quietness and good governance of the people there, and for speedy and indifferent administration of justice to be had between party and party, intendeth to continue his right honourable council called the King's Council in the North Parts. ... (2) And further, his majesty by these presents giveth unto the said lord president, in all counsel where things shall be debated at length ... a voice negative, to the intent nothing shall pass but by his express commandment, consent, and order. . . . (3) To which president and council the king's majesty by these presents doth give full power and authority, as well to punish such persons as in anything shall neglect or contemn their commandments, as others that shall speak any seditious words, invent rumors, or commit any such offenses, not being treason, whereof any inconvenience might grow, by pillory, cutting their ears, wearing of papers, or otherwise at their discretions; and to poor suitors having no money, at their discretions to appoint counsel and other requisites without paying of any money for the same.[16]

Institutions: The three sections of the Order here quoted provide a new institutional means for solving the problem of governing the hitherto separatist and rebellious northern part of the country. A central royal council, with legislative and judicial

---

[16] *Ibid.*, pp. 321–23.

as well as administrative powers, sets up an adjunct council with similar, although dependent powers. The reliance of sixteenth-century English royal government on concentric circles of conciliar jurisdiction is evident in this document. The student who is generally familiar with English constitutional history will note that the format for the adjunct new king's council in the north—a president and council responsible to the Privy Council with the lord president to have an absolute veto over the other members of the Council of the North—is virtually identical with the government of most overseas British colonies in the seventeenth and eighteenth centuries. And therefore in examining the institutional aspects of this document you should conclude that this is an experiment in the government of distant provinces, and as it turned out, a successful experiment, which became the model for overseas colonial administration. Another point of institutional significance is that it is evident from (1) that this order is made under the King's prerogative and without a specific piece of parliamentary legislation to support it. This will be seen as a typical example of a sixteenth-century royal proclamation and use of the royal prerogative.

Policy: The aims and policies of Henry VIII's government are clear from this source, namely nationalization and centralization, what one historian has called "the Tudor revolution in government." *Values and theories:* There are, furthermore, fascinating theoretical assumptions and values implied in this passage. The government adopts a rhetoric of public welfare in (1) and gives plausibility to this claim by a paternalistic attitude toward the poor in (3). The government is very sensitive to seditious speech as well as acts and by no means believes in the free trade of ideas. It is also important to consider the punishment that is stipulated in (3) for seditious acts short of treason: public humiliation and torture. It is fascinating to speculate on the theory of human nature held by the authors of this document. Your reading in secondary sources will tell you that the sixteenth-century English monarchy had few police officials and only a very small standing army. You can then speculate that this is an instance of a government sounding severe and oppressive because its lack of military and police power makes it hypersensitive to the smallest hint of sedition. *Social change:* Finally the selection offers only sparse information on social change but does indicate the possibility of the ultimate pacification of the bellicose tribal nobility of the North and the integration of northern landed society into the ordered and controlled society of the southern half of England.

We have subjected specimens of two of the five categories of public records to quadruple analysis under the headings of institutions, policy, values and theories, and indices of social change. Documents in the other three categories can be similarly "tortured" by this kind of questioning and explication. The yield of historical information in each of the four analytical columns will vary from category to category; but some knowledge, insight, and meaning can be elicited from any kind of public record in response to each of the four types of topical explication.

IV. Private Letters and Journals

This variety of primary source consists of private correspondence and diaries. In some instances private letters and journals will have been written with an eye to future publication, but essentially *this kind of source gives us a view of people in their personal commitments and in their private involvements with family, friends, and acquaintances rather than in their public or broadly social capacities.* Private letters and journals can be an extremely illuminating source for both the intellectual and institutional historian, but modern scholarship in attempting to construct a picture of the past has made only moderate use of this kind of material in comparison with public records, treatises, and contemporary formal accounts. There are two reasons for this relatively slight reliance on private letters and journals—the actual material is often either nonexistent or inaccessible, and secondly, historians are not as sure of the right method of explicating this kind of material as they are of the other kinds of primary sources we have examined.

Private correspondence and diaries can be divided into three groups according to their authorship. The first group comprises the private letters and journals of public figures, what German scholars have called "world-historical individuals"—statesmen, politicians, famous authors, artists, musicians, scientists, etc. The second group is the writings of genuinely obscure and private people who as individuals left no impress on the course of history. The third group is the private letters and journals of what might be called semi-public people—local big shots and men and women on the fringes of power who had relations with the great and famous but who themselves did not achieve prominence. It is unfortunate that very little of the writings of the second group, the genuinely ordinary people, was thought worth preserving before the nineteenth century and that only an occasional fragment of this kind of primary source has survived the ravages of time for any period before the last 150 years. We even have little in the way of the genuinely private correspondence of public figures for the period before 1800. Even then, modern public figures' private letters and journals usually come down to us in heavily edited versions published by their heirs or literary executors; and this edited correspondence, voluminous as it may be, is designed to make the great man appear in as favorable a light as possible. We often get a more balanced and rounded view of the famous and prominent from the remarks in the surviving correspondence and diaries of semi-public people who knew them, than in the version of their own private writings that is made accessible to historical investigation. Because the impress of the experience of childhood on adult personality is a quite recent idea, we have very little circumstantial material on the childhood and youth of even the most famous and prominent people who lived before 1900.

The availability of private letters and journals for historical study is also determined by changes in the level of literacy and education, by intellectual and social fashions, and by technological factors. Before the eighteenth century only a very small number of what we would call ordinary and obscure people were sufficiently educated to write letters that tell us anything significant about their feelings and way of life. During the late eighteenth and the nineteenth centuries there was a tremendous increase in private correspondence because of improved education and the introduction of cheap postage, and also because, especially in the late nineteenth century, it became a middle-class fashion to write long personal letters and keep detailed diaries. During the last four or five decades the historical information to be gained from private correspondence has probably *decreased* because the telephone and air travel have made possible alternative methods of personal communication. In any case the private papers of a great many public figures of the twentieth century are still closed to the public, and the sensitivity to historical judgment of the families of great men is now such that these papers are likely to remain for a very long time in this sealed condition. The private papers of David Lloyd George, the British Prime Minister during the First World War, who died in 1945, have still not been opened to historical researchers.

The limited use made of private materials by historians has also been caused by a failure to develop systematic methods of explication. Since the middle of the nineteenth century intellectual historians have drawn most of their knowledge from formal treatises and contemporary histories; and institutional historians have worked out the development of government, society, and economic organization from public records. They have made use of private papers mostly to confirm or highlight the knowledge already derived from these other kinds of material, and they have been slow to develop distinctive ways of questioning and explicating private sources. Personal records have been mainly of interest to biographers, but even for this purpose there has been no consistency in method. A majority of biographers simply try to give as full an account of the subjects' lives as the sources allow, proceeding in straightforward fashion from birth to death. A minority of twentieth-century biographers have experimented with the application of psychoanalytic theory to the explication of their sources. But this remains an extremely controversial method among academic scholars; and in any case, even among biographers who attempt to employ psychological interpretation, there is little in the way of commonly accepted categories of explication. Psychological biography is still largely based on the particular writer's intuition.

The ever-increasing popularity of biography as a form of historical literature and the new interest that institutional historians have recently evinced in using private letters and journals will undoubtedly lead in time to the elaboration of academically orthodox methods of eliciting subtle shades of meaning from this kind of material. In the meantime the novice student of history should at least be aware of the questions and motifs that prevail at present in explicating this kind of primary source, however meager and unimaginative these may seem. *There are five such common questions and motifs, two of which relate private materials to the general pattern of historical development, and three that are of particular use to the biographer.*

a. Confirmation of General Historical Developments

EXAMPLE: Material from private correspondence is frequently used to confirm and illuminate the general pattern of historical development elicited from public records by bringing it down to the personal level. Thus we know from public records of the prevalence of social disorder and lawless violence in mid-fifteenth century England. This political and social breakdown becomes more real and significant to us when we find it referred to in a private letter by a lady who belonged to a family of prominent gentry in Norfolk about the year 1450:

God in his holy mercy give grace that there may be set a good rule and a wise [one] in the country in haste, for I heard never say of so much robbery and manslaughter in this country as is now with a little time.[17]

The only difficulty with this kind of personalization of the general course of historical change is that the contemporary writer may simply be expressing a typological motif rather than reacting to actual social change. In this case the student will have to ask whether our midfifteenth-century lady, Margaret Paston, was actually witnessing new violence and disorder or reflecting a new concern on the part of the gentry about social conditions that had existed with little or no change for several centuries.

b. New Perspectives on General Historical Development

EXAMPLE: Private materials can reveal attitudes and conduct that run somewhat counter to, or even directly contradict, the general pattern of historical development indicated by formal sources and public records. Private materials can show us the underside, the more dark and grotesque aspects, of a society and allow us to get a rounded view of the mores and standards of a particular era. The traditional picture of austere and reserved upper-middle-class Victorians is called into question when we find the following passage in the diary of a famous nineteenth-century English headmaster:

I had a little boy named _____ in to speak to who had been lying, and I spoke to him very seriously. When I had finished I held out my hand to him and he took it, and on my shaking hands and drawing him forward he fell on my neck weeping and kissed me, and I him.[18]

[17] J. Gairdner, ed., *The Paston Letters* (Edinburgh: John Grant, 1910), Vol. II, No. 435, p. 83. Modern English version in H. S. Bennett, *The Pastons and their England* (New York: Cambridge University Press, 1922), p. 185.
[18] G. R. Parkin, *Life and Letters of Edward Thring*, Vol. II, p. 166 (2 Vols., 1898). Quoted in W. L. Burn, *The Age of Equipoise* (New York: W. W. Norton & Company, Inc., 1965), p. 42.

A brilliant historian, W. L. Burn, has used this and similar material derived mostly from private sources to conclude that among the Victorians "the combination of a rigid moral standard with the sanction of force behind it and impulsive emotionalism could produce some grotesque results."[19]

An historian who made use of psychological theory would go further and would say that this statement from a private diary, along with similar passages from other sources, indicates a deep sado-masochistic streak in Victorian middle-class character. In any case this example shows how private material can be used to reveal the dark underside of life, those aspects of society that are rarely proclaimed by governments and applauded by theorists. It is unfortunate that so little of this kind of material is ever available to the historian.

c. The Impact of Personality

EXAMPLE: One of the hardest tasks of the biographer is to penetrate the posthumous reputation and to establish the complexity of a real human personality as it impressed itself on contemporaries. For this purpose the private letters and journals of people on the fringe of power can be extremely valuable; their reports on their day-to-day encounters with great public figures allow us to observe these famous men with the wondering, hesitant appraisal of contemporaries and not through the filtered stereotypes of modern textbooks. Here, for example, are two entries in the diary of Charles Greville, a writer on the periphery of political life, giving his views of Benjamin Disraeli, the British Prime Minister. The fact that Greville's two descriptions of Disraeli, entered in his diary twenty-four months apart, are somewhat contradictory and show Greville's change in attitude does not make it easier for the historian when he attempts to gain a con-

---

[19] Burn, p. 41.

sistent view of the Prime Minister's qualities. But Greville's contradictions and hesitancies when making a judgment on his great contemporary bring home to the student the paradoxical and enigmatic nature of Disraeli's personality and the strange combination of distaste and awe he elicited from most upper-class Englishmen of his era:

January 23rd, 1858. On arriving in town yesterday, I received a visit from Disraeli, who said he had come to consult me *in confidence,* and to ask my opinion, by which his own course would be very much influenced. I was not a little surprised at this exordium, but told him I should be glad to hear what his object was, and that he was welcome to any opinion he wished for from me. He then began a rather hazy discourse, from which I gathered or at least thought I gathered, that he thinks the present state of affairs very serious, and the position of the Government very precarious; that he is meditating on the possible chances there may be for him and his party in the event of Palmerston's fall, and knowing that some sort of coalition with some other party would be indispensable to form any other Government, an idea had crossed his mind that this might be practicable with some of the most moderate of the Whigs, especially with the younger ones, such as Granville and Argyll, and he wished to know if I thought this would be possible, and whether I could be in any way instrumental in promoting it, and if I did not think so what my ideas were as to the most advisable course in order to avert the threatened Reform, and to give the country a better Government than this. This, with a great deal of verbiage and mixed with digressions about the leading men of the present day, seemed to me to be the substance and object of his talk. He professed to speak to me of his own sentiments without disguise, and with entire confidence about everything, but I cannot call to mind that he imparted to me anything of the slightest interest or importance. . . .

London, December 25th, 1859. Disraeli raised himself immensely last year, more, perhaps, with his opponents and the House of Commons generally than with his own party, but it is universally acknowledged that he led the House with a tact, judgement, and ability of which he was not before thought capable. While he has thus risen, no rival has sprung up to dispute his pre-eminence. Walpole and Henley are null, and it is evident that the party cannot do without Disraeli, and whenever Parliament meets he will find means of reconciling them to a necessity of which none of them can be unconscious, and I have no doubt that whenever any good opportunities for showing fight may occur the whole party will be found united under Disraeli's orders.[20]

d. Confirmation of the Public Man

EXAMPLE: The biographer finds it indispensable to have the private papers of a public figure in order to confirm whether the man's public image and professed ideals are also paramount in his private and personal thoughts. As an example of the use of a diary to confirm publicly professed idealism, we have this entry in the diary of the great Victorian liberal Protestant statesman William Gladstone, which was made on his sixty-ninth birthday:

Why has my health and strength been so peculiarly sustained? All this year, and more, I think, I have not been confined to bed for a single day. In the great physical and mental effort of speaking, often to large audiences, I have been, as it were, upheld in an unusual manner; and the free and effective use of my voice has been given to me to my own astonishment. Was not all this for a purpose? And has it not all come in connexion with a process to which I have given myself?[21]

The political historian can argue that Gladstone's aims and policy were imprudent and misguided; a psychoanalytic biographer could find subconscious motivations derived from Gladstone's repressed middle-class Victorian upbringing. If Gladstone was self-deluded or motivated by compulsions of which he was not consciously aware, there is no evidence in his private papers to charge him with hypocrisy or fraud. He sincerely and passionately believed in the religious and political ideals he publicly professed.

[20] Louis Kronenberger, ed., *The Great World; Portraits and Scenes from Greville's Memoirs* (*1814–1860*) (New York: Doubleday & Company, Inc., 1963), pp. 344–45, 358–59.
[21] Quoted in Philip Magnus, *Gladstone* (New York: E. P. Dutton & Co., Inc., 1964), p. 256.

e. Contradiction of the Outer Image

EXAMPLE: Alternatively the private papers of a public figure can contradict the image derived from his public acts and writings. This contradiction need not be to the discredit of the famous man. For example we may take the case of the nineteenth-century German statesman Otto von Bismarck. His public image is that of the "Iron Chancellor," a dour and calculating power politician and diplomat. We are rather surprised to find that his letters to his wife are full of unblushing sentimentality:

My Beloved Heart— . . . I long to be with you, although I have nothing else to complain of, and am leading a life which is mentally very restful. At about eight I bathe; that is best of all; royal waves, high as a tree, and like a waterfall when they break; soft sand and no stones. It is always hard to leave them, to climb around them for about two hours among the miles of sand-dunes, to frighten the rabbits and birds, and to lie in the warm sand among the wild whortleberry bushes, smoking, dreaming, or thinking of Interlaken.[22]

Sentimental passages as this one in Bismarck's private correspondence will soften the traditionally harsh public assessment of him. But these letters can do more than that; they can lead the student to reconsider his view of Bismarck's motivation and policy. The unrestrained feeling that runs through his letters to his wife shows how fully the young Bismarck had absorbed the Romantic ethos of the early nineteenth century. Since not only personal sentimentality but adoration of the power of the state was central to this ethos, his personal letters make it plausible to view the Chancellor not as a cold and calculating Machiavellian but as a fervent ideologue, completely loyal to the traditions of early nineteenth-century German culture.

[22] Bismarck, letter to his wife, Sept. 5, 1853; *The Love Letters of Bismarck*, tr. C. T. Lewis (New York: Harper & Brothers, 1901), p. 295.

V. LITERARY AND NONVERBAL SOURCES

It is an opinion widely held today among the younger generation of scholars that historians should not confine themselves to the traditional varieties of primary sources. Historical scholarship has achieved great things in the past hundred years in the way of constructing a view of the past from public records, treatises, contemporary formal accounts, and, more recently and to a lesser degree, private letters and journals. But if history is the explanation of all that man has done in his social capacity, then it surely follows that the historian must cast his critical nets beyond these sources and make use of literature, art, and music—the finest accomplishments, along with science and technology, of Western civilization. To understand a particular era the historian cannot afford to ignore anything that has survived to us from that time; and among the artifacts and products of a previous age, literary and nonverbal materials are directly available to us. These have to be explicated along with other primary sources if we are to achieve the proper perspective on the world of the past and its significance for our present era.

There is no more reason why the historian should leave literary sources to the professional students of literature; painting, sculpture, and architecture to the art critic; and music to the musicologist than that he should leave the records of governmental institutions to the political scientist and the materials for social history to the sociologist.

It is a counsel of perfection to say that the student of history should make use of literary and nonverbal sources. It is quite another matter to define the method that he might use to explicate the significance of these kinds of sources and relate them by disciplined questioning to the general course of political, social, and cultural change. The fact is that historians have traditionally left literature, art, and music to specialists in these fields. This was partly due to the self-restraining principle that institutional history had to be the hard foundation of historical knowledge and therefore was to be built up first, and partly due to scholars' personal inclination and taste. But now that the framework of institutional history has been worked out by the enormous labor of the past three generations of historians, and now that a new generation of scholars has come on the scene who have a strong liking for literary, artistic, and musical materials, this traditional neglect is bound to be slowly overcome; and the literary and nonverbal sources of history are likely to be as carefully investigated in the later twentieth century as public records have been up to now.

Because of this self-imposed limitation on the variety of primary sources, which has thus far generally prevailed, historians have done very little in the way of working out special methods and distinctive motifs for the explication of these kinds of sources. *The student who seriously wishes to do advanced work in literary and nonverbal sources should undergo intensive training in departments of literature, art and art history, and musicology.* This is not to say that he will always be thoroughly enlightened by these studies. He may find that several of his teachers of literature, art, and music are indifferent to any kind of historical inquiry and that even when they undertake historical inquiry they often fail to relate the products of literary and artistic imagination to the social context, with results that seem meager and narrow. Nevertheless it is the professional scholars at work on literary and nonverbal material who have the intensive knowledge needed to make good judgments on these sources, and it is to such scholars that the historian has to turn if he wants guidance and preparation in the use of this material.

Eventually it is possible that now unknown and unforeseen dimensions of historical insight will arise from such studies, but for the moment the undergraduate who comes to explicate literary and nonverbal sources finds that *there are only two commonly used questions and motifs for explicating this material.* Literary sources are used to provide confirmation and highlighting of political, social, and economic change that we know about chiefly from public records. Secondly, literary and nonverbal sources communicate the values, ideas, and feelings prominent in a given society; in other words this kind of primary source provides valuable evidence for the historian of ideas.

a. Confirmation and Highlighting of General Historical Developments

Literary works can be treated as contemporary formal accounts and may be quoted to illuminate general trends in social history. In much the same way as a statement in a private letter or journal provides a graphic personalization of a general pattern of historical development, a selection from a novel, drama, or poem can powerfully evoke the tenor of life at a particular period. An obvious example of this use of literary sources is the account of the sufferings of the German peasantry at the hands of mercenaries during the Thirty Years' War in the midseventeenth century given in Grimmelshausen's *The Adventurous Simplicissimus:*

Although it was not my intention to take the peaceloving reader with these troopers to my dad's house and farm, seeing that matters will go ill therein, yet the course of my history demands that I should leave to kind posterity an account of what manner of cruelties were now and again practiced in this our German war. . . . The first thing these troopers did was, that they stabled their horses: thereafter, each fell to his appointed task: which task was neither more nor less than ruin and destruction. For though some began to slaughter and to boil and to roast so that it looked as if there should be a merry banquet forward, yet others there were who did but storm through the house above and below stairs. Others stowed together great parcels of cloth and apparel and all manner of household stuff, as if they would set up a frippery market. All that they had no mind to take with them they cut in pieces. . . . Houseware of copper and tin they beat flat, and packed such vessels, all bent and spoiled, in with the rest. Bedsteads, tables, chairs, and benches they burned, though there lay many cords of dry wood in the yard. Pots and pipkins must all go to pieces. . . . Our maid was so handled in the stable that she could not come out; which was a shame to tell of. . . . And now they began: first to take the flints out of their pistols and in place of them to jam the peasants' thumbs in and so to torture the poor rogues as if they had been about the burning of witches: for one of them they had taken they thrust into the baking oven and there lit a fire under him, although he had as yet confessed no crime: as for another, they put a cord around his head and so twisted it tight with a piece of wood that the blood gushed from his mouth and nose and ears. In a word each had his own device to torture the peasants, and each peasant his several tortures.[23]

In using this confirmatory highlighting by a literary source, the student has to consider the conditioning role of typology, as in the case of contemporary formal accounts. In addition you have to be aware of the fictional quality of literary sources and to recognize the possibility of dramatization and rhetorical exaggeration. Historians very rarely draw any important conclusion on social conditions from literary sources alone. Recognizing the selective and symbolic character of the belletristic author's work, they use socially descriptive passages to provide dramatic examples but not as evidence for determining fundamental changes in the social structure. Just about every historian of eighteenth-century England refers to Henry Fielding's compelling portrayal of Squire Western in his novel *Tom Jones*, but this literary evidence never stands alone. Our knowledge of the eighteenth-century English squirearchy is mainly derived from public records.

b. Communication of Values and Ideas

EXAMPLES: *Literary and nonverbal sources are important to the historian of ideas for two reasons.* They communicate values

[23] H. J. C. von Grimmelshausen, *The Adventurous Simplicissimus*, tr. A. T. S. Goodrick (Lincoln: University of Nebraska Press, 1962), Bk. I, i, pp. 8–9. Reprinted by permission.

and ideas with an intensity of feeling not usually present in formal treatises. Secondly, for long periods of history, literacy and education were largely the preserve of a small elite; literature, art, and music intended for a wide audience can be used as indices of the popular ideas, feelings, and assumptions held by the middle and lower orders of society. Thus all the tragedies of Shakespeare have in common the theme that whoever tries to upset the hierarchic order of the universe will be brought low in the end. There is a fixed balance of order in society that must not be attacked. We can cite this theme in Shakespeare's plays as evidence for the continued profound impact of the medieval idea of hierarchy in the late sixteenth-century popular English mind.

As an example of the way in which a belletristic writer communicates the values and ideas of his era, even when he is apparently trying not to, we can examine a passage from the beginning of the novel *Henry Esmond* by the midnineteenth-century English novelist William Thackeray. In this novel Thackeray intends to describe for us the thoughts of a gentleman who lived in the early eighteenth century and who is passionately loyal to the now-fading Stuart conception of divine-right monarchy. And yet Thackeray has his hero write in his journal sentiments that clearly reflect the liberal and democratic values of Thackeray's own day.

The Muse of History hath encumbered herself with ceremony as well as her Sister of the Theatre. She too, wears the mask and the cothurnus, and speaks to measure. She too, in our age, busies herself with the affairs only of kings; writing on them obsequiously and stately, as if she were but a mistress of court ceremonies, and had nothing to do with the registering of affairs of the common people. I have seen in his very old age and decrepitude the old French King Lewis the Fourteenth, the type and model of kinghood—who never moved but to measure, who lived and died according to the laws of his Court-martial, persisting in enacting through life the part of Hero; and, divested of poetry, this was but a little wrinkled old man, pock-marked, and with a great periwig and red heels to make him look tall—a hero for a book if you like, or for the brass statue or a painted ceiling, a god in a Roman shape, but what more than a man for Madame Maintenon, or the barber

who shaved him, or Monsieur Fagon, his surgeon? . . . I saw Queen
Anne at the latter place [Windsor] tearing down the park slopes, after
her stag-hounds, and driving her one-horse chaise—a hot, red-faced
woman, not in the least resembling that statue of her which turns its
stone back upon St. Paul's, and faces the coaches struggling up Ludgate
Hill. She was neither better bred nor wiser than you and me, though we
knelt to hand her a letter or a washstand-basin. Why shall History go on
kneeling to the end of time? I am for having her rise up off her knees,
and take a natural posture: not to be forever performing cringes and
congees like a court-chamberlain, and shuffling backwards out of doors
in the presence of the sovereign.[24]

This passage can be used in two ways to illustrate mid-Victorian liberal thought. Its contempt for monarchy and hierarchy
certainly reflects a dominant tendency in Victorian liberal thinking. It also is important for the very way that Thackeray misunder-
stood the outlook of an early eighteenth-century royalist, attributing ideas to him that he could not possibly have held. Thackeray
thus typifies the liberalism of his era, which measured all things
against itself and anachronistically interpreted earlier history in
the light of its own values.

Nonverbal sources have the same twofold use for the historian
of ideas, that of communicating intensity of feeling and of reflecting popular values. Because of problems of illustration, we will
have to confine ourselves to visual artifacts, but *music can also be
used as a primary source for intellectual history.* It should be
noted, however, that in dealing with music the historian has to
avoid the pseudoemotional metaphors of the kind commonly
found on record jackets. Such language is usually both ahistorical
and nonmusical jargon. Mozart is not to be thought of as characteristic of eighteenth-century culture because he is "sweet." In
using literary and nonverbal sources, the historian has to learn an
analytical language that is precise and significant and that reflects
some acquaintance with the critical categories established by professional students of literature, art, and music. Otherwise the his-

[24] Wm. Makepeace Thackeray, *The History of Henry Esmond,* in *Works*
(New York: Jefferson Press, n.d.), Bk. I, pp. 1–2.

torian will merely be engaging in the futile exercise of enunciating tiresome clichés and banalities.

The first two examples from artistic sources are Figure 1, Bernini's "Ecstasy of St. Theresa," a sculpture dating from the mid-seventeenth century that is in the Cornaro Chapel of S. Maria della Vittoria in Rome, and Figure 2, Gros' "Napoleon at the Pest House at Jaffa," which is in the Louvre Museum and is a painting of the early nineteenth century. Both works reveal a high level of technical excellence, and both helped to establish the main style for their period—high baroque in the case of Bernini, academic grand style in the case of Gros. (See pages 86–87.)

The significance of these art works for the history of ideas and values can be elicited by examining the central figure in each case. Theresa is presented as an individual, with attention given to every detail of her appearance, her facial structure, her hands and wrists, and so on. Napoleon, in contrast, is presented not as a unique individual, but as an idealized type, a figure—who could possibly be anyone—in a heroic pose. These differences lead to a distinctive quality of feeling or ethos in each case. With the Bernini sculpture, one experiences a situation that generates a genuine emotional response, while in the Gros painting one experiences only the pathos of the ill—balanced by the abstract exoticism of the Islamic setting—whom only Napoleon can revive into normal, healthy life. The pathos is heightened by the lighting and use of color in this painting, in that most of the figures are swathed in darkness and only Napoleon is highlighted. Theresa, in contrast, is suffused with light from a window above; and even more, behind the statue there are explicitly placed gilded rods to catch this light and thus to manifest the heavenly light that informs her experience.

Napoleon is depicted as a world leader. The artist emphasizes Napoleon's power to save the world, to bring the "unworldly" or near dead back to life. In the representation of Saint Theresa, on the other hand, the whole aim of the artist's design and technique is to show that she is apart from the physical world of events.

FIGURE 1.   GIAN LORENZO BERNINI (1598–1680):
"ECSTASY OF ST. THERESA."

FIGURE 2. BARON A. J. GROS (1771–1835):
"NAPOLEON AT THE PEST HOUSE AT JAFFA."

/ 87

Having established the main theme of these art works, the student can use them as primary sources for seventeenth-century and early nineteenth-century culture. In the case of the seventeenth-century example, one encounters a religion that is highly emotional in the quality of its faith, that emphasizes a moment of experience more than an eternity of truth, and that is mystical and extra-worldly in its tendencies and in its motivations. The Bernini sculpture is designed to inspire this attitude in the observer. In the example from the Napoleonic era we encounter a religiosity that is focused on a charismatic person who is very much of the world, who organizes society around him and is its leader, and who is able to "heal" the diseases that beset mankind and restore order to that world. All the observer can do is to join the crowd that admires the sublime Napoleon.

This interpretation of these representations only achieves plausibility because we know from literary sources, formal treatises, and contemporary formal accounts that the ideas we believe are found in these artistic sources were central to the thought-world of midseventeenth-century Italy and early nineteenth-century France. In using nonverbal sources the student must follow the rule worked out by the great German art historians of the early twentieth century: artists do not live in a rarified world of their own. The motifs in their paintings reflect, in an intense and vivid way, ideas and emotions that prevail in their intellectual milieu; and we know these ideas and emotions in the first instance from verbal sources. *In using works of art as primary sources, you must relate the representational imagery of the picture* (what art historians call iconography or iconology) *to standard written sources that provide textual evidence for the artistic motifs.*

As a further example we can examine Figure 3, the illustrated title initial in a twelfth-century book of Psalms (Morgan Library MS. 43, f. 33v). This miniature represents the standard iconography for the theme of the "Tree of Jesse," the motif that the Middle Ages associated with the prophecy in Isaiah xi, 1–2. The

FIGURE 3. MORGAN LIBRARY MS. 43 f. 33ᵛ:
"TREE OF JESSE."

miniature shows Jesse reclining in bed, and from him rises a "tree" in which one sees, among other figures, King David (playing a harp), the Virgin Mary, and Christ. We might simply assume that the "tree" has the design it has for genealogical reasons, David being present because he is the ancestor of the Virgin and hence of Christ. But research in medieval texts permits a much deeper analysis of the theme that the artist intended. The up-and-down design of the composition suggests at once a possible hierarchical significance, with important figures superior to lesser figures. Study of verbal primary sources supports this inference and even refines it in subtlety, suggesting that the figures in the hierarchy are thematically related to each other. By looking at allegorical interpretations of Scripture prepared in the Middle Ages, at about the time of the miniature, the historian finds that in the traditional allegorical interpretation of the Tree-of-Jesse passage in Isaiah, only the Virgin is symbolized by the "rod of Jesse" and only Christ by the "flower," and that no mention of David is made at all.[25] Why, then, is David present in the hierarchy of this miniature? Not because he is an ancestor of the Virgin but rather, as medieval theorists tell us, because he is himself a "type," a prefiguration of Christ who is the culmination of the Tree of Jesse.[26] His inclusion in the tree, then, reinforces the idea that the line of Jesse leads to Christ in a highly significant way, in that it produced a king who was a type of Christ and so prefigured the eventual coming of Christ. David's presence is meant to suggest *the theme of kingship as an imitation of Christ* that was central in medieval thought.

From the analysis of this and the previous examples, nonverbal sources are seen to be very useful in giving us an immediate and sharp sense of the world view of past eras. But nonverbal

[25] Herveus, *Commentariorum in Isaiam,* J. P. Migne, ed., *Patrologia Latina,* clxxxi, coll. 140, 144–5.

[26] Hrabanus Maurus, *Commentaria in Libros IV Regum, Patrologia Latina,* lix, col. 52.

sources can legitimately serve this purpose only when they are part of a total context of proof obtained by analyzing and evaluating all possible varieties of primary material.

The explication of literary and nonverbal sources is a difficult task. But in working with this kind of material, the principles and methods to be followed are generally the same as those followed in studying more conventional and commonly used primary sources. Whatever the variety and quality of the record, this most important and indispensable form of historical work requires your undivided attention and the fullest commitment of your critical intelligence. Primary sources cannot be studied in an offhand and superficial manner while your emotional energies and the best part of your mind are directed elsewhere. You have to involve yourself completely in the explication of the source in order to discover its meaning. You have to subject every sentence, every word—or, in the case of artistic material, every detail of iconology —to the most careful scrutiny. You must assume that, however refractory it may appear, the source ultimately has something immensely important to tell us about the shape and meaning of the era and society from which it stems. Often at first reading the source is obscure and unintelligible, insignificant and confused; but under critical analysis it eventually reveals to us the deeds and thoughts, the loves and hates, the hopes and disappointments, the glories and the agonies of a generation that has preceded our own.

What historians call primary sources alone provide the means of awakening our insight and imagination to the triumphs and the tragedies of the countless men and women who have disappeared forever into the remorseless silence of the past. As a great twentieth-century scholar, Marc Bloch, has said, the sources show us the "tracks" of the generations that have preceded us on this earth. In studying these tracks, the people and the cultures of past eras are recreated in our minds.

5 / How to Read Secondary Sources

After the great emphasis we have placed on the fundamental importance of primary sources, the student may by now be wondering why he should read any secondary sources (treatments of the history of a subject) at all. If critical analysis of secondary books makes it so obvious that such books always represent a "point of view," a particular slant on their subjects, and if primary sources can supply "facts" that will be useful in historical proofs, then why bother with secondary books: what is their use?

While a question of this sort is frequently heard—indeed, is most often heard from the most serious students—it reflects a disproportionate value judgment, a failure to understand exactly what the historian is trying to do. As we have repeatedly suggested, it is absolutely essential for an historian to be very familiar with his "facts," with the "what" of his history. To discover and present such facts is, however, not the goal or the aim of historical work. Rather, the analysis and explication of primary sources should lead to the all-important step at which "history" begins to be created, *viz.*, the ordering of facts and the explanation of their importance by identifying and defining relationships of cause and effect among them. The goal of history is to explain "how" or "why" the facts came to be, to demonstrate the "meaning" of the facts. Put another way, the aim of the student of history is to create a secondary source himself, and at that, a secondary source which has a historiographical theme, or point of view, not merely to report the contents of primary sources. If the student will recognize this as his proper aim, then other secondary historical sources can be of great assistance in facilitating his work and in giving him insights and information that would otherwise be very difficult to obtain.

First of all, secondary books can often be very useful mines of primary material. It is of course to be expected that any good work of historical study is going to be based on considerable research in primary sources, and that such sources will be cited, described, and selectively quoted by the historians who use them. The latter will be the case if the primary sources are unusual, hard to obtain, or unpublished. Very frequently—indeed, more often than might perhaps be desired—the student is going to find himself totally dependent on such reports of primary sources and excerpted quotations. A student of eighteenth-century politics in England who lacks access to great family archives in Britain is quite grateful to be able to study such books as Lewis Namier's *The Structure of Politics at the Accession of George III*, not only because of Namier's theories but also because of the lengthy quotations he provides from documents in such archives. Again, students of medieval thought may find that a useful aspect of Beryl Smalley's *The Study of the Bible in the Middle Ages* is the footnotes, which offer lengthy quotations from treatises that are unpublished and available only in unique manuscripts in Europe. Such use of cited excerpts of primary source materials in secondary books need not be confined to unpublished or hard-to-obtain sources; a student pressed for time, who concentrates on one field in his primary source reading is fully justified if he depends on outstanding historical scholars to summarize the primary sources of another field for him.

Only two warnings need be offered to the beginner in this respect. Both are restatements of our earlier remarks: (1) It is better to read full-length sources when they are available than excerpts, to prevent distorted emphasis; this is even more true if the source is well known or can be easily obtained. One would expect any student to make direct use of a standard edition of Machiavelli's *The Prince* or Mill's *Utilitarianism* rather than an excerpted form of such works in secondary sources. (2) When using primary sources as presented in a secondary work, one is subject to the selectivity imposed by the particular emphases and point of view of the modern author, who has reported what is useful to the theme he is developing. This means that if one is going to cite a primary source quoted in a secondary work, one should be certain that the secondary author is accurate in his transcription or quotation of the primary source and that he is at least competent and careful enough to give a balanced conception of his sources in his choice of the materials he excerpts.

The factual material to be found in secondary sources is of several kinds. Besides the citations and quotations from primary sources, one may find statistical facts of great usefulness: lists of supplies, records of harvests, descriptions of the amount of time a given military operation required, the amount of goods manufactured at Manchester over a given period of time, and so on. What is more, the student should be aware that such facts can be determined inferentially. To give an obvious example, if we read that "between 1499 and 1501 Caesar Borgia conquered most of the Romagna and was created its Duke," we could use such a passage to support the "factual" claim that during that three-year period Borgia was in Italy and spent most of his time in the Romagna.

But in using the inferences of other historians as if they were facts, you must recognize that your source material is really someone else's judgment and not the "simple truth." It is very common for students to make such reference to major historical theories as if they were axiomatically correct, like the "given" in a geometric proof. Consider the following statement:

Such efforts were sustained by an enthusiasm for the increase in knowledge about classical civilization which for the extent of its appeal had few parallels in the history of Europe. The new learning was taken up by kings and princes and its findings were communicated to an ever-widening circle of the educated public.[1]

The author has assumed as obviously true that the classical learning of the fifteenth and sixteenth centuries is somehow "new"; in effect, he is presenting a view of the revival of learning or "new learning" in Renaissance Italy held by many historians. It is a plausible thesis; but in citing or quoting this statement, the student is not quoting or citing a fact. He is quoting or citing an interpretation, an inferential hypothesis; and he must remember that there may be other, possibly contradictory, views of the relationship between facts in the works of other modern historians.

The easiest way the college student of history can indicate that he does not accept a secondary source as inevitable truth is to note that he is following so-and-so's interpretation on the subject. The student should exercise critical judgment about the interpretation that is being followed, indicating if he has some doubt about part of the interpretation. Such an approach will show that he understands the difference between primary fact and inferential judgment.

The best antidote to uncritical acceptance of one historical interpretation is to read as many of the major works of interpretation as possible on a particular era or problem in history. When a student reads several secondary sources dealing with the same subject, he will readily see that there is more than one way, and sometimes several ways, of perceiving the relationship between the same basic facts. Advanced students are required to master the "literature of the field"; that is, they must read all the major works of interpretation in a given historical field and be able to assess the strong and weak aspects of each interpretation. While students in survey courses can certainly not be expected to have achieved such mastery—far from it—they should be aware that there is more than one interpretation of every important historical subject.

[1] Myron P. Gilmore, *The World of Humanism* (New York: Harper & Brothers, 1952), p. 183.

Freshmen should immediately take note of conflicting interpretations as they come up in lectures and readings; this awareness is the beginning of the long and arduous but delightful task of mastering the great interpretive themes of modern historical thought.

During the last four or five decades history has not attracted nearly as many first-class minds as have the physical sciences; nevertheless there have been many men of great learning and wisdom and writers of high literary skill (sometimes these qualities were combined in the same historian) who have devoted themselves to the great questions of history. Reading secondary sources should be on the whole a delightful experience because in these works students will encounter the thoughts of writers of great humanity and compassion who have concerned themselves with the heroic and tragic destiny of mankind. In the hands of a writer of great learning, humanity, and wisdom, history can become a compelling and persuasive form of literature; in fact in the last decade historical books have come to equal or surpass novels in popularity among college-educated readers. One of the benefits of studying history is the opening up of a wonderfully rich storehouse of literature. Since historians interpret the significance of human conduct, and since men and women who lived long ago in a very different kind of society still resemble us enough so that we recognize our kinship with them, the student will find that some secondary sources—that is, modern works of historical literature—not only illuminate the past but also offer a new perspective and meaning to the reader's own experience.

A vast and profound world of intellectual excitement and illumination is available to the student in modern historical literature; but to enter into this world, he must read constantly. *History is a reading subject:* teachers of history are forever surprised to find how few students seem to be aware of the truth of the point. We have emphasized over and over again that history is not merely the collection of facts which are the events and happenings of the past, but is rather the explanation and interpretation of relationships among those facts. *Learning history implies becoming familiar with the varieties of history offered by the hundreds of writers whose books constitute the major secondary literature in the subject.*

At the very outset, the student who is thinking of carrying on any advanced work or professional activity in the field of history should acquire the habit of constant and considerable daily reading in history, both of primary and of secondary sources. Only by so doing will he eventually have that firm and thorough grasp of the field of his interest that will mark him as really competent. If you are a beginner, the reading of one secondary book in history each week should be enough—but *just barely* enough—to enable you to build up the necessary skills of reading quickly, which include finding the thesis of a book in a few minutes, learning to recognize the devices of various fundamental interpretations, and finally storing in your memory some approximate awareness of the contents and subjects covered in the book so that you can use it later as a reference. Such practice will become the start of a lifelong habit of constant reading and preparation for advanced historical research and writing. The student should try, as the years of his education roll on and as practice in dealing with books makes him more skillful, to increase the pace of his reading until by the time he starts graduate school he is prepared to read one secondary book a day in addition to his other studies and courses. Only a graduate reading program of such intensity will offer a serious student a really sound preparation for his examinations within a prescribed period. To be sure, once the pressures of graduate work ease and the new pressures of writing, teaching, and having a deeper and closer interest in primary sources take over, the professional scholar's reading of secondary sources will decrease with time. But even so, most good scholars still try to read at least one secondary source each week and to keep up with the periodical literature, and in general try to stay abreast of the literature of their own fields of interest.

Since reading—and quick, facile reading at that—is of such major importance in a student's development, what are some of the skills that might enhance his ability to read secondary books properly and find what is useful in them without becoming bogged down in pages of details?

First of all, you must remember that while the book will naturally offer you some new factual information, you are reading it to obtain some view of the facts, some statements about the meaning of the facts. This suggests that the *first aim in reading any secondary work should be to determine as soon as possible what the main point of the book is*—to find the central conclusions the book is trying to prove, and to recognize the historiographical point of view represented in the book, i.e., the assumptions and value judgments upon which the author bases his conclusions.

There are several ways of approaching a book that facilitate the achievement of this goal. *To find the main point of a book, you should read the introduction, the first chapter, and the last chapter before you read any other part of the book.* Very often, in introductions or prefaces authors will give an explicit statement of their exact aims and ways of achieving those aims. This is frequently even more true in a second edition of a work, where in the preface an author will take up the various arguments that have been adduced against his thesis and state his views countering such arguments, all of which of course helps to make the author's basic intention very clear. But also in the first or the last (or both) chapters it can be expected that the author will give some definitive statement of the aims and conclusions of his entire work.

The value for the student in beginning his study of a book with a knowledge of its thesis is enormous. With the main point as a central focus, everything else to be discovered by the student as he reads the book will have a frame of reference. There will be an organization of ideas into which each new item will fit, permitting greater comprehensibility of the thread of the author's argument, and even greater retention of the key points, because they will not seem random or unrelated. Thus, immediate perception of the thesis should always be the first task in encountering and mastering any new book.

There is a peculiar form of literary immaturity that we often encounter in beginning students, especially those fresh out of high school. This is the claim that they find it "impossible to understand a book unless every word is read directly from beginning to end; skimming or reading in sections conveys nothing." The very form of most historical writing, which is expository treatment leading up to, and organized in terms of, a central conclusion, would contradict the value of such an approach to reading history books; and it is no surprise that it is the very students who make this claim who become bogged down in detail and fail to discover the point of the books they are reading. Indeed, several such students admitted to us that the attitude was a prejudice developed in high school as a result of dire warnings "not to read the last chapter of a book first." But except in a few cases, history books are *not* novels (even when they are narratives), and the main emphasis is not to find out "how it comes out." The events of history have already happened, and they will "come out" whether or not the student reads the last chapter first. Indeed, if the student does not already know for the most part what the events of the subject being studied are, he is not yet prepared to read the book. Remember, it is not *what* happens that is of interest in most history books, but rather the explanation of *why* events come out as they do.

Hand-in-hand with recognizing the main point of a book is the primary purpose of discovering the historiographical emphasis in the book—the author's assumptions and values. We cannot underscore this point strongly enough, because unless the book has some startlingly new primary source material, the only significant contribution it can have, the only validity the book can claim as a study of its subject is due to the originality and depth

of its explanations—its historiographical analysis. To grasp historiographical points, the reader of a book should look for a number of clues. One is the emphasis in subject matter; if the book is
full of references to agricultural production, commercial data,
impact of business on society, and the like, the chances are good
(although not certain) that the emphasis will be on an economic
form of historiography. Again, if the examples in a book seem
to come primarily from sermons or works of literature, one might
anticipate a cultural emphasis; and the extensive use of personal
letters may indicate a psychological approach.

Thus a preliminary skimming or glance over the contents of a
book will help you to know what to expect when studying it more
closely. In this skimming process two tricks to employ are to study
the table of contents carefully and to read the key paragraph of
each chapter, which in most cases will be the last one. The table
of contents, if it is at all systematic or orderly, will frequently be
close to an outline of the book and will thus reveal a great deal
about the patterns of development and the organizational logic of
the book at a glance.

The "key paragraph" concept may need more explanation. It
is a tendency with most writers to have the overall organization of
every section of a large work (e.g., the chapters of a book) be the
same, so that in every chapter the conclusions will be explicitly
stated either at the beginning or at the end, most often at the end.
The preliminary reading of the first and the last chapters plus a
quick glance at a couple of other chapters should be enough to
give the reader an awareness of where the major conclusions and
basic points of the chapters will be found. You should search for
these conclusions, and compare them with the main conclusions of
the whole book and with the general tendency of the argument in
the book found from skimming it and from the table of contents:
this should be enough to lay bare the heart of the book.

Since we have emphasized that the major concern in a secondary work is to find the author's point of view, in reading conclu-

sions of chapters and main conclusions to evaluate the significance of a book, the student should always be looking for clues to the author's system of values. Again, a slight familiarity with each author's individual style will make clear that he has certain "signal words" that telegraph, so to speak, his major assumptions. It would be impossible to list all such words here, of course; and this is a matter in which only practice—which means constant, thoughtful reading—can make perfect. But the more the student looks for the concepts and facts with which an author associates words and phrases like "causes," or "led to," or "was the result of," or "it is obvious that," "fundamental," "significant," or "turning-point," the more adept he will become at recognizing historiographical nuances and emphases.

It is these nuances and implied assumptions that the student must constantly be looking for because they often tell us more about the author's assumptions than more explicit statements of the governing principles of his work. Therefore *the student has to be as creative about reading books as about writing his own papers.* Reading must be an active process of analysis and recognition, not merely a passive process of absorption. You must use the same critical power on secondary as on primary sources. Again, you must question your sources. To do this properly, you must know something about the author. If you are given a six-teenth-century treatise to interpret, you will want to begin by knowing at least an outline of the author's biography. Similarly, given a work by a twentieth-century writer, you will want to know the salient facts of his nationality, education, family and cultural background, and career. These facts will often prove extremely valuable in ferreting out the implied assumptions and nuances of meaning in the secondary source.

To obtain the fullest understanding of a secondary as well as a primary source, the student would have to read the book in the language in which it was written. Only in this way would he fully recognize the connotations of meaning intended by the author.

Such connotations are frequently distorted by even the best translations. Reading historical works in foreign languages is not demanded of freshmen. But history majors in good colleges are required to read historical works in at least one foreign language. Frequently freshmen who enjoy history courses neglect their required language work. This is a great mistake. For students of any field of history outside of the history of the United States, and possibly England, a knowledge of foreign languages, beginning with French and German, is as important as mathematics to the potential physics major. Even a single year of study of a European language is enough to let the student read short essays and chapters of history books in that language. Fortunately historical prose in modern European languages is rather simple and straightforward and is much easier for the novice than poetry or novels. Once the student has mastered the basic grammar and vocabulary of French and German he can develop skill and fluency in reading history works in these languages through a half an hour a day of practice; but he must devote himself to this task daily, so that he slowly learns the common vocabulary of historians writing in French and German.

Once you have mastered the heart—the essential concepts and principles—of the book you are studying through reading introductory and concluding chapters, surveying the contents, and searching out the conclusions and points of each chapter, further reading of the book and use of the book as a source of information should be fairly easy for you, a matter of a few hours of concentrated reading. Not every word of the book will be important. Rather than painfully considering every sentence, the student should try to read the book rather quickly, recognizing and remembering the most important facts and inferences needed to sustain the thesis; and only *after he finishes the book should he make notes* for use in a general note file. Waiting until finishing the book before taking notes will enable you to remember the main thread of the argument more successfully because you will not be constantly interrupted by details. Furthermore the notes you will take will include only the fundamental points and leave out the less significant. To be sure, if the student is looking for information about a specific subject, he will take more detailed notes about that subject. But since most of a student's historical reading is for general interest and information, it is more important that he remember in general that certain subjects will be covered in such-and-such a book, which he may later turn to as a reference, than that he acquire an encyclopedic knowledge of the detailed contents of a single book. *It is a wise practice for a student who is reading for general information to compel himself immediately upon completing a book to attempt to digest the main points, arguments, and subjects of the book onto a single note card or sheet of paper, which can become part of a bibliographical file.* In this way, the student will find that he has "internalized the book," made it part of his knowledge and understanding. He should, in his memory of the book, be able to characterize it *briefly* by describing its historiographical point of view (the author's assumptions and value judgments), its major conclusions and themes, and the general contents and *kinds of facts* it contains. Such knowledge will always enable the student to turn to and use the book handily if he needs detailed information on a particular problem.

To make the reading of historical books easier, we urge the student to know the basic facts of the subject in advance. Unless the student is aware of the pattern of events, the whole significance of most interpretive arguments will be lost on him, especially if the arguments have any degree of subtlety or complexity at all. Most history books will demand such a prior, "textbook" knowledge from their readers, and it would be a very great mistake for students to assume that simply because interpretation is the only really *meaningful* aspect of history, that facts and data can be ignored. Indeed, it is the meaning *of the facts* that the historian is trying to present, and lack of fact in the student's background will reduce his understanding of historical meaning to the vanishing point. We are not persuaded by students (especially students in required survey courses) who protest that they would enjoy history if they were only allowed "to read" and "think" and not also required to know basic facts—dates, names, etc. You cannot think unless you have something to think about. To be sure, the emphasis in history courses is all too often (especially in survey courses) the other way; and far too often students are simply asked to remember a great deal of factual information without seeking any insight into these facts. It is partly because of this common failing in history courses (and in graduate programs) that we have placed our emphasis in this book so heavily on the absolute primacy of interpretation and explanation. But the student should never assume an ability to offer, or even to read, such explanations without any grasp of the factual material into which such interpretation seeks to provide insight. Instead, before beginning any program of reading or study, the student should make himself *thoroughly* aware of the major events, and dates, and issues, and people that constitute the facts of the subject he is studying; and he should also have a thorough understanding of the geographical background of the subject, i.e., of the physical setting, of the economic setting, of problems of transportation, barriers and aids to communication, relative roles of sea and land in the course of developments, and the like. Only thus will the understanding and insight to be gleaned from the study of history books be at all mature or profound.

While we have, for pedagogical purposes, separated our discussion of how to use primary and secondary sources, ultimately this distinction is somewhat artificial. The interrelated, interacting use of primary and secondary sources is fundamental to the actual process of historical thinking. From primary sources, the historian learns about the complex course of events at a certain moment in time and gets an indication of the crosscurrents of values, aspirations, and motives underlying these events. From secondary sources, the historian learns plausible interpretations of the interrelationship of events and causes of events, and obtains new questions that he can use for a more penetrating and imaginative study and questioning of his primary materials. The study of history is thereby a continuous process of greater perception and more subtle understanding, in which the events and ideas of the past, and the theories and insights of the present, are bridged by the creative historical imagination. No wonder that with some students history becomes not only a subject or discipline but a passion and a narcotic, a form of psychoanalysis, a way of life itself.

6 / A Practical Lesson
in How to Read
a History Book

It is time again to become more specific and practical and to show the student through actual examples the methods he should follow. We have therefore chosen three books that are very frequently assigned to students in European history survey courses; and we propose to show how they should be read, analyzed, and remembered.

The first work is Roland Bainton's *The Reformation of the Sixteenth Century.*[1] It is a characteristic example of the kind of book that presents an introductory survey of its subject and serves primarily as a valuable source for information and for reports of facts, with explanations and interpretations highly generalized in nature.

Bainton's book does have one general point to make—remember that any book or paper must attempt to establish a point or else it is useless except as a list of facts. This thesis can be easily seen in the first chapter and is reinforced by the final paragraphs of the book. On the first page, Bainton begins by discussing a number of movements that he claims are parallel to the Reformation rather than identical to it—worldliness, nationalism, commerce—but in the second paragraph he states very explicitly what he feels to be the main aspect of the Reformation: "The Reformation was above all else a revival of religion."[2] In making

[1] Roland H. Bainton, *The Reformation of the Sixteenth Century* (Boston: The Beacon Press, 1952).

[2] *Ibid.*, p. 3.

this statement, Bainton is not only defining the subject of his book but is also clearly revealing his main point, his particular contention or thesis about the meaning of his subject. The student should note how after stating his thesis, the author proceeds to reinforce it by dissecting it into a series of detailed subpoints, each of which examines an aspect of the main point. He states that the Reformation split the ecclesiastical structure of the Middle Ages, and yet that the Reformation was "the renewer of Christendom" in terms of religious spirit.[3] Finally, he makes the subpoint that the reformers did not think of themselves as innovators, but as restorers of older Christianity.[4] These, then, seem to be the main themes that we will expect to see explicated by the detailed discussion in the book.

The conclusion of the book confirms this analysis by restating in one short paragraph the paramount importance of the themes extracted above:

To close merely by observing the effects of the Reformation on politics, economics, and domestic relations may be quite misleading, because all these were only by-products. The Reformation was a religious revival. Its attempt was to give man a new assurance in the presence of God and a new motivation in the moral life. How far it succeeded no one can ever tell. . . . This only one can say, that the Reformation at once rent and bound. The external unities were shattered, but the Christian consciousness of Europe was renewed. . . .[5]

Thus we have identified the major conceptual bases for the book; and if it is well-constructed, we should expect that most of the details of the book will serve to elaborate, explain, exemplify, and prove those points. It would be well to make a few mental notes about style and quality, so that we have some preliminary judgment of the book, which we can confirm or deny by further reading. Thus it is clear that these points offered by Bainton are rather sweeping, generalized rather than specific; and the terms in the points are not very well-defined. What are "Christian consciousness" or "religious spirit" as historical concepts? Are they

[3] *Ibid.*, p. 4.   [4] *Ibid.*, p. 5.   [5] *Ibid.*, p. 261.

absolute, so that our modern understanding of the terms will suffice, or do we need some special sixteenth-century definition of the terms? Bainton offers no clues in his introduction, so we should suspect that his values may prove to be rather modern ones, that he is a present-day religionist interested in his subject personally because it helps him to shed some light on the generalized problem of faith and Christianity. Two quick checks add some weight to this preliminary historiographical judgment. The last sentence of the book states that "if there is still surviving any consciousness of the Christian culture in the West, the Reformation of the sixteenth century is one of those periodic renewals to which it is due."[6] This statement reveals the emphasis in Bainton's mind on the generalized nature of "Christian consciousness" and his conception of the Reformation not merely as a sixteenth-century phenomenon, but as part of the general history of Christian faith. Second, a quick look at any standard biographical encyclopedia of modern authors reveals that Bainton was, until his recent retirement, a professor of ecclesiastical history at Yale University and that he is himself a devout Protestant. This information offers the reader some insight into Bainton's methods and emphases, and some hint of what to anticipate in the book. Of course, these observations are still preliminary and must be confirmed or denied by further study of the book.

Another preliminary observation of great importance is to note a characteristic stylistic feature of Bainton's writing; he has a tendency, in the passages already read in the book, to place the topic sentence, the main emphasis of each paragraph, at the very beginning of the paragraph. This will be a useful feature to remember later when we are skimming the book to discover its general range of ideas and points.

Since the first chapter is called an "Introduction," we should expect that it will either suggest in summary the contents of the whole book or else provide basic historical background for the main subjects to be discussed later. Reading the chapter shows

[6] Ibid., p. 261.

that the latter is more the case. After the few paragraphs of statement of theme, which we have already analyzed, Bainton immediately proceeds to give a very cursory summary of the history of Christianity, especially of medieval Christianity, as a means of showing what the issues and problems of the Reformation were.[7] This is, of course, a perfectly valid task for an introduction, although it does leave the reader a bit in the dark about what the main threads of the book proper will be. Since Bainton is emphasizing the medieval background in terms of establishing the problems with which the Reformation had to cope, the reader can guess by indirection what kinds of subjects will appear in the main body of the work. Thus the introductory chapter concentrates on papal authority in the world,[8] on philosophical aspects of dogma,[9] on faith and salvation theology,[10] and on the nature of the sacraments.[11] We can assume that in the rest of the book we will find the same subjects treated, with an analysis and explanation of the Reformation views on these subjects.

Three other preliminary observations result from this reading of the first chapter. First, we note that once any general point has been made, Bainton's writing tends at once to become narrative in its expository form. Rather than taking up the topics of his chapter in order, he takes up the sequence of events as it unfolds century by century, with his discussion of the topics scattered throughout the narrative. Thus we will expect to find a similarly chronological narrative approach in the main body of the book. Second, Bainton's explanations are easily comprehended and seem plausible, but he has a tendency to sacrifice complexity for clarity. We now realize that this book is extremely introductory and more useful for beginning the study of the subjects it treats than for any definitive treatment of a subject we might wish to research.

---

[7] "This was the situation on the eve of the sixteenth century." *Ibid.*, p. 21.

[8] *Ibid.*, pp. 8–13, 14–18.   [9] *Ibid.*, pp. 11–12, 15–16.

[10] *Ibid.*, pp. 13, 16–17, 18–19.   [11] *Ibid.*, pp. 10, 19–20.

Finally, we note a stylistic point: Bainton sums up the chapter with a general statement of the contents of the chapter and a clear presentation of the themes and issues, whereas at the beginning of the chapter he tends to leave issues vague, to be suggestive rather than explicit. What is more, we note that the summarized conclusion offered at the end of the chapter is given with a certain dramatic flair, almost a tendency to overstate:

This was the situation on the eve of the sixteenth century. All serious spirits were disturbed and recognized the need for reform. But one party wanted to go back to the heyday of the high Middle Ages when the new monastic orders flourished and the Papacy wielded theocratic power. Such was the ideal of the Catholic Reformation. Others felt that theocracy and monasticism at their very best constituted abuses, and the return must be to the simplicity of a much earlier time. This was the view of what came to be known as the Protestant Reformation.[12]

We now suspect that a quick outline of Bainton's views can be found from reading the concluding paragraph in each chapter, if indeed this tendency to summarize at the end is characteristic of his style. Checking another chapter chosen at random, we find this to be almost the case,[13] although Bainton's extremely narrative approach often overpowers any synthesizing or summarizing tendencies in his writing by concentrating on transitions to the next chapter and the next development. Recognition of this stylistic quality of the ends of chapters will be of great assistance later when skimming the book for its broad outline.

Digressing from the analysis for a moment's reflection, we would emphasize to the student that *all of the preceding observations and discoveries about the book have been the result simply of a careful, thoughtful, and analytical reading of only the first*

[12] *Ibid.*, p. 21.

[13] Any final paragraphs of chapters will illustrate these two points, but see especially the ends of Chapters 1 and 3, pp. 34–35 and 74–76, the former revealing a tendency to summarize, the latter a tendency toward transition.

chapter, the last page, and the concluding paragraphs of a few more chapters. Even for one totally unfamiliar with the subject, the maximum amount of time required for this reading plus the analysis is only a half hour, and yet that half hour of thoughtful, *creative* use of the book has produced almost all the major insights necessary for a thorough grasp of the whole work. Bainton's main points are clear; the subjects he will emphasize and treat are evident; the terms and values of his historiographical argument have been suggested; and the style and content of his book are fairly predictable. All that remains for the student is to read the rest of the book quickly in order to confirm the accuracy and validity of these preliminary conclusions and to find out the specific contents of the book, so that he can use it in the future as a reference or as a source of information. *The student should master the entire work in not more than two hours.* Furthermore, the main impact of the book on his attention will be in terms of its arguments, its principles, and its ideas, which means that the book will stimulate the student's own thoughts about the subject. Study of the book will have been truly profitable rather than a passive attempt to absorb the contents without any analytical thought at all. That so much is to be gained from creative reading is the primary argument in its favor.

To be sure, not every book will be as clear or as simple in its structure as *The Reformation of the Sixteenth Century,* and the preliminary analysis of a more complicated or more specialized book may take longer and be more subtle. *But every historical work is susceptible to a similar approach,* and such an approach will always make a book understandable, not only in a minimum of time, but in a more useful, thoughtful way, giving the reader a knowledge of the book in terms of its main arguments, ideas, and historiographical views as well as in terms of its information content should it be used later as a research tool. Provided that the student is reading books in a language with which he is familiar, we feel that two or three hours spent on such active, creative reading of history each day would make even a beginning student master of two secondary works each week; and this in turn will enable a student quickly to acquire a bibliography that is rich and well informed.

To continue our analysis of *The Reformation of the Sixteenth Century:* what remains, now that the basic structure of the book has been suggested, is to skim the book as a whole to confirm our first impressions and to reveal the particular subjects treated in the body of the book. Since no prefatory note about the contents is offered, the first step should be to glance over the Table of Contents. Here we see at once that the basic outline of the book is chronological. The sequence of topics passes from Luther to Switzerland to Calvin, and then the chapters deal with the subsequent history of the Reformation movements ("The Struggle . . ."). Also, it can be seen that any relationship between the Reformation movements and other aspects of historical interest, e.g., politics or economics, is reserved for the final chapters. This information elicited from the Table of Contents supports earlier suggestions that the basic approach in Bainton's work is chronological and rather narrative, and that his primary concern is not with the Reformation in relation to sixteenth-century society but rather with Reformation thought itself, perhaps in connection with larger questions of Christian faith.

Skimming through the book, we find confirmation of these and our other preliminary points. After the first chapter, which treats the principles of Luther's theology—again, we note, in rather simplistic fashion—the events of Luther's reform and of the spread of the reform to other countries and to other thinkers are taken up in a step-by-step, almost year-by-year narrative. But at the mention of each major event, and especially at the mention of each new publication or liturgical development, Bainton pauses to give a simple, direct digest of the major ideas and doctrines involved so that the reader gains a clear understanding of the steps in the development of the content of Reformation thought, as well as a knowledge of the sequence of events involved in the ongoing

Reformation.[14] As each new movement or thinker comes into the narrative, Bainton emphasizes certain central subjects; in Chapter 4, on the spread of the Reformation to Switzerland and the thought of Zwingli, the topics singled out for emphasis are the philosophical (humanist) origins of Zwingli's theological views,[15] the relationship between Zwingli's reform and his ideas of military power and theocratic authority in the world,[16] Zwingli's conception of Scripture as the basis for faith,[17] and sacramental and liturgical changes.[18] Again, as our footnotes suggest, these subjects are not treated topically; rather, reference to them is scattered throughout Bainton's narrative of the course of events in Zwingli's reform. The subjects and the manner of treatment will be found to be similar in almost every chapter of the book; and it can be seen that they are approximately the same general subjects that we identified above in our analysis of the introductory chapter. Thus our preliminary view that these subjects constitute the primary focus of interest in the book seems to be correct. Moreover, one finds throughout the book that discussion of these particular subjects is related ultimately to establishing Bainton's main point, that the Reformation is a religious revival and renewal.[19] The only chapters that show a categorical, topical treatment rather than the standard narrative approach just discussed are the two on the political and economic-social consequences of the Reformation (Chaps. 12–13). Here Bainton has been primarily concerned with discussing the various views on these subjects that have been presented in the secondary literature; but even so, he does not fail to repeat his basic idea of the primacy of

[14] To cite only two examples, see the references to the Lutheran treatises of 1520 on pp. 52–54, 58, and the description of the activity of Muentzer on pp. 66–67. The treatment of every subject throughout the rest of the book is quite similar.

[15] *Ibid.*, pp. 80–81. [16] *Ibid.*, pp. 81–82, 84–85, 88–89, 90–94.

[17] *Ibid.*, pp. 82–83, 85–86. [18] *Ibid.*, pp. 83, 86–89.

[19] See for instance p. 140; even a chapter whose main subject is the course of events, e.g., Chap. 8, concludes with an emphasis on the primacy of faith in the Reformation spirit (p. 159).

the problem of faith as the most important characteristic of the Reformation movement.[20]

Finally, to make a few brief observations about bookmaking in general, Bainton does not use footnotes, which again confirms our initial impression that the aim of this book is primarily introductory and that the book is not very useful for scholarly purposes nor will it lead the reader into specialized historical problems. This is also suggested by the bibliography, which is limited and with one exception only lists works in English, again connoting the desire to be introductory rather than thorough and exhaustive. Finally, this point is once more suggested by the illustrations, which are decorative and interesting as examples, but which are not precisely related to the text of the discussion, and usually not even referred to in the text.

Now the only task remaining to complete our study of the book is to prepare a bibliographical note and a précis of the main points and the content of the book, to be put into some sort of bibliographical file. Such a note will look something like the following:

Bainton, Roland H., *The Reformation of the Sixteenth Century* (Boston: The Beacon Press, 1956; unaltered paperbound reprint of the original 1952 edition). *Author:* Yale U. scholar, Protestant.

Main thesis: While the Reformation has political, social, and economic dimensions, and while it is related to other aspects of the sixteenth century such as the humanism of the Renaissance, it is primarily a movement in terms of Christian faith, a renewal of the spirit, and an attempt to correct what it regards as abuses by a return to an earlier, Apostolic and patristic Christianity (see pp. 3, 261).

Historiographical observations: Periodically, and at the beginning and the end, Bainton states his thesis and his subsidiary points explicitly. For the most part, the rest of the book is narrative historiography, taking up events and people in chronological order, with points interspersed as they occur. Mostly just introductory survey,

---

[20] "To close merely by observing the effects of the Reformation on politics, economics, and domestic relations may be quite misleading, because all these were only by-products. The Reformation was a religious revival." (p. 261).

with very few value judgments, except in terms of the very general main point above. When values seem implicit, they certainly reflect Bainton's Protestantism and his greater interest in questions of religion than in social questions (see p. 261, last sentence).

Summary of arguments and subsidiary points: Essential problems of the period are worldly authority, especially in relationship to ecclesiastical authority (p. 8ff), philosophical aspects of dogma (p. 11ff), faith and salvation theology (p. 13ff), and sacramental theology p. 10ff). Lutheranism has many relationships to preceding period (p. 22); he shows both affinity and change (p. 23). Chap. 1 gives aspects of Luther's faith, especially doubt in man's ability to participate in salvation (pp. 29–31), influence of mysticism (pp. 31–32), and salvation by faith (pp. 34–35). Chap. 2 treats of early steps of Luther's reform; says Luther an Augustinian not a Thomist (p. 36), emphasis on Scriptural authority (p. 44), anti-sacramentalism (p. 46ff). Luther thus wrecked medieval pattern of Christianity (p. 51). Chap. 3, on the breach, says after Leipzig debate, Luther well known (p. 57). Muentzer's ideas important in subsequent Protestantism (p. 67). Humanism different from Lutheranism; humanism elevates man, Lutheranism elevates God (p. 69)
  [*and so on, listing the major conclusions and emphases of the course of the argument of the book; pages may be added for quick reference*].

Subjects on which there is important factual information in the book: Medieval bases for Reformation issues (Introduction); aspects of Luther's ideas (Chap. 1 and *passim*); early stages of Luther's break with Rome and early councils and meetings (Chap. 2–4); Zwingli's reforms and actions and relationship to Luther (Chap. 4); Anabaptism (Chap. 5)
  [*and so on, listing the major subjects treated for which the book would provide useful research information or study helps*].

Bibliographical references, etc.: No footnotes; small bibliography lists both primary and secondary sources, in English. Some illustrations, unimportant.

This précis provides more than enough points and examples for a thorough historiographical and critical analysis of *The Reformation of the Sixteenth Century*. Any student who had read and analyzed the book in this manner would certainly know it well enough to remember its main ideas and the place it holds in the historiography of the subject. He could use the book in any of the situations that normally face a student: he could refer to it in preparing for an examination; he could write a book review with not many more than the examples our illustration has provided; and if he needed to use the book as a reference in a research paper he could find what he was after in the book with a minimum of effort because of his familiarity with its basic structure and contents. The student who reads every book in this way will certainly have a far greater command of his bibliography than the student who has heedlessly slogged through every book assigned to him page by page, not relating the book to the broader problems of historiography or of historical investigation.

Our model analysis of *The Reformation of the Sixteenth Century* was sufficiently detailed that it would serve little purpose to discuss other books as thoroughly. It is, however, worthwhile to examine two other well-known historical works in more cursory fashion in order to illustrate further the method of reading we have advocated and to indicate the variety of possible organizations of secondary sources.

The first of these books is *The Waning of the Middle Ages*,[21] a justly celebrated study by the Dutch scholar Johan Huizinga. This work is characterized by an emphasis and organization that are directly opposite to Bainton's book, and Huizinga's style is also radically different from Bainton's.

This difference is clear from the very beginning of Huizinga's study. His first chapter gives no statement of any theme or central idea; instead, it offers what at first seems a bit like a random series of examples or vignettes from various fifteenth-century primary sources. But all the examples are of extreme emotion and violent activity, in keeping with the theme suggested by the

---

[21] J. Huizinga, *The Waning of the Middle Ages* (Garden City, N.Y.: Doubleday & Company, Inc., Anchor Books, 1954). The first Dutch edition of this book was published in 1919. The English translation, with changes in the text made by Huizinga, was published in London in 1924 by Edward Arnold Ltd. The Anchor paperback edition of 1954 is the same translation, with different pagination.

chapter heading, "The Violent Tenor of Life." Only at the beginning of the second chapter is any synthesis or summarizing statement given, which brings into focus all of the examples of the preceding section:

At the close of the Middle Ages, a sombre melancholy weighs on people's souls. Whether we read a chronicle, a poem, a sermon, a legal document even, the same impression of immense sadness is produced by them all.[22]

We have here, then, an example of a different approach to introducing a book, a style of organization that in a later chapter we will call the "impressionistic" style, in which the author first beguiles the reader's attention by offering a few arresting examples, and then synthesizes those examples into a generalized conclusion from which he can proceed with his argument. The technique can be extremely successful in introducing a subject when it is used by a master stylist like Huizinga (our reading of the first chapter has already revealed, even in the English translation, Huizinga's gift of narration and his ability to turn a phrase).[23]

Since the first chapter provides no clue about the main thesis or premise of the book, we must turn to the introduction ("Preface") and to the last chapter; in both places we find Huizinga's explicit commitments. In the Preface he states his intentions: "the present work deals with the history of the fourteenth and fifteenth centuries regarded as a period of termination, as the close of the

---

[22] *Ibid.*, p. 31.

[23] See such passages as "The contrast between silence and sound, darkness and light, like that between summer and winter, was more strongly marked than it is in our own lives. The modern town hardly knows silence or darkness in their purity, nor the effect of a solitary light or a single distant cry. All things presenting themselves to the mind in violent contrasts and impressive forms lent a tone of excitement and of passion to everyday life and tended to produce that perpetual oscillation between despair and distracted joy, between cruelty and pious tenderness which characterize life in the Middle Ages" (p. 10). Or such phrases as "So violent and motley was life, that it bore the mixed smell of blood and roses" (p. 27).

Middle Ages."[24] This is confirmed by the conclusion, which also states the exact main thesis of the book:

The fifteenth century in France and the Netherlands is still medieval at heart. The diapason of life had not yet changed. Scholastic thought, with symbolism and strong formalism, the thoroughly dualistic conception of life and the world still dominated. The two poles of the mind continued to be chivalry and hierarchy. Profound pessimism spread a general gloom over life. The gothic principle prevailed in art. But all these forms and modes were on the wane. A high and strong culture is declining, but at the same time and in the same sphere new things are being born. The tide is turning, the tone of life is about to change.[25]

This statement reveals the overriding ideas that the particular discussions in each chapter will try to prove. What is more, this passage also provides, one would think, a summary of the general contents of the body of the book. A quick check of the table of contents proves this supposition to be correct, for it can be seen that the chapters deal with exactly the subjects described in the quotation: pessimism, hierarchy, chivalry, symbolism and religious thought, and artistic expression. The main theme of the book, that the fifteenth century has a strongly medieval dimension and is not "Renaissance" or modern in character, becomes a central thread that recurs constantly as an explicit reference throughout the discussion of each particular subject[26] and thereby binds the whole book together as a discussion of one central idea.

The survey of the contents just offered plus the theme of the book itself suggest that the book is an essay in "cultural history";

[24] *Ibid.*, p. 5.   [25] *Ibid.*, p. 335.

[26] See for example p. 70: "The thirst for honour and glory proper to the men of the Renaissance is essentially the same as the chivalrous ambition of earlier times, and of French origin. Only it has shaken off the feudal form and assumed an antique garb. The passionate desire to find himself praised by contemporaries or by posterity was the source of virtue with the courtly knight of the twelfth century and the rude captain of the fourteenth, no less than with the beaux-esprits of the quattrocento."

it is concerned with the literary, artistic, philosophical, and theological products of the culture of the fifteenth century. That Huizinga's interests lie primarily in cultural history, in the sense of relating monuments of thought to social life at large, is explicitly confirmed by the introduction, where the subject is closely bound up with the main theme of the entire book:

The present work deals with the history of the fourteenth and fifteenth centuries regarded as a period of termination, as the close of the Middle Ages. Such a view of them presented itself to the author of this volume, whilst endeavouring to arrive at a genuine understanding of the art of the brothers Van Eyck and their contemporaries, that is to say, to grasp its meaning by seeing it in connection with the entire life of their times. Now the common feature of the various manifestations of civilization of that epoch proved to be inherent rather in that which links them to the past than in the germs which they contain of the future. The significance, not of the artists alone, but also of theologians, poets, chroniclers, princes and statesmen, could be best appreciated by considering them, not as the harbingers of a coming culture, but as perfecting and concluding the old.[27]

Our suppositions have been confirmed early in the book, but had we skimmed the contents of a few chapters, we would in any case have realized that the book's main concern is with cultural history. The book is full of quotations from primary sources; these consist of poems, chronicles, treatises by churchmen and sermons, devotional literature, and iconology. The very full bibliography adds further support to this point, because it lists all of these primary sources conveniently. (This bibliography, by the way, can readily be seen to be useful, because it gives the works in the best edition and in the original language.)

In our preliminary examination of the book as we search for Huizinga's value judgments and interpretations, it becomes clear that his historical assumptions have strong psychological overtones. He is continually discussing states of mind and emotions and feelings; his real interest is in "that perpetual oscillation be-

[27] *Ibid.,* p. 5–6.

tween despair and distracted joy, between cruelty and pious
tenderness which characterizes life in the Middle Ages."[28] The
book abounds with explanations that depend on his description of
the mental or psychological state of people of the time.[29] This
hypothesis is strengthened when we examine Huizinga's way of
using his primary sources closely. He does not analyze chronicles
or narrative descriptions to find implicit ideas and values, as
would be true of an historian of ideas; but rather he takes such
material as offering literal and explicit description of what people
did and how they felt and responded to situations. For instance,
in attempting to show that people were becoming more irreverent,
Huizinga uses several chronicles and a religious treatise in just
this way:

Vigils likewise, says Clemanges, are kept with lascivious songs and
dances, even in church; priests set the example by dicing as they watch.
It may be said that the moralists paint things in too dark colours; but
in the accounts of Strassburg we find a yearly gift of 1,100 litres of wine
granted by the council to those who "watched in prayer" in church
during the night of Saint Adolphus. Denis the Carthusian wrote a
treatise *De modo agendi processiones,* at the request of an alderman,
who asked him how one might remedy the dissoluteness and debauch-
ery to which the annual procession, in which a greatly venerated relic
was borne, gave rise. "How are we to put a stop to this?" asks the
alderman. "You may be sure that the town council will not easily be
persuaded to abolish it, for the procession brings large profits to the
town, because of all the people who have to be fed and lodged. Besides,
custom will have it so." "Alas, yes," sighs Denis; "he knows too well how
processions were disgraced by ribaldry, mockery, and drinking." A
most vivid picture of this evil is found in Chastellain's description of
the degradation into which the procession of the citizens of Ghent,
with the shrine of Saint Liévin, to Houthem, had fallen. Formerly, he

[28] *Ibid.,* p. 10.
[29] One example can represent the whole: "Rarer than processions and
executions were the sermons of itinerant preachers, coming to shake people by
their eloquence. The modern reader of newspapers can no longer conceive
the violence of impression caused by the spoken word on an ignorant mind
lacking mental food" (p. 12).

says, the notabilities were in the habit of carrying the holy body "with great and deep solemnity and reverence"; at present there is only "a mob of roughs, and boys of bad character"; they carry it singing and yelling, "with a hundred thousand gibes, and all are drunk."[30]

When we look at the date of publication of *The Waning of the Middle Ages,* we discover that the original Dutch edition was published in 1919. This is quite early in the twentieth century for an historian to be concerned with psychological themes. Therefore we realize that this book is not only a work of great importance for the interpretation of fifteenth-century culture; it is also a pioneering work in the application of psychological theories to historical understanding and represents a milestone in twentieth-century historical thought.

But Huizinga can be criticized on the ground that his psychological insights depend on a very literal, almost naive interpretation of late medieval documents. He does not seem to consider that there might be present some mode of expression other than the literal one; for instance, the sources he is quoting might be expressing conventional rhetorical figures rather than explicit descriptions of "real life." Thus the psychological method used by Huizinga requires careful consideration by the reader. On the one hand, it is challenging and original. But on the other hand, it can be held to be somewhat insensitive to the typological mode of thought of the era with which it is concerned.

The preceding discussion has been enough to show that even with a complex and subtle work like *The Waning of the Middle Ages* preliminary thoughtful analysis, which seeks from the first to lay bare the vital structure of the book, can in a very short time enable the reader to discover the most significant features of a secondary source: its main point or major thesis, its historiographical attitude and values, the kind of evidence and factual material it provides as a research source, and a general notion of the topics discussed in the book. Indeed, in the case of a book as complex

[30] *Ibid.,* p. 160.

and as rich in detailed examples as *The Waning of the Middle Ages,* such preliminary analysis of the structure and major point of the book is not merely helpful but is *absolutely essential* to prevent even an experienced student from losing the thread of the argument in the welter of detail.

Further close analysis of the chapters and body of the book would here be supererogatory; from the example of our analysis of *The Reformation of the Sixteenth Century* the student can judge how he would proceed from the stage to which we have led him. A complete study would involve the confirmation of our preliminary analytical hypotheses by searching for evidence of their validity in all of the discussions of particular subjects throughout the book. It is necessary, however, to dwell on the difference in technique of organization between Bainton and Huizinga. In Bainton's work, it will be recalled, there is a continuous narrative style; presenting his material chronologically rather than topically, Bainton sought to touch upon every major figure, writing, and issue of the period and to show the sequence in which events follow one another in time. His general points, analyses, and conclusions thus became almost like asides or pauses within his narrative of facts. Huizinga's approach is altogether different. His organization, as reflected in his table of contents, is topical rather than chronological; and the thread in his book is provided not by a chronology of fact or example but by the continual elaboration of his central idea, topic by topic. His factual examples and primary source references are superimposed on this flow, inserted into his exposition as illustrations of the theme he is developing. Because of this technique, his book cannot offer the reader any useful sense of the course of events in the fourteenth and fifteenth centuries, nor even any sense of the total significance of a single primary source of the period. It is typical of his method that the discussion of a given primary source may appear in two quite separate places because the source is related to two different topics under discussion.[31] While this technique heightens the profundity and the interest of Huizinga's book as an interpretive, provocative study, it also decreases the usefulness of the book as a research source providing factual or primary source information. And yet, paradoxically, Huizinga's technique requires many more examples and primary source references than does Bainton's chronological narrative, because it is only through showing the application of his thesis to a wealth of examples that Huizinga can establish its validity. It is much easier in a narrative work to show the connection of examples—based on simple sequences of events —than in a topical kind of historiography.

A brief examination of one more source, Isaiah Berlin's *Karl Marx*,[32] will not only give a further example of how preliminary analysis can expose the general theme and central core of ideas in a secondary work, but will also illustrate that the format of an introductory chapter can indicate the organizational structure of the rest of the book. Moreover, this work exemplifies an approach to organization that combines the methods used in the two previous examples. It alternates sections of chronological narration with sections of topical analysis.

The very beginning of Berlin's text might lead the reader to suspect that the intention in the book is to create a narrative biography: the first few pages offer paragraph after paragraph of summarized features of Marx's character. Since only two or three pages suffice to make clear that Berlin, in an almost tedious way, usually makes the topic, or key, sentence of the paragraph the

[31] For instance, Huizinga twice refers to the description in Chastellain's *Chronicle* of a judicial duel between two burghers of Valenciennes in 1455, the first time to illustrate that bells were a common feature of town life (p. 10) and the second time to show the absence of chivalry among the lower classes (pp. 101–102); no cross-reference is given to remind the reader that this is the same source in both cases.

[32] Isaiah Berlin, *Karl Marx: His Life and Environment* [New York: Oxford University Press, 1963; Galaxy Book (paperback), 1963].

first one, our point can be exemplified by a string of such topic sentences from the opening pages of the book:

No thinker in the nineteenth century has had so direct, deliberate, and powerful an influence upon mankind as Karl Marx. . . . Marx totally lacked the qualities of a great popular leader or agitator. . . . His public appearances were neither frequent nor notably successful. . . . He was endowed with a powerful, active, concrete, unsentimental mind, an acute sense of injustice, and exceptionally little sensibility, and was repelled as much by the rhetoric and emotionalism of the intellectuals as by the stupidity and complacency of the bourgeoisie. . . . This sense of living in a hostile and vulgar world, intensified perhaps by his latent dislike of the fact that he was born a Jew, increased his natural harshness and aggressiveness, and produced the formidable figure of popular imagination.[33]

And so on. Nonetheless, before we are satisfied with an initial impression that in this book we are dealing with biographical historiography, with a "personality" approach to explaining the genesis and development of Marx's ideas, there are several other clues to the major emphases of the book which bear consideration, and which lead to a slightly different conclusion. We get one clue when after a few minutes' research in the library, we discover that Berlin is an Oxford professor, not of history but of political theory and social philosophy. Another is provided by the preface to the revised edition ("Note to Third Edition"). When an author revises a book, he very frequently puts in a note of preface explaining what the revisions were; such notes can be very revealing, because they suggest which aspects of the book have received the greatest attention and consideration, and hence which aspects probably have the greatest importance in the eyes of the writer. In the present case, Berlin states:

I have taken the opportunity offered by a new edition to correct errors of fact and of judgment, and to repair omissions in the expositions of Marx's views, both social and philosophical, in particular of ideas which were neglected by the first generation of his disciples and his critics

[33] *Ibid.*, pp. 1–4.

and came into prominence only after the Russian Revolution. The most important of these is his conception of the relation between the alienation and the freedom of men.[34]

From this statement, we would gather that Berlin's first interest in his writing is to give an explication of Marx's theories and ideas rather than of his life, and to trace the history of his ideas in the world of his time and afterward. This hypothesis is confirmed by the conclusion of the entire work, always a most revealing source of insight into the primary emphasis of a book, in which Berlin confines his entire discussion to a consideration of Marx's main doctrines and the relationship between those theories and the general history of political, economic, and social thought:

Others before him had preached a war between classes, but it was he who conceived and successfully put into practice a plan designed to achieve the political organization of a class fighting solely for its interest as a class—and in so doing transformed the entire character of political parties and political warfare. Yet in his own eyes and in those of his contemporaries, he appeared as first and foremost a theoretical economist. . . . All those whose work rests on social observation are necessarily affected. Not only conflicting classes and groups and movements and their leaders in every country, but historians and sociologists, psychologists and political scientists, critics and creative artists, so far as they try to analyse the changing quality of the life of their society, owe the form of their ideas in large part to the work of Karl Marx. . . . Its effect was, and continues to be, revolutionary. It set out to refute the proposition that ideas decisively determine the course of history, but the very extent of its own influence on human affairs has weakened the force of its thesis. For in altering the hitherto prevailing view of the relation of the individual to his environment and to his fellows, it has palpably altered that relation itself. . . .[35]

If the reader now performs an analytical reading of the body of Berlin's book, similar to the model analysis we provided for Bainton's *Reformation of the Sixteenth Century*, he will find that in this summarizing conclusion Berlin has not only outlined the

[34] *Ibid.*, "Note to Third Edition," n.p.
[35] *Ibid.*, pp. 282–84.

basic contents of his book, but has also, in the first and last sentences quoted, offered an explicit statement of his main thesis. Once again, a little biographical information on the author and preliminary analysis of key portions of a book have made clear at the beginning of the reading of the book what are its most important features and ideas.

But what of the apparent disparity between the theoretical interests of the preface and the conclusion, and the seemingly biographical emphasis of the first chapter? One possibility, of course, would be that this book is organized in such a way that it is narrative throughout, only reaching its final conclusions at the very end. Further reading of the first chapter, however, shows that an altogether different style of organization is being used by Berlin. We jumped to the conclusion that his emphasis is biographical because we only read the initial pages of the first chapter; had we continued, we would have found that in this "Introduction" Berlin also offers a summary of the essential points of Marx's theories,[36] the relationships between Marx's theories and other ideas current at the time,[37] the relationship between Marx's ideas and earlier social and philosophical theories,[38] and finally the contemporary historical setting into which Marx's ideas were introduced.[39] In the course of this analysis, Berlin offers some summarizing introductory statements that give as complete and explicit a statement of his main thesis as did the paragraphs at the end of the book:

He [Marx] concluded that the history of society is the history of man seeking to attain mastery of himself and of the external world by means of his creative labour. This activity is incarnated in the struggles of opposed classes, one of which must emerge triumphant, although in a much altered form: progress is constituted by the succession of victories of one class over another, and that man alone is rational who identifies himself with the progressive class in his society. . . . The

[36] *Ibid.*, pp. 5–12, 16–17, 20–21.   [37] *Ibid.*, pp. 5, 19.
[38] *Ibid.*, pp. 12–16.   [39] *Ibid.*, pp. 17–18, 20–22.

war must be fought on every front, and since contemporary society is politically organized, a political party must be formed out of those elements which in accordance with the laws of historical development are destined to emerge as the conquering class.[40]

In this way a full reading of the introductory chapter corrects our first impression and reveals that the main emphasis in Berlin's argument is on the contents, genesis, and impact of Marx's thought in the context of contemporary thought and society. This example should serve as a warning not simply to accept one's first reactions to a book or one's first hypotheses as necessarily correct. Only a thorough, perceptive analysis that looks for a variety of clues and indications can give sufficient or satisfactory insight into the contents of a book. However, thoroughness does not, we repeat, mean reading every single word for fear that one might "miss something"; rather, thoroughness is achieved by perceptive analysis, by constantly seeking insight into the nuances of emphasis offered by the writer throughout the reading of the book.

The balance between biographical narrative and analysis of Marx's ideas is presented by Berlin through the use of an organizational structure rather different from those encountered in the works of Bainton and Huizinga. Even in the first chapter, Berlin's approach to organization of his writing is clear. He alternates biographical or narrative sections (pp. 1–4, 12–13, 17–18, 20–21) with analytical discussions of general, theoretical points (pp. 4–12, 13–17, 19–20, 21–22). In considering the structure of the book as a whole, it is interesting to note that Berlin follows exactly this same pattern of alternation in his sequence of chapters: a study of Marx's early development (Chap. II) is followed by a general consideration of idealist and Hegelian philosophy in the eighteenth and nineteenth centuries (Chap. III). The next chapter (Chap. IV) is once again a biographical study of Marx's formative years, but the context of discussion is widened, so that Marx is seen in relationship to other thinkers of his time. Chapter V

[40] *Ibid.*, pp. 7–8, 10.

continues this pattern, but is then followed by a purely analytical chapter on the question of historical materialism (Chap. VI). Chapters VII and VIII are once again primarily biographical narrative, but they are followed by a chapter discussing generally the movement of the socialist International (Chap. IX). Finally, in the last two chapters, Berlin is able to combine the two types of material. Because his account of Marx's life is primarily an exposition of the development of Marx's thought, narrative description and theoretical analysis can in these chapters be combined into one continuous discussion. This alternating of narration and analysis permits Berlin to present his material smoothly and coherently; and the clever way in which the organization of the first, introductory chapter implies the overall structure of the book gives the reader a feeling of great cohesiveness about the whole work that is pronounced and satisfying, and reflects thoughtful planning in the writing of the book.

We have dwelt at rather great length on these three examples, not only to provide the student with models that help him learn how to become a skillful and thoughtful reader of secondary sources, but also to emphasize and to urge over and over again our major point: historical works are really only useful if approached creatively and actively. If a student claims that he does not understand a certain book—and how often have we heard this woebegone complaint from students who have given up in despair—the probability is overwhelming that the fault lies in the student himself rather than in the book. The student has been waiting for the book to "tell him the answer" instead of using the book as a means of finding an answer. The chief use of a secondary historical source—a book written to prove a point—is to provoke, to stimulate, to lead the reader on to new insights of his own; and only thoughtful, analytical reading of secondary sources will make this possible.

The one theme that has recurred, again and again, thus far in our guide to the study of history has been the need for active perception, for creative and imaginative interpretation in the use of all types of historical materials. Neither primary sources nor secondary sources will offer any significantly meaningful insights to a passive reader who seeks merely to recognize their contents. But the student who has acquired the basic principles of analyzing sources, and who through diligent study learns by practice and by observing the work of other historians to apply such principles fluently, will find himself fully prepared and well informed for the next major step in his development—the writing of his own original historical papers.

7 / Excursus on Auxiliary Disciplines

Primary and secondary sources and their study and explication are the basic materials and techniques of the historian, whether he is a freshman or an eminent professional scholar. But the historian is also heavily dependent on what the nineteenth-century German scholars who founded modern historiography called *Hilfswissenschaften,* or auxiliary disciplines. This term is usually applied to the ancillary materials and studies which the undergraduate begins to encounter as a history major and which the graduate student is required to master. But at all levels of historical study, beginning with survey courses, there are auxiliary disciplines whose methods the student should follow in order to maintain his commitment to excellence. The purpose of this excursus chapter is to introduce the student to these helpful techniques and materials at each of the three levels of academic historical work—at the level of survey courses, at the level of potential and beginning history majors, and at the level of advanced undergraduate and graduate work.

For Students in Survey Courses: How to Use a Textbook and Take Lecture Notes

In about 70 percent of American and Canadian colleges and universities the introductory European history survey will, through the academic year, cover the whole development of Western civilization, from prehistoric man to the present. In some institutions, in addition to European history, glimpses of Asian and African history will be offered; and the course will attempt to survey the whole of "World History." In the remaining 30 percent of American colleges, the introductory survey covers a shorter period and provides a more intense examination of the period from the late Middle Ages or Renaissance (fourteenth-fifteenth centuries) to the present.

In these survey courses a *standard core textbook* is usually assigned to the students. In the required weekly reading assignments the textbook is supplemented by a readings or documents book and some paperbacks on special topics of crucial importance. Book reviews are nearly always demanded of the students. The essays and research papers which are usually required in more advanced and specialized history courses are also sometimes assigned to freshmen in the survey courses. In any case there is a long procession of quizzes and tests confronting the novice history student in the survey courses. The teaching in survey courses usually comprises two formal lectures a week and a discussion class.

In the next chapter we will discuss the technique of writing good exams, but for now we wish to delineate some helpful information on how to use the textbook and how to take notes on lectures.

It is the function of the textbook in a history course to provide the basic factual information and interpretations upon which the student can draw in explicating primary sources and evaluating secondary works. *You should use the assigned textbook in the following way:*

1. At the beginning of the term read through the whole textbook quickly to get a general view of the pattern of events you will be studying.

2. Each week, before going on to the study of the assigned primary sources and interpretive secondary sources (the "collat-

eral reading" of the course), study carefully the chapter or two from the textbook assigned for the week in the course syllabus. Underline the most important names, dates, and generalizations made in the textbook. Summarize in the margin of the book the thesis or theme of each paragraph.

3. Before each test reread the underlined sentences and your marginal notes.

4. Before the final examination read the whole textbook through to get a general view again. This time, as a result of lectures, source study, and the reading of interpretive works, you should be able to supplement the summary statements in the textbook at several points with much more detailed and sophisticated knowledge. If you have been using your primary and secondary sources correctly, you should, at the end of the term, know much more than the textbook provides on several key historical problems.

Lectures are always a prime source of knowledge for the history student. The lecturer draws upon years and even decades of professional training and intensive study to illuminate problems and summarize the state of current knowledge in his field. For the introductory student lectures are indispensable and should be attended and listened to with a clear mind and undivided attention. Some college lecturers are more eloquent and brilliant than others, but all can open up the many-sided dimensions of an historical era for the student.

Taking and filing notes on lectures is important, not only for the immediate purpose of preparing for course exams but also for the long range use of research on papers. You may recall dimly while working on an essay that three semesters ago one of your instructors mentioned a book dealing with the subject you are now investigating, or offered an interpretation that at the time seemed incisive and original. But this dim recollection will be of no use unless you can quickly put your hands on specific information. Even if the European history survey is the only college level history course you intend to take, you should make and file your notes with great care, not only for exam purposes, but also because the ideas and material of the Western civilization course will be extremely valuable for whatever field of the humanities and social and natural sciences becomes your speciality.

The following method of lecture note-taking will enable you to take the fullest advantage of your instructor's teaching:

1. During the lecture listen carefully to what is being said and *write down only* (a) the bibliographically important information; (b) the major points of interpretation; (c) phrases that seem particularly evocative and original, and points that are strongly stressed; (d) material not in the reading assignment—it is absolutely necessary that you do the week's reading before the lecture, or else you will simply be taking notes on material fully discussed in the assignments.

This method will allow you to comprehend and enjoy what your instructor is saying. Nothing dismays a lecturer more than to see row after row of students bow their heads as soon as he utters a syllable and keep them down for a whole hour while they try to make stenographic reproductions of what he is saying. Stenography is exhausting labor; and students, who are in any case rarely trained in professional shorthand, become so preoccupied with the motor skill involved in getting down every sentence of the lecture, they cannot make any sense out of what the instructor is saying. Hours, days, or even weeks later they struggle through their semiverbatim notes and try to figure out what were the theme and the main points of the lecture. It is far more efficient to do this while listening to the lecturer than to try to evoke his ideas from cold and incoherent notes. The same stricture applies to the latest method of the amateur stenographers in the student body—taping the lectures. Unless there is some physical reason why you cannot take notes, taping lectures will prove an extremely inefficient procedure. You will have to play the whole tape, lasting an hour, in order to get the main points of the lecture; whereas proper note-taking will recall these points for you in two or three minutes.

2. As the lecture comes to an end, before slamming your notebook shut, take thirty seconds to summarize in three or four lines the main theme of the lecture.

3. As soon as possible after the lecture, and certainly within twenty-four hours, go to a quiet place and write down *in your own words* a one or two page summary of the lecture, incorporating your class notes on those aspects listed in 1 and 2 above. Striking or important phrases used by the lecturer which you have noted down should be signified by quotation marks. Any details of the lecture on names, dates, events, etc., that you cannot recall can be derived from the textbook and collateral reading.

4. Leave at least a two-inch margin on the left side of your notes, both those taken in the class and those made afterward on the lecture. As you go over these notes, you can enter subject headings describing the main topics considered, your own comments, and reference to discussions of the same subject in secondary sources. If you wish to find, a year or two later, bibliographical material and interpretive points, all you have to do is run your eye down this left-hand margin, and the information will be found after a few minutes' search. The most conscientious student will make entries on note cards of the bibliographical material and interpretive points presented in the lectures and will file these away for future reference.

When making notes on lectures, always jot down in the upper right-hand corner of the sheet or card the name of the instructor and the date of the lecture. This practice will allow you to refer to the lecture in a later essay in the proper manner, such as: Professor X. Y., Europe Since 1500, "Lecture on the Causes of the French Revolution," March 10, 1966. Lecturing is a form of publishing; and you may—if your instructor allows this practice—cite a statement made in a lecture in the same way that you cite a page from an interpretive book. But remember that a lecture has the same quality as any other secondary source; it is not per se author-itative proof. You must evaluate an interpretation offered in a lecture in exactly the same way you evaluate the validity of any thesis presented in a secondary source.

FOR POTENTIAL AND BEGINNING HISTORY MAJORS: PLANNING AN UNDERGRADUATE HISTORY PROGRAM

The student in a survey course who finds that he has a marked aptitude for explicating primary sources, evaluating secondary works, and for critically examining and discussing the main themes in the development of Western civilization or of American history will begin to consider concentrating in history in his upper-class college work. There is every good reason for choosing history as a college major. As a field of concentration, history has three distinct uses:

1. History is probably the best field for the student whose main aim in college is a sound liberal education. History is concerned with all that man has thought and done, and a history major combined with individual courses in literature, philosophy, art, music, and the social sciences introduces the student to all facets of human culture and experience.

2. Deans of law schools and schools of journalism believe there is no better undergraduate preparation for postgraduate professional study in their fields than the knowledge and methods acquired by the history major. For most branches of government work historical study offers the best preparation; and for students who intend to go directly after graduation into management training programs offered by business corporations, history also offers an excellent background.

3. Students who wish to become college teachers of history will need a quite heavy undergraduate concentration in history, combined with specialized work in languages and the social sci-

ences. There is every reason nowadays to choose an academic career in history. The historical profession offers the unsurpassed intellectual and emotional satisfactions of college teaching, and attractive remuneration as well. Most new Ph.D.'s in history start at about the same salary offered to graduates of the better law schools when they begin work in a legal firm in one of the larger American cities. No profession equals the academic one for economic security. Most college teachers nowadays obtain permanent tenure (which means they can only be fired for gross immorality, felonies, or extreme incompetence) a half dozen years after they begin their academic careers. A college teaching career can, furthermore, be combined with many opportunities for writing, publishing, and consulting; and it can lead to high posts in academic administration.

The student in a survey course who thinks he is a potential history major should follow a definite procedure:

1. Before you make your final decision, you should have taken two survey courses, one in European and the other in either American or non-Western history. You should also have taken at least one specialized history course dealing with a relatively short period, in which extensive use has been made of primary sources. There are some students who enjoy history at the survey level, and get good grades in this kind of course, but who find more advanced work to be either too difficult or unsatisfying.

2. Before you become a history major, you should become proficient in at least one foreign European language; and you should have taken survey courses in economics, sociology, and if possible, also in psychological theory (*not* experimental psychology, which is mainly concerned with rats and of little use to the historian) and in the principles of cultural anthropology.

3. As early as possible in your sophomore year (or even at the end of your freshman year) you should have a long conference with the member of the History Department who is responsible for advising majors and concentrators (he is usually called the

departmental representative or student adviser). Tell this departmental adviser as succinctly as possible your secondary school background, your reasons for becoming a history major, your professional ambitions, what courses in history you have taken, the level of your grades, and the areas of history you wish to make your specialty.

The departmental adviser will be able to tell you if there are any prerequisites that you still need to fulfill for admission into the history majors' program. He will at this time or later in the year work out with you a program of courses for your junior and senior years.

While majors' programs are dependent on the student's needs and the offerings of the department and university, we think it is a mistake for the undergraduate history major to specialize too narrowly. The purpose of a major's program is to introduce the student to the concepts and methods of the humanities and the social sciences in general, and to several eras and varieties of history in particular. Narrow concentration on special areas and techniques are the province of graduate study. The history major should study two distinct fields of history and should do extensive work in at least one other department of the humanities and social sciences.

The following program is designed to give only a general impression of the kind of program the potential and beginning history major should work out in consultation with his departmental adviser.

Freshman year: European History Survey
                 Foreign Language
                 Introduction to Philosophy
                 Introduction to Economics
                 English Literature
                 Introduction to History and Philosophy of
                        Science

Sophomore year: American, Asian, African, or Latin American Survey

Introduction to Cultural Anthropology

Foreign Language and Literature

Art History; Musicology

Introduction to Sociology; Psychological Theory

Specialized History Course

Junior year: Specialized history course in first field of concentration

Specialized history course in second field of concentration

Second Foreign Language

Specialized work in one of the social sciences or humanities

Seminar or supervised independent work in history (involves writing of a long paper making extensive use of primary sources)

Senior year: Specialized history course in first field of concentration

Specialized history course in the second field, or in a third field

Seminar or supervised independent work on a senior thesis

Specialized work in one of the humanities

Specialized work in one of the social sciences

You should aim at a balanced program that offers specialized work in at least two major fields of history; introductory work in several of the humanities and social sciences, and specialized work in at least one of these subjects; sound training in at least two foreign languages; and extensive experience in the writing of long papers. Remember that at all levels of academic historical study your teachers, who are well-trained, experienced, and conscientious people, are ready to help you in any way they can. You should confer extensively with your professors during their designated office hours on the progress of your work.

FOR HISTORY MAJORS AND POTENTIAL GRADUATE STUDENTS: ANCILLARY MATERIALS AND DISCIPLINES

As you get into advanced work as a history student, you will realize that the preparation necessary for serious research and writing includes a great many materials, disciplines, and techniques derived from ancillary fields and from subjects not usually part of the offering of standard history courses, or included in standard history department curricula. This fact is important, and not merely in terms of satisfying academic requirements. Even to think in a sophisticated way about historical problems, you have to command this additional knowledge. In its most ideal form, history is the synthesis of all knowledge, for history seeks to explain everything that has happened.

Even at an immediately practical level, the student will need to have a mastery of a number of ancillary techniques to cope with problems that will come up in his work. The most obvious of such techniques is a firm and sure reading ability in languages pertinent to his particular field, both the original languages of the primary sources and the languages in which the major secondary scholars in the field have written. It is worth repeating here our earlier point that to understand primary sources from an earlier age, the student should have some philological awareness of changes in language patterns and meanings of words. Otherwise he will be misled by attributing modern meanings to older words that have an altogether different sense.

Anyone who knows anything at all about graduate programs in history is aware that advanced work will involve the reading of foreign languages. But students who come from an historical

training narrowly political, social, and economic in emphasis—as
is all too frequently the case—fail to recognize that there are a
number of other fields that contribute not only other approaches
to historical study and other points of view but also additional
factual information of great importance. While we have offered
below some suggestions about specific subjects to accompany the
study of particular periods of history, in general *the study of
religious thought, of art history, of literature, of geography, and of
the social sciences will be of great value no matter what your field.*
Indeed, some of the greatest insights into history have begun with
the consideration or at least the contemplation of works of art or
literature. For instance, Jacob Burckhardt's conception of the
Renaissance to a great extent had its roots in his attempt to understand what caused certain drastic changes in the style and content
of literature and art in fifteenth- and sixteenth-century Italy, and
recent attempts at forming a concept of the Renaissance have paid
careful attention to the views and contributions of noted art historians like Erwin Panofsky.

Of all such ancillary fields, geography is the one most immediately and universally central to the historian. The science of
geography includes a great deal more than simply physical geography, although physical geography—the knowledge of topog-
raphy, rivers, plains, and the like—is the basis for all geographical
insight. In addition, the geographer seeks to understand such matters as population distribution, patterns of fertility and barren-
ness, climate distribution, trade patterns in relationship to physical
geography, and many other aspects of the physical world in which
the events of history took place. A firm grasp of such knowledge is
absolutely indispensable for gaining a full and realistic perspective
on the course of historical change. Students of European history
should make every effort to gain an early and profound acquaintance with the map of Europe and the Mediterranean basin, and
at least a basic knowledge of the geography of the whole world.

Auxiliary knowledge for the historian involves much more

than specific academic disciplines. Only through reflection on his own experiences can the historian adequately understand and imagine the experiences of men in the past as described in primary sources. If he has not experienced something like the emotional responses indicated in his sources, the historian will have little or no success in achieving an empathy with the people of the era he is studying and of communicating to his readers the quality of past thoughts and feelings. The gaining of experiences that illuminate the past for the scholar is part of the process of growing up rightly, of developing an integrated personality, and of living a happy and full life.

There are, moreover, many obvious and immediate experiences that can consciously be sought for in order to provide insight into the human condition in a previous age. For the medieval historian, a visit to a Catholic cathedral on a high feast day can convey an awareness of the impact of liturgical practice on thirteenth-century society. The student of modern political or economic history might do very well to try to gain some experience in actual work with a government office, in order to get a taste of the workings of a modern bureaucracy; or he might follow the stock market and associate himself with businessmen and others connected with modern commerce in order to experience their way of looking at the world of finance and trade. Even the student interested in the ancient city-state can gain a certain insight into the social problems of life in ancient Athens of the fifth century B.C. or in Rome of the Principate by becoming aware of the problems and the activities involved in modern city planning and urban redevelopment in crowded metropolitan areas.

Travel to the places which will be the setting for the area which he is studying is indispensable for the serious historian. If you were writing about the Renaissance in Italy, a visit to Florence would allow you actually to tread the streets and feel around you the walls that were the physical environment of the Renaissance poets, artists, and princes. The physical remains of past ages are invaluable in giving concrete dimensions to old insights and in connoting and suggesting new ideas. The places of Europe are full of such monumental incarnations of past ideas—the nineteenth-century imperialism of the Paris Opera house, the order of the Athenian Acropolis, the paranoid walls of medieval towns in Flanders and southern France, the royal microcosm of Versailles. Any student interested in European history should certainly plan to spend at least one year in Europe. Indeed, if the student can manage it, two years might be better—one year of general travel and observation, perhaps early in his career, and a later year specifically devoted to the region connected with his advanced research, perhaps while completing a doctoral dissertation. Students of United States history should "see America first" and this includes experience of life in small towns and on farms in the Midwest and South.

The various periods of European history each require some special training and mastery of particular materials.

Ancient History

Almost all graduate programs in ancient history will require a reading knowledge of Latin, Greek, French, and German. These languages will certainly be the basic tools needed for work in this field—Latin and Greek for the primary sources, and French and German to cover the major scholarship. Other languages will certainly be necessary, but the specific choice would depend on the student's area of concentration. If he is interested in the Ancient Near East or in the Biblical period, he would probably first want to master the languages of the primary sources, especially Hebrew or some languages from the near-eastern regions, either ancient (Akkadian, Egyptian in its various forms, Hittite, Sumerian, Ugaritic, and the like) or Hellenistic (Syriac, Aramaic, Old Persian, etc.). If, on the other hand, the student plans to concentrate on Greek and Roman history, a knowledge of an ancient language, such as Egyptian, might aid him in explicating Greek primary sources (e.g., Herodotus), but a more useful language for him to master first might be Italian, because important secondary scholarship in classical studies has been written and is being written in Italian. As for ancillary subjects, it should go without saying that a very thorough knowledge of classical literature, Greek, and Roman, and a full acquaintance with all of the monuments of ancient art and architecture are *sine qua non* for classical studies, and a comparable knowledge of literary remains and artistic monuments is indispensable for understanding the Ancient Near East. In addition to general literary and art-historical study, the student of ancient history would be very well advised to learn not only the information but also the techniques and methods of the fields of archeology, numismatics (the study of all aspects of coins), and epigraphy (the study of inscriptions carved in stone or metal monuments)—all of which will provide a considerable amount of factual evidence of great value in reconstructing a conception of the ancient world.

Medieval History; Renaissance and Seventeenth-Century History

Most graduate programs in medieval or Renaissance history will require a reading knowledge of French, German, and Latin. Again, this accords with the patterns to be found in the literature. Latin is necessary for the reading of primary sources, and most medieval scholarship has been written in French and German, with a certain amount in Italian. Beyond these basic languages, concentration on some topic of medieval or Renaissance history will certainly require further knowledge of languages to facilitate reading of primary sources. Students concentrating on Byzantine studies would certainly have to know Greek (in its Scriptural and medieval form, not ancient), and probably a knowledge of Arabic would help as well. The great growth of Byzantine studies in the twentieth century has also made clear that no student of this field can succeed without some knowledge of East European languages, first Russian and then some of the languages of the Balkan countries; this is true not only because of primary sources but especially because of a great deal of secondary scholarship in those languages. For intellectual history of the Byzantine period one might also add Old Church Slavonic to the list of needed languages. Students of medieval and early modern Spain will need to know Spanish and Portugese in their various dialectical forms, not only for analyzing primary sources but also for reading secondary scholarship, since in this field there is a substantial bibliography in Spanish, Portugese, and Catalan. Even more, the study of medieval Spain would be greatly facilitated by a knowledge of Arabic, Hebrew, and Gothic, especially Arabic, since many of the primary sources for this history are Arabic records. Students of medieval England or of the early Middle Ages in the North should expect to learn the various medieval Germanic languages, especially Anglo-Saxon; also, students of medieval England might want to add the Celtic languages (Welsh and Old Irish) and Old Scandinavian forms (Old Norse and Icelandic), or for a later period, Middle English and Old French (including Anglo-Norman French). Students of the high Middle Ages in Europe will certainly need to know Old French and also would need some specialized study of medieval Latin. Students of medieval intellectual history should ideally know Greek, Arabic, and Hebrew to have a complete grasp of the primary sources in their fields. Students of Renaissance and seventeenth-century intellectual problems will certainly have to know Italian and Latin in order to have full view of two of the major streams of thought and culture of this period; beyond that, the student should plan to become very familiar with the Renaissance and early modern forms of the languages of the countries in which he is interested.

As for ancillary fields that will aid in the study of medieval and Renaissance problems, besides the general fields of art history and literature already considered, particular emphasis might be placed on the study of theology, philosophy, and liturgy as especially relevant to understanding "the medieval mind." In Renaissance studies a knowledge of the technology of commercial processes is of great help in reference to many aspects of life in the period. In the study of art in these periods, particular attention should be paid to acquiring a close knowledge of iconography (the use of standard, commonly recognized images, postures, gestures, settings, etc., in pictorial representation), because many concepts important to the age were manifested visually in major works of art; and such concepts can only be grasped by an understanding of iconographic techniques. For research in archives and for the use of manuscripts a good course in paleography (the study of styles of writing) and some knowledge of diplomatic (the understanding of standard forms and patterns in public documents such as commissions, writs, charters, and the like, including standard abbreviations used) will be indispensable. Finally, to aid in dating an unknown manuscript, both paleographical knowledge of style in handwriting and art-historical knowledge of styles of manuscript illumination and of page decoration would be of great assistance. For all aspects of medieval and Renaissance studies, it is absolutely indispensable for students to have a thorough knowledge of classical literature (mostly Latin literature for the Western Middle Ages, but also Greek literature for Byzantine studies and for Renaissance studies) and of the entire Bible, Old and New Testaments, because this material was a central part of education in these particular eras. Finally, for intellectual history in these periods, knowledge of ancient philosophy (especially of Plato, Aristotle, and of the Hellenistic schools of philosophy) and of basic scientific problems (especially in the fields of biology and physics) will have considerable bearing on several of the key intellectual questions found in medieval and Renaissance philosophy.

Modern History

Generally, most graduate programs in modern history will require French and German, as the languages in which the major secondary scholarship is written. Beyond this, the student should acquire a thorough grounding (probably even a fluent speaking knowledge) in the languages of the countries in which he is interested, since these will be the languages of his primary sources. In addition, the student should have some degree of knowledge of the languages of nearby or of historically related countries, since events in modern history inevitably involve some interaction between neighboring people and countries. But by and large, it must be said that the language problem is not as great for the study of modern history as it is for either ancient or medieval history. However, in considering ancillary disciplines in modern history, perhaps more than in earlier periods, one must cope with the insights and the facts provided by the social sciences. The student should be thoroughly familiar with theories and methods of economics, sociology, and statistics; and study of political theory and the institutional functioning of administration and law in modern states will be very valuable as well. Knowledge of literary and artistic developments is, as always, necessary; and of particular importance is some understanding of modern concepts and developments in science, engineering, and technology. Certainly as part of any sociological approach to modern history, the student should try to learn as much as he can about modern ideologies and mass movements. A firm grasp of modern philosophical doctrine is almost as necessary for the intellectual historian.

The most recent innovation in historical methodology has been the programming of computers to solve problems involving a hitherto indigestible mass of material. These computer techniques have been most useful to institutional historians, as for example, in analyzing electoral results along class and group lines. But also intellectual historians have found use for the new technology, as in distinguishing linguistic and rhetorical patterns in a large mass of literary material. Public lectures and courses on computer techniques are coming to be offered on the campus, and serious students should take advantage of these opportunities to comprehend the working of these new tools of historical research.

Finally, any historian, no matter what his field, will need some grasp of the rudiments of psychology. No matter how institutional or impersonal the historian's subject may be, history ultimately concerns people and what they have done; and one cannot avoid interpretations that include consideration of the views on the nature of man that modern psychology has provided. Again, as we have already suggested, anyone interested in intellectual history of any period will have to acquire a very strong background in philosophy, religion, and art; but it is important to go even further than this and to assert that *every* historian needs some background in these areas if he expects his insights to be at all mature. Similarly any historian whose approach involves a categorical and comparative treatment of history rather than a period or regional approach (the study of "constitutionalism" or "the rise of the working class in the nineteenth century," rather than "England from 1603 to 1689" or "France from 1789 to 1848") will have to be particularly well-informed on current sociological and anthropological theories.

The sharp lines formerly drawn between academic disciplines are slowly dissolving. The historian sees himself more and more as part of a great team of humanists and social and behavioral scientists working together to understand the nature of culture and society. This trend toward academic synthesis is reflected in the increasingly broad and many-sided character of advanced historical work.

8 / Forms of Historical Communication

You now know that historical writing is always a matter of judgment, of commitment, and of values; and you should be prepared to seek such values constantly, not only in the work of others but in your own work as well. You are now ready for the most crucial step in your development as a history student—the preparation and writing of your own historical works.

We cannot emphasize enough how very significant this step really is in the scholarly life of a student. While acquiring information, constant reading, and informed study are vital to mature and thoughtful understanding, *the student should never forget that the final aim is for him to create a history.* In almost every circumstance this means the creation and presentation of some formal type of historical communication, such as a paper, a book review, or an oral report. In the most concrete sense, then, the immediate goal for the history student is to learn how to write history himself (nearly all oral reports are organized exactly like written papers). The only clear test of a student's *knowledge* of history is found in his ability to *communicate* his knowledge. It is beyond doubt that the active profession of history is founded entirely on written communications, on historical books and articles; and every professional historian is keenly aware of the obligation he has to channel his work into published writing. In order that an academic historian gain professional recognition, his ideas must be available for other scholars to evaluate. Similarly, in order for the undergraduate to attain distinction, he must be able to write well.

From previous chapters you have learned analytical and conceptual methods that underlie mature historical thinking. These methods must now be applied in your actual historical writing. The aim of this and the following three chapters is to guide you in a highly practical way to learn how to write skillfully, with great precision and clarity of communication.

In the courses that most history students take, three basic types of historical writing will be required again and again: *written examinations, book reviews,* and *full-length essays.*

EXAMINATIONS

In all probability, written examinations will climax the study in almost all lecture courses, and sometimes such examinations are required in seminars as well. It is perhaps unfortunate that examinations will constitute so large a part of your creative effort as an historian and will thus inevitably provide the main means by which an instructor can evaluate your progress. But exams, if approached with the right attitude and prepared for in an efficient and intelligent way, can be of real value to you in your study of history. *You should regard exams as milestones in the development of your studies* and as the opportunity to undertake careful review of the basic facts and reconsideration of the major problems in the course. Exams should be thought of as the time for critical stock-taking of how well you have mastered the primary and secondary materials and lectures. Exams should be viewed as an intellectual challenge and a high-level game, not as a grievous and annoying burden.

There are two general types of exams—written and oral. While *oral exams* are always required of graduate students, undergraduates only encounter this type of test as advanced history majors, and even then only rarely in American and Canadian colleges. The purpose of an oral exam is to assess the limits of your knowledge and the way in which you think under the pressure of direct questioning by a panel of examiners. When you do take an oral exam, you should listen very carefully to the question and take a few seconds to frame the answer clearly in your mind. Remember that the examiner in an oral test can immediately challenge you on any point. Therefore you should be ready for the examiner to probe more deeply on any subject or theme you raise in your answer. Your initial response to the question should be such as to indicate to your examiner the themes you are prepared to explore more fully in subsequent discussion.

Written exams fall into two categories—short-answer quizzes and essay exams. These are frequently combined as separate parts of a single written examination paper. *Students in survey courses will have several short-answer quizzes. The purpose of this kind of exam is merely to see whether you have thoroughly read the assigned reading and fully comprehend the lectures.* Short-answer questions are factual in nature rather than analytical—you are usually asked to identify a name or define an institutional term— and hence what they require is an answer that is brief, precise, and *to the point:* you should avoid the temptation to say too much and to give needless detail. However, if you have sufficient time, it is better to use whole, grammatical sentences rather than awkward phrases. If you follow the methods we have outlined for taking notes on lectures, reading the textbook, analyzing the other assigned secondary sources, and explicating primary sources, you will find short-answer questions to be very easy. In preparation for possible short-answer questions on the final exam, it is advisable to run through all the entries in the index of the textbook of the course (if there is a textbook) and make sure you can precisely identify each name succinctly and describe each institution listed.

Essay exam questions require an answer that is in substance a short paper. Consequently essay exams require creative and imaginative historical thinking and skill in literary exposition.

The student will only begin to achieve first-class work in examination-writing when he realizes that the underlying historical values in an examination essay must be no different from those in any other historical writing. Unless a teacher is one of those rare pedants who insists on simple parroting of his own lectures or reading assignments, *what will generally be sought in an examination essay is precision and detail in information, thorough grasp and assimilation of the subject matter, which in turn should lead to precise and obvious organization of the finished essay around some central core of ideas, and finally originality of insight and evaluation on the part of the student.* The student's preparation for the examination should equip him to produce an essay that exhibits such mastery, not a formless regurgitation of crammed-in materials.

Creative exam-writing requires thoughtful and careful preparation. We have already stressed that the teacher's lectures should be listened to attentively and critically. The student should not merely copy down and memorize the contents of the lectures but should evaluate them as historical communication, seeking an understanding of the kinds of value judgments and opinions that reflect his teacher's personal historical commitment and assumptions. Understanding them will help the student to develop his own point of view toward the subject matter. As a consolation to the inexperienced and frightened neophyte, we would like to emphasize that almost all teachers definitely prefer to encounter *thoughtful* originality in student essays rather than unthinking repetition of the contents of lectures or readings. The next stage of preparation is in thorough mastery of the textbook. Such mastery will provide the student with the factual information he will need to command in the examination and with a frame of reference and overall context for the interpretations in other secondary sources.

Once these preparatory stages are completed, the student is ready to approach the secondary sources and primary sources he read for the course. He should at once seek to reduce these sources to essential ideas and points, with some key examples—on the one hand avoiding needless detail, but on the other hand trying to be very precise in his summaries. One of the commonest errors in preparation on the part of inexperienced students is to attempt to master some secondary source in total detail, reading word by word so as "not to miss anything," and hence failing to grasp the significance of the source as a whole or as a point of view. What is more, such a plodding approach to reading sources will slow down a student's preparation enormously and make his reading program seem much too heavy. His aim, as a beginner, should be to master historical books as representing overall points of view and historiographical methods, not as containing an infinity of minute evaluations of many small points about very detailed, specialized subjects. Of course, the student should plan to be much more detailed and thorough in his mastering of any primary sources found in his reading program, which will provide him with the facts needed in developing arguments in his essays.

Once you have completed your mastery of the various sources read, you should prepare a *collation*, a comparison of the material of the lectures, the textbook, and the sources, and should try to recognize the various points of view possible about different topics and subjects that were emphasized in the course. You must evaluate these interpretations, or points of view, and decide to what extent you are in agreement or disagreement with each of them. Ultimately it will be only your own point of view, informed and carefully thought out, to which you must be committed: even in an examination essay the student himself is the historian, and no one else.

Finally, just before the examination, *a very good form of preparation would be for the student to prepare outlines of arguments for discussion of twenty or so standard topics in connection with the course.* Not only will this benefit him if such topics form the basis for one or two of the examination questions, as is often the case, but even more the experience in organizing answers to essay topics will give the student confidence and control in writing about any given topic, even an unfamiliar one.

After thorough and careful preparation, the actual writing of essays in the examination itself will give the student no difficulty; it should in fact be a challenging and pleasant game. *Always answer that essay question first about which you have the most knowledge and in which you have the greatest interest;* this will enable you to get over the initial panic that afflicts some students when they first see the exam questions. After you have answered one question well, your anxiety will decline and you will be able to turn calmly to consideration of the other questions. If there is more than one question to be answered, you must allot yourself adequate time to deal with each required question. Many students believe that "running out of time" is a valid excuse for not finishing an exam. Put such a consideration entirely out of your mind. It is assumed when you write an exam that you are a mature and intelligent person who can allot his time adequately so as to finish the paper.

Your examination answer must be a finished and self-contained piece of work. You cannot expect the grader of your exam to have any previous knowledge about your work or yourself; indeed in freshman courses a grader will frequently not be your teacher, but a graduate student hired to read exams. You should not assume anything on the part of your reader, including his knowing by intuition which question you have chosen to answer, if there is a choice. The essay should clearly define the subject and problem at the outset. Never let your essay degenerate into a series of random observations and unrelated facts on an unspecified subject—this is a sure road to failure, and it is a road taken by thousands of American college undergraduates every year. Also never use your exam as an opportunity to write personal notes to your teacher. This is not the time or the place to tell him that you immensely enjoyed his course and that you consider him a combination of Albert Schweitzer and John F. Kennedy. Nor is the exam paper to be used to inform the reader that you were ill during the exam or deeply depressed by your grandmother's death. Such personal references in an examination are in exceedingly bad taste. If you are ill, go to the campus infirmary and get medical attention. If you come to write the exam, do the work that is expected of you.

You should above all remember that *a history examination essay is no different from any other essay* and that your compositional form should be identical with that used to write any essay or paper. Organization around one main point, good paragraphs with topic sentences and clear transitions, full and developed sentence structure, and a sense of summary and conclusion all help to make the difference between an examination essay that is a pleasure to read and one that is merely routine. The tenor and frame of reference of the answer should reflect the question: if the question is detailed and precise, so too should the essay be precise; while if the question is sweeping and all-inclusive, the essay must of necessity be more broadly spaced in its topics and discussions. But in every case *the student should use facts and examples to support his conclusions and general statements,* remembering however, to avoid needless detail and *never simply to list unrelated or irrelevant facts without reference to some generalizing point.*

Careful organization and relevant presentation of all material in the essay is so important that we always advise our own students taking essay examinations to use 30 to 40 percent of the time alloted for each essay for preliminary thinking, preparation, and organization and only the remaining part of the time for writing. Inevitably, this method is far more successful than that used by the student who begins to write immediately and spends the entire exam time incoherently spilling out all the information he has that might be vaguely related to the given topic.

We can illustrate all these points by consideration of two sample essay answers, one successful and one of rather poor quality. The set question was: "Evaluate the importance of the conversion of Constantine for the development of, and periodization of medieval Europe." Notice that while part of the subject matter of the essay—the conversion of Constantine—is carefully specified by the question and hence would certainly have to be part of the discussion, the other aspects of the subject are purposely undefined in the question, so that the student has considerable latitude in setting the frame of reference of his discussion for himself. One student succeeded quite well in recognizing that this was the organizational problem of the question, and immediately set about to define a precise subject for his essay. This is his answer (the sentences are numbered for convenient reference in the critical analysis that follows):

(1) While most scholars attempt to view the "conversion of Constantine" as a crux, a turning point in the transition from the ancient world to the medieval world, no agreement on the definition of any of the terms of the discussion exists. (2) Where some will date the conversion from the vision before the battle of the Milvian Bridge in 312, others focus on the Edict of Milan in 313, still others on Constantine's leadership at the Council of Nicea in 325, and some emphasize Constantine's deathbed baptism in 337. (3) Still more, it is impossible to find any agreement on what is to be regarded as the definitive sign of a change from late Roman society to medieval society. (4) Thus my discussion of the problem of the significance of the conversion of Constantine for periodization of European history will necessarily hinge on a consideration of each of the terms of the proposition.

(5) As for conversion itself, one must relate an evaluation of the religious and political import of any such occurrence to the general pattern of late classical culture and intellectual values. (6) Cumont has emphasized that salvation, ecstatic and mystical inspiration, and a personal saviour were propounded by Mithraism and a number of other mystery cults as well. (7) Among these last, one—the cult of the unconquered sun—had official sanction from the time of the Emperor Aurelian on, and was followed by Constantine himself before his Christian conversion. (8) Thus the transition to what Constantine may have regarded as

one more such salvation religion would not require any tremendous adjustment of values; and in this sense, I believe that one can say that Constantine was converted from the time of his vision onward (assuming, of course, that the vision as reported by Christian apologists such as Eusebius is a true event). (9) Constantine's confusion about theological values and his use of heretical advisors at the time of the Council of Nicea support this conclusion, because it reveals the relatively unintellectual quality of Constantine's religion, and also shows that his assumed headship of the Church is very similar in kind to the association between the emperor and the cult which was characteristic of earlier imperial religion. (10) As for the deathbed baptism, this was also common in the early Christian period. (11) In this sense, I will regard Constantine's conversion in 312 as genuine, and I cannot accept the critical views of either Jones, who regards the incident of the vision as mere superstition, or of Burckhardt, who sees Constantine merely as a shrewd power politician converting cynically.

(12) Similarly, the impact of the conversion upon the organization of Roman society is a problem of definition. (13) The central and authoritarian position which Constantine assumed as a result of his triumph in the name of Christ is certainly nothing new. (14) Again one may say that the institution of Christianity as a state religion demanding the loyalty of all is no different from the earlier imperial cults or cult of the unconquered sun: most of the persecutions of Christians stemmed from the refusal of the Christians to give homage to a state cult. (15) Thus the issue of transition or change rests on two points; first, is there a significant change resulting from the official recognition of Christianity itself as a religion different from any preceding religion, and second, is there a change in the nature of Christianity itself, transforming early or primitive Christianity into a new, medieval type? (16) Each of these points must be discussed in turn.

(17) Despite Cochrane's brilliant attempt to recognize a difference between the "classical mind" and the Christian self-consciousness, I do not feel that there is really a great difference between the worldly ambitions of the emperors before and after the introduction of official Christianity. (18) The emperors have a world view altogether different from St. Augustine's emphasis on the "City of God" as the real goal of Christian living. (19) To the emperors, Christianity was a source of power for the state; their

rule was *justified* by their support of Christianity, but the aims of that rule remained unchanged: universal dominion, absolute authority for their office, and the ultimate need for all the world to be subject to the Roman law. (20) Worship of the true God and support of his Church merely assured that they were in accord with proper order in the universe, and their aims are clearly worldly in direction. (21) This pattern can certainly be seen not only in Constantine himself, but in his successors right on to the world-conquering schemes and recodification of the law under Justinian. (22) Thus the particular values of Christianity do not create any significant change in the political, social, or legal goals and structure of the Empire.

(23) In contrast, the other question, whether there is a change in the nature of Christianity itself, is I think provocative and suggests a clue to the emergence of what might be called a medieval conception of society and world organization. (24) With Constantine's efforts, especially with the Council of Nicea, one can say that for the first time, the Church had a recognizable, defined institutional structure, and in the future the Church would exist not only as a salvation doctrine, a community of believers, but also as a political entity, an institution, would need rules, laws, a government, a tangible authority structure. (25) From this time on, one begins to look for the rise of governmental and institutional thinking within the Church, as suggested by Ullmann's study of the rise of papal government, and even doctrinal theology starts to take on a new, formalized tone—as in the treatises of Augustine —and doctrinal issues are settled by Councils, conferences, and papal pronouncements, all of them institutional or governmental procedures. (26) This new spirit, which one might argue is the fundamental characteristic of the medieval Church, would thus suggest that with the official position of Christianity, which stems from the conversion of Constantine, one can identify a transition from an early, "late antique" phase in Christianity to the later central and institutional position of Christianity in the medieval world.

(27) In sum, then, I must conclude that while the events and details of political, social, and religious life created by the conversion of Constantine do not reveal any important changes or new features which would suggest a change from the late Roman world to the medieval world, the new spirit which the official position of

Christianity creates does become a basis for later, medieval developments; the transition created by the conversion of Constantine is not external, but internal, and is only made manifest by the slow unfolding of centuries.

Despite the fact that the student left several aspects of the problem unanswered or even unmentioned, and despite the frequent lack of detail, we think that all teachers would agree that this is a truly first-rate answer for an essay examination. First, although the student is never pedantic or detailed merely for the sake of including information, it is clear that he is extremely well-informed and has mastered his reading well enough to relate it to the problems about which he thinks (see sentences 2, 6–7, 11, 17, 25); this information is never irrelevant, but always appears as part of, and in reference to, the point the student is discussing. That there is a problem to be examined is constantly emphasized (sentences 1, 4, 8, 11–12, 17, 23, 27). Moreover, the whole essay is dominated by one overriding theme, which is examined step by step; but each step is always related back to the final conclusion required, which at the end is related in summary form. Each problem is discussed in terms of precise issues and examples that make clear not only the student's grasp of the particular problem, but also his general ability to reason and argue historically (sentences 5–10, 13, 14–15, 17–22, 23–26). The student's excellent writing style helps to preserve the thread of continuity between these various particular discussions and adds greatly to the pleasure of reading his essay; one should particularly note his use of long, graceful sentences, his ease of expressing himself, and his very good emphasis on the transition from one discussion to the next (sentences 4, 5, 11–12, 16–17, 23, 27). As for the failure to be very detailed or to discuss many side issues and questions that in another context would certainly come up, one should remember that this is an essay test, under restrictions of time; and the student's problem is not to settle all issues of the question but to show his mastery of a particular subject, the extent of his information and grasp of his reading, and his general ability to think and discuss in historical terms. All of these ends the student brilliantly accomplished in his essay; indeed, his success was *enhanced* by his carefulness not to become sidetracked or to wander, and by his clear emphasis on a central idea of his own, which he discussed fully.

The clearest demonstration of the worthiness of the preceding essay can be found by comparing it to the following answer to the same question. We would like to say that this is an example of an exceptionally bad essay, but unfortunately from what we have seen in our experience, it is representative of a larger percentage of exam papers than the earlier sample. To spare the reader, we have abbreviated the example, which ran on for three full exam blue-books, all of them similar in nature:

> (1) Constantine was a very great ruler. (2) He was converted in 312 when, before he was going to fight a battle with Maxentius at the Milvian Bridge, which is just outside Rome, he saw a vision of a flaming cross in the sky. (3) Not everyone agrees on what Constantine really saw. (4) Some think he was just superstitious and when he saw a weather phenomenon he thought it was a cross. (5) Anyway he put Christian symbols on his standards and made his men pray to Christ; and when he won the battle, he began to make the worship of Christianity required all over the Empire. (6) Pretty soon Constantine was the sole ruler of the Roman Empire, and then he comes out into the open and really established the Church everywhere. (7) This was shown by the Council of Nicea (320) in which, after all was said and done, Constantine was the head and made all the important decisions. (8) This shows that Burckhardt was right in calling Constantine just another oriental despot. (9) In 337 he dies and is baptized by Eusebius.
>
> (10) When did the Roman Empire end? . . .

When, indeed? It is clear that no meaningful answer to the question will emerge from this essay, despite another twenty-five pages of the same kind of stuff. The real tragedy of this example is that it is obvious that the student did study and prepare. He has some information (sentences 2, 4, 9) and has done some secondary reading (sentences 3-4, 8), although he is not explicit about what he has read. The essay fails at the level of thought, organization, and communication. There is no sense or central point at all in the essay, which is merely a random collection of scraps of knowledge expressed in rather hearsay fashion. The first sentence is meaningless and vague, and reveals that the student has made no effort at all to get to the point, to analyze the issue implied in the question. True there are details and facts, but no order, no idea is imposed on them; and there is no sense of selectivity—does it really matter in terms of the original question whether Constantine's vision was meteorological or not (sentences 3-4)? How does such a detail relate to a main point, if at all? This student is simply trying to put down everything he knows, with a vague generalization at the beginning to suggest a semblance of main point. Even the factual information is imprecise (sentence 7); the student's understanding of what he has read is imprecise and inaccurate (sentence 8); and those original conclusions the student presents are expressed in vague terms that make the conclusions meaningless *non sequiturs* (sentences 4, 7). The essay is terribly difficult to read; not only is the style loose and the usage too general and nonspecific (sentences 5-7), but at best the sentences have an ugly, awkward structure or else are short, choppy, and immature (sentences 1, 2, 4, etc.). At worst, the student is ungrammatical (sentence 6, shift of tense; sentence 9, shift of tense from sentence 6, the last one dealing with Constantine). As for overall organization, summary, or transition, this essay is utterly devoid of any sense of form (sentences 9-10). The mark of a unified, coherent essay is absent here because the student never defined his problem precisely. And thus the student's whole preparation appears meaningless and unthoughtful because of his failure to communicate his study in the form of creative historical writing.

BOOK REVIEWS

Besides essay examinations, the other chief forms of historical writing required of the student are book reviews and original historical papers or essays. While we separate them here in our discussion, the student should realize that the two are not really very different in kind at all. A book review is an essay that critically evaluates an historical work, or two or more works in relation to each other. We have emphasized repeatedly that history as a form of thought is a series of value judgments about, and analyses of, primary sources. In a book review, the primary source is the book to be considered; and this primary source is measured just the way any primary source is measured, according to a series of certain analytical questions that reveal its accuracy, its validity, its relationship to other primary sources of similar kind.

In other words, a book review must always be "critical." No matter how famous the book being considered is, no matter how learned the author may appear and how uninformed about the subject the student himself may feel, *it should always be remembered that the desired goal is an evaluation, a critique of the book and not merely a report of the book's contents.* Unless directed otherwise by his instructor, the student should *never summarize the full contents of the book or outline its points chapter by chapter.* Rather, he should assume as the audience for his essay a reader who knows something about the book and the subject, and is interested in what contribution the book makes to the historical understanding of that subject.

Let us put this point another way. In our opening discussion, we suggested that the writing of history involved an explanation of facts (of "what") in terms of answers to the questions "why" and "how." In this sense, the writer of the book review is not satisfying the requirements of proper history writing if he merely digests the book in his review. He will only be presenting the "what" of the book in simple, unassimilated form. Analysis involves an emphasis on the historical values to be found in the book, whether explicitly or implicitly, and a consideration of the success or validity of those values for a study of the subject matter with which the book deals.

The preceding point would suggest, of course, that it is important to give the reader of the book review some sense of the "what" of the book. But rather than a summary of the book, the student should begin his essay with an introduction to the book in terms of its main point, the kinds of facts to be found in the book and the kinds of facts omitted, the nature of the author's argument and some of the main conclusions he reaches. This will permit the student to give a fairly complete profile of the "what" of the book in a few sentences, and indeed such a profile will probably be a much clearer presentation of the book as a whole than three pages of detailed summary of the entire contents.

After such an introductory description, you can then concentrate the bulk of your discussion on an evaluation of the book. The precise questions to be asked of a book, of course, vary with the individual subject and its treatment, but in general, the reader would expect to be told why the author follows a particular historiographical method. This should be illustrated, as always, by reference to facts, which in the case of a book review means reference to examples in the text of the book which show how the author makes value judgments and reaches conclusions because of his particular assumptions. Also, some attention should be given to the kind of factual information the author musters in proof of his points. Does he attempt to account for a wide range of fact, or does he dwell only on a narrowly restricted range of information, such as economic data? Certainly the review should also assess the quality of the author's writing and his success in communicating his ideas in a clear and persuasive way.

The central question a book review should answer is whether or not the author's methods and interpretations are valid for the study of his subject. Given the subject and material, what degree of success has the author attained in eliciting meaning and significance? Has he adopted the best approach for exploring the subject and explicating the primary sources? Has he put the right questions to his sources? Do the author's assumptions and methods illuminate the subject and contribute considerably to an understanding of it? If so, how? If not, why not?

These tests of validity raise a vexed issue among professional historians—is it legitimate in a book review to criticize an author adversely for failure to deal with an important subject? *An author has the right to choose his own subject,* and to condemn a book because it deals with a field of inquiry that does not interest the reviewer is extremely unfair. To dismiss a work on economic history for not being the biography of a statesman, or a work on institutional history for not studying the history of ideas is absurd and pointless. The question of whether the author has chosen a good subject to study is a matter extraneous to a book review. Unfortunately this is a very common error, even in the review pages of academic historical journals.

But given the author's right to choose his own subject matter, it is a reviewer's task to decide whether the theme or thesis the author propounds does anything to advance the understanding of the subject. If an author chooses to deal with a given body of material in a way that precludes or limits insight into the significance or meaning of this material, it is the reviewer's right and duty to say so. An author whose subject is the biography of Oliver Cromwell, the seventeenth-century English Puritan statesman, and who makes no effort to assess the impact of Cromwell's Protestant piety on his career and policy, should be severely criticized. Similarly, an author who sets out to explain the causes of the First World War and who ignores the increasing proclivity to violence as the means of solving social and political problems in the years before 1914 has neglected a major aspect of his subject and failed to elicit full significance from his sources.

The whole of this discussion could really be summed up in one basic principle: *the goal of a book review is not a summary, but an historiographical critique.* If the student always keeps in mind the principle that in history significant statements are always personal value judgments on the part of historians, then the need for historiographical orientation in a book review should be readily apparent to him; and he will see that his aim in writing a review is to place the book properly into the whole context of historical knowledge, especially about the particular subject.

You should never forget that a book review is an essay, and that much of the interest on the reader's part will come from the quality and clarity of your writing. You should always try to have a *main point or thesis* in your review. This is not as obvious as it might seem; all too often book reviews consist of only a random series of paragraphs that make one observation after another about the book without ever reaching some clear conclusion. There are many possible main points in a book review—indeed, some points need not even be about the book in question directly, but may be broader considerations of historiography or of the implications of the author's subject—and the writer of a review should be careful to give his essay the sense of cohesion and organization that is the result of having an overriding theme. This is perhaps even more true when the reviewer is examining more than one book in his essay; failure to achieve a unifying main point or simply taking up the books one after another will certainly make the essay incoherent, and its value will be small.

Papers and Essays

The third kind of historical writing that college students are required to produce is variously called an essay, a paper, a term paper, or a research paper. This involves the formal presentation at some length (usually 5,000 to 10,000 words) of an historical theme. It involves wide reading in both primary and secondary sources; extensive problems in organization; firm command of an effective prose style; and, usually, employment of footnote paraphernalia. This is the most serious and important kind of historical communication.

The technique for writing history books is only a large-scale extension of the principles involved in preparing a good short essay. The presentation of oral reports for seminars and talks is only a vocal form of a written paper. While there is no doubt that the oral aspect of a talk gives it a special, of-the-moment quality that can be an important part of the pleasure of hearing a skillfully delivered address, nonetheless the approach to organization of the materials of a talk is in every respect identical to that required for the organization of a paper. Far too many speakers overlook this point and seem satisfied with a rambling, disorganized thought pattern in oral presentations, as anyone who has suffered through graduate seminars or historical conventions is all too aware of. Knowing this to be the case, the student who takes the trouble to prepare an oral presentation adequately and thoughtfully can expect to find his reward in the grateful and interested attention of his hearers, not the least of whom is his teacher.

There are two broad categories of history papers, determined by their subject matter. Generally, *historical subjects fall into two types, which we can call open subjects and closed subjects.* The latter is by far the most common and is also the easier of the two to write. A *closed subject* is one whose total dimensions are clearly and exactly defined by the topic, as is the case in papers on such topics as "Techniques of Diplomacy in the Sixteenth Century," "Origins of the British Cabinet System," "Formation of the German Zollverein," or "Lloyd George's Policy at the Versailles Peace Conference." The titles fully indicate what the reader can expect.

Papers on subjects of this kind are almost inevitably analytical-expository in nature, presenting a subject, reviewing the primary materials available and solving all questions of precision or factual accuracy that occur, stating judgments and relationships directly and simply, often only by giving a chronology of the facts, or by generalizing from the facts to some sort of categorical pattern of events or institutions.

There is only so much the author can do with a closed subject—it is a finite, self-limiting problem. Usually in the treatments of such subjects the number of sources is directly limited by the definition of the topic, and the amount of factual material to be considered is kept small by the severe limitations on the kinds of facts that the topic allows. One benefit of this for the writer of such a paper is the relative ease of proof permitted by the limitation on material and on frame of reference, because "extraneous" points need not be considered or discussed; this can result in a very clear and direct narrative or presentation in the finished essay and can also give the writer very firm control over his material. Therefore choosing a closed subject is a quite safe procedure—especially for a total beginner in history—but on the other hand it is very difficult to make papers on such subjects seem intellectually distinguished or highly original. This is especially true because the only possible originality in such papers is to find new primary sources for the subject, which have not been previously made part of the general historical knowledge of the subject. As a result, the best approach if one intends to write a paper of this type is to find a subject that is completely untouched in the secondary literature; but such subjects are rare, and interesting subjects of this kind are still rarer. The college student can achieve excellence in treating a closed subject only by exhausting the material available to him, by being extremely clear and coherent in presentation, and by straining his mind to come up with a conclusion that is at least personal if not highly original.

In contrast, the *open subject* is an infinite one; it permits unlimited chains of connection among a wide variety of factual materials and sources, but the organization of the subject is a priori unclear. Indeed, one might say that in this case most of the originality is going to result from the organization that the historian will seek to impose on his materials, which need not be unfamiliar at all. Typical open subjects are such topics as "Constitutionalism in European History," "The Aristocratic Nature of Seventeenth-Century Government in Europe," "Rationalism and Romanticism in the Eighteenth Century," "The Nature of Medieval Heresy," "The Origins of Totalitarianism," and "Eastern and Western Factors in the Culture of Hellenistic Greece and the Roman Empire." Fundamentally, such a paper is always a re-examination or a redefinition of significant terms; for instance, in the first sample above, the historian would have to make clear just what he means by "constitutionalism" and in the next topic what he means to identify by the term "government"—theories or practices? The burden of proof in such a paper is heavy and rests primarily on the logic of organization and the originality of the insight the historian has into his materials. Frequently, such a paper can be only a re-examination or re-evaluation of very well-known materials; the originality is all in the historian's own thought. The quality of writing here is very important in helping to convince the reader of the validity of the historian's point of view, because, as opposed to the closed subject, establishing proof of one's own insight or evaluation of materials is very difficult. The historian is almost compelled to employ a wide range or variety of subject matter in order to convince the reader of the accuracy of the patterns he seeks to demonstrate in the history he studies.

Given a choice of both closed and open subjects, you will have to make your decision as to which is preferable in terms of your estimation of your own ability. The closed subject is best for the student who does not have a talent for highly abstract conceptualization but is more of a down-to-earth facts kind of person. This is also the best kind of paper for a highly technical, detailed problem, such as those often found in institutional history. The open subject can be successfully handled by the imaginative person who is also a very good writer, but the result will be calamitous if the author lacks either of these qualities. Put in the most mundane terms, it is not hard for a student to get a B on a paper with a closed subject provided he is thorough and careful. On open subjects the grades tend to be what sociologists would call polarized—either A's on the one side or C's and below on the other.

9 / Shaping an Historical Essay

CREATIVE HISTORICAL THINKING

Whatever kind of historical paper you are undertaking—examination, book report, or formal essay—the difficult problems of analysis and organization must be resolved if you are to achieve a very thoughtful and accomplished final draft. It is important to read extensively, sometimes even exhaustively, in the primary and secondary sources; it is also necessary for you to command the techniques of writing good English prose. The *intermediary step* of thinking your way through the material, of organizing your ideas in coherent form, and of bringing your knowledge and insights to shape the material toward a persuasive conclusion—this difficult, painful, agonizing process—will make all the difference between a first-class essay and an extremely mediocre one.

All professional historians will tell you that they find it pleasant to read books, and many will also say that the writing of the final draft, which involves purely literary problems, is also a delightful exercise. But between these initial and final stages is the *intermediary agony of creative historical thinking,* which demands the fullest commitment of the historian's intellectual resources and emotional energy. It can be a long and a frustrating struggle until finally the material begins to reveal its secrets, until finally the historian is able to glimpse an interpretation that makes sense out of the facts, until finally an illuminating idea takes hold and drives the historian toward a synthesis of his material and a powerfully argued thesis.

A college student of history must undergo the same agonizing struggle in shaping his own historical essay. Except in rare instances your conclusion will not be truly original, a fully novel interpretation. It could not be, because it is most unlikely that you will command all the primary sources for any given problem. *But your conclusion must be a personal one.* You must make the material and the problem part of yourself, and you must solve the problem in terms of your own understanding of the dimensions of the subject. The ultimate success or failure of the final draft, assuming that you have read the right books and can write reasonably well, will depend on the thoroughness with which you have attempted to think through the material and solve the problem for yourself. Furthermore, you must take all possible pains to organize your thoughts so that your understanding of the problem is communicated in an effective and persuasive way. Remember also that any piece of historical writing is in actuality an expository essay, and the general remarks we are now making about writing formal papers should be applied to book reviews and exams, and to oral reports as well.

Your understanding of the nature of historical thought will only become sophisticated and sure through strenuous and even painful efforts to exercise the historian's craft. As you work and rework your outlines, trying to give meaning and shape to your material, as you attempt to find the best organization for communicating your insight into the problem you are concerned with, you are thereby refining and developing the sensitivity and complexity of your historical method. *Profound insight into history comes to the student through the writing of historical works rather than from abstract airy speculation about the philosophical nature of historical truth.*

In coping with any historical problem, the student will probably begin by asking some questions, by postulating certain tentative hypotheses, by searching the available primary sources with an eye toward answering the questions his subject raises in his imagination.

That each subject has its own unique set of analytical questions is obviously clear. Nonetheless, there are some generic historiographical questions that bear on any possible subject, and the beginning student would do well to fix these firmly in his mind. Indeed, sometimes when the student is very confused about finding a proper approach to a complicated or obscure subject, starting with such general questions can often give him a first wedge, to assist him in breaking open the problem. Inevitably, the first such question should be to ask what primary sources are pertinent to the subject to be discussed; i.e., which sources contain ideas, information, factual references, and the like that connote the subject of the proposed paper, either directly or indirectly. From this first question a host of related analytical questions will follow. Are the pertinent primary sources all of one sort, or is a diverse conglomeration of materials useful in treating the subject? From this last, is there a suggestion that the main point to be made must be very general and broad, or should it be specific and narrow? Do the primary sources offer any critical values that might be useful to the writer in establishing his own final conclusions? What is more, do most of the primary sources suggest the same conclusion over and over again, or do they exhibit a conflict in ideas? If the latter, how is the conflict to be resolved; what criteria of significance do the primary sources suggest? Do these criteria of significance make clear the main organizational points of the essay; i.e., in their totality are they broad enough to encompass, and yet permit a precise treatment of, all the primary source material pertinent to the topic at hand? Does one basic, main point emerge as fundamental to all other points, so that the essay can achieve a clear, coherent organization?

In this way, proceeding from one analytical question to the next, the student will build toward a recognition of the organizational form his essay will finally assume. Of course the questions we have suggested are not all of the possible generic problems involved in any historical writing, and a number of further questions should occur to each student as soon as he begins serious thinking about some particular problem. But he should strive to make all the questions he raises lead toward a coherent outline that can develop into an expository essay.

Again, while the precise form of organization will certainly derive from the exact subject being treated, it is possible to recognize *certain fundamental types of organization that are characteristic of almost all historical essays.* That these types can vary widely from the most "scientifically" rigorous formalism to a loose and subjective evocation should not be surprising, because form in historical writing is essentially literary rather than objectively logical. English-speaking historians write in plain English and not in any special language or style.

Among the generic forms of organization of historical papers one possibility is the logical or *"scientific" organization,* which follows a completely explicit, patently logical exposition in clearly defined sections: an *introduction* that states the aims and thesis of the paper, a section of *discussion* that adequately proves the thesis by examining primary sources and discussing other secondary views, and lastly a *conclusion* that offers a summary of the major points of the discussion in relation to a succinct restatement of the main point. Perhaps the chief advantage of such a procedure, and an advantage which all beginners should certainly keep very seriously in mind, is that it is very safe. With so much explicit statement of purpose and clear demonstration of method there is little chance that the reader will miss the point or lose the subtlety of the argument, because the form of the paper is intentionally designed to make these aspects of the historian's thinking manifest. But it is the straightforward and manifest nature of this form that is also its chief drawback. Papers written in this way, even by skilled professional writers, are often banal and uninspiring. Scientific organization is safe but rather dull. What is more, the strictness of logic that is suggested and encouraged by the rigor of the form often has the effect of being highly restrictive of the discussion, not allowing much "free play" for subsidiary discussion, flashes of insight and intuition, or even for a wide range of subject matter in a given paragraph. For these reasons, this *scientific organization is best suited for the discussion of closed subjects,* which, as already pointed out, have exactly the restricted content that suits this style.

An organizational approach, which is the exact opposite of the scientific method, is also sometimes found in outstanding works of history. This second method might be called *impressionistic organization.* Its technique involves a dramatic narrative consisting of a series of very precise, detailed, particularized discussions, almost *a series of descriptive pictures, which at the very last moment are drawn together* and are all shown to manifest an inner thesis or main point. For success, this method depends on the ability of the writer to create a number of very precise, evocative impressions that will arrest the reader's attention and make him feel that there is some importance in the details being narrated; only ultimately does the discussion pass from the level of the particular to more general conclusions. To use the impressionistic form of organization, the writer must have very great historiographical insight, because he needs to present to the reader those details which are attractive and exciting by themselves but which also can be fitted into a mosaic pattern of general significance. The impressionistic approach must therefore be regarded with extreme caution by beginners, because it is fully successful only in the hands of a master of literary style and one completely versed in all aspects of the subject. Two such masters who come to mind are Johan Huizinga, whose impressionistic *The Waning of the Middle Ages* was analyzed in a previous chapter, and Garrett Mattingly, whose book on the Spanish Armada of 1588 is a magnificent *tour de force* in the impressionistic vein. When not in the hands of a master, there is the danger that this approach can degenerate into slick verbalizations and metaphors;

and its content can lapse into a mere fascination with detail for detail's sake, overlooking the fact that detail is significant in historical writing only when it contributes to the establishment of a thesis. These two faults have in our experience very frequently marred and made insignificant several otherwise competent student essays, not to mention dozens of second-rate professional papers.

The scientific method is, then, a safe but dull extreme, and the impressionistic method is a dangerous but intriguing extreme. *A third, intermediary method of organizing papers, a combination of the two,* is also possible. In this style, a writer might *begin* by capturing the interest and imagination of his reader by offering a few flashes of aspects of his subject, or perhaps one or two leading questions, a detail here and a detail there; but *immediately* thereafter the writer should make clear the organization of his thought by revealing his main thesis, stated in terms of his broad historiographical principles and the conclusions resulting from those principles. Then his discussion can return to details, perhaps first the formerly unclear ones of the introduction and then all the remaining details of his argument, now analyzed in terms of, and in relationship to, the thesis stated. The paper can then conclude with a summary. This intermediary approach is especially useful when the subject being treated is unusual or very complicated, because in such cases it is a great help to the reader to have an explicit thesis or main point as a steady frame of reference for following the lines of an elaborate presentation or argument. But in addition, the nature of this organizational style helps to give a work life and sparkle where a more cut-and-dried scientific approach would seem pedantic.

In shaping your material and thoughts into a coherent and well-argued essay, you must follow some definite rules of the historian's workshop:

1. You must realize that a full development of the subject, a proper balance between stating your thesis and documenting it

adequately, will be possible only after a long process of trial versions and the evolvement of successive drafts, which will enable you to eliminate all unnecessary matter and include all relevant aspects.

2. A point you are trying to prove, either your main theme or a part of it, should always be stated in the form of a contention, a firm statement of truth. Repeated contentions spread throughout the paper will provide for the reader a clear and firm outline of the steps of your argument. This method will allow the reader to understand fully what you are trying to prove and to judge whether your material supports your thesis.

3. Your writing should reflect a constant balance between (a) primary fact, (b) the interpretations of the problem made by modern historians, and (c) your own inferences and judgments. Of these three the primary fact and your own inferences are the most important. Supporting an argument by relying largely on the opinions of modern scholars puts you in the position of being nothing but a camp follower. Students who merely collate the great ideas found in secondary sources are inevitably and justifiably marked down as unoriginal. On the other hand, secondary sources are necessary in any discussion because they represent important points of view, ideas about the subject which should be taken into account by the student in order to broaden and develop his own insights. In no wise do you have to agree with the secondary sources for your subject, but you must show that you are aware of their views and indicate in what way you disagree with these previous interpretations. This is especially the case when a treatment of the subject is an historical classic, a well-known work by a scholar of great reputation. The more renowned previous writers on your subject are, the greater care you must take to indicate your stand with regard to such well-known viewpoints.

4. Secondary sources are extremely useful as ancillary discussions of subsidiary topics, freeing the student from having to develop personally every single detail of his subject. For example

if you were writing a paper on Catholic religious thought in the midsixteenth century, you would not have to refer in detail to the proceedings of the Council of Trent. You could simply state the general point you wish to make about the relationship between the theology and the Council and cite as evidence the authoritative work on the Council of Trent by Hubert Jedin.

5. You are writing a work of history, not publishing a collection of sources. By themselves the primary sources tell the reader nothing. The primary sources require your constant explanation and evaluation to make their meaning clear. Take great care to indicate to the reader *your* understanding of every quotation in your paper. Limit quotations to statements needed to prove your argument.

6. After all the reading, thinking, organizing and writing of the main themes, the lines of argument, the critical points in dispute, and the illustrative examples should come together to form one well-organized and synthetic whole. A history paper should be as coherent and as consistent as a Mozart symphony. If after all your efforts to shape your essay you still find awkwardness, irrelevancies, and inconsistencies, then you must reluctantly assume the inadequacy of some aspect of your technique. Either your assumptions are not relevant, or you need further or different primary sources, or your anticipated hypothesis is wrong and will have to be re-evaluated in the face of the evidence. When you sit down to shape your material and organize your essay, as in the case of any creative work, it will not be easy to anticipate whether the forming of your paper will go smoothly or not. This is one of the strongest reasons why you should never put off the writing of papers until the last moment, but should plan and begin actual *writing* long in advance of scheduled deadlines.

THE NATURE OF HISTORICAL PROOF

A question that bothers the novice historical craftsman is: What is the nature of historical proof? Or put more practically: When can I be satisfied that I have proved my point? These questions are similar in nature to the great conundrums of the universe: What is truth? When is a picture beautiful? How long is a piece of string?

During the past two decades analytic philosophers have attempted to define the nature of historical proof. As yet they have not come up with any widely accepted answers, but even if they do their solution is likely to be too abstract to be of much use to the practicing historian.

The historical craftsman, as distinct from the philosopher, knows from the experience of his work that there are *two kinds of historical proof:* (1) demonstrable proof, and (2) inferential, or synthetic, proof.

Demonstrable proof can be achieved in specific, narrow, specialized problems, such as are offered by most closed subjects. Problems that can be answered yes or no from a finite body of primary sources lend themselves to demonstrable proof. As an example: Did King Edward I of England, who ruled from 1272 to 1307, get as much money from customs receipts as he got from income and property taxes levied with consent of parliament? The historian can go through the financial records of King Edward's government and demonstrate whether it was parliamentary taxes or customs that produced the most income for the monarchy. Or take another example: Did lords still predominate in the membership of the British cabinet in the 1860's? Once he has established a definition of what a lord is in the England of the 1860's, the historian can go through lists of cabinet members and demonstrate whether the lords still predominated among the ministers of the crown. Demonstrable proof is possible on these kinds of particular questions, provided of course the primary sources are sufficient to give a clear answer one way or another.

The other kind of proof may be termed *inferential, or synthetic.* It may not satisfy logicians, but the more general problems of history can only be answered by this kind of proof, which is much less logical and much more intuitive than the demonstrable variety. A great American historian of the French Revolution once remarked to his students that *the really important questions of history cannot be proved in an absolute sense. They can only be answered in a probable and plausible way.* In trying to answer some general interpretive problems, such as whether the English civil war was the consequence of the rise of the gentry, or whether the French Revolution was triggered by aristocratic reaction, the historian must take into account a large number of variables ranging in quality from specific facts to general trends in society as a whole. He must relate these to each other and in the end decide that the weight of probability lies more in one direction than another. He must infer from a large number and range of variables a general thesis that seems to explain what happened in a more plausible way than any other possible thesis. *This kind of proof therefore achieves its validity by the extent to which the thesis can synthesize a large number of particular facts into a consistent and coherent whole.* It is unlikely that any thesis proposed as a solution to one of these large problems will fully account for every fact and draw every variable into the total picture. If there are thirty variables that must be related in answering a problem, at least one, and probably three or four, will not fit perfectly into the total view offered as an explanation by the thesis. But a thesis that relates 90 percent of the variables is obviously more true than one that relates only 70 percent. Eventually another historian will come along and claim that he has discovered some new facts that cannot be accounted for by the prevailing interpretation. Or he will argue that certain relationships that the prevailing thesis seemed to establish can be shown on closer examination to be either very weak or nonexistent. At this point an historical "revision" will occur, and a new inferential synthesis will be proposed to relate the variables in the problem.

To students with a dry, logical bent of mind the use of somewhat intuitive inferential proof by historians will seem disappointing. But the student must realize that history deals with the complexities of human life and the freedom and variety of individual personality. Human relationships cannot be demonstrated in many instances in a finite and absolutely certain manner. They can only be inferred in at best a highly plausible way.

If it is a limitation of history that its most important general interpretations cannot be absolutely proved, it is also one of the glories of historical study. For it makes history an ever-changing, ever-growing creative subject. It is a fact that a general interpretation rarely goes unchallenged for longer than a generation. Frequently within a decade after a thesis has been widely held to have plausibly synthesized and related the variables on a given historical problem, further research or reflection leads to the undermining of the thesis and its replacement by a new explanation. While revolutions in scientific thought occur very rarely, fundamental shifts in historical interpretation are carried out with exhilarating swiftness. In every important field of history, at least half of the widely accepted interpretations current in 1940 have either been overthrown or are in the course of being vigorously challenged today.

But let us return to the student's question that inspired this discussion of the nature of historical proof: When have I proved my point? *You have proved your thesis when you have mastered the primary and secondary sources for the subject, and have so thoroughly examined all dimensions of the problem that a consistent pattern of relationships leading to a precisely stated thesis has emerged in your mind.* As you reconsider the evidence and go through the steps of the argument again and again, the same pattern and conclusion should inevitably appear. When you can see in your mind's eye a firm structure of relationships and when you can state your thesis in a sentence or two, you can feel confident that you have reached that stage of demonstrability and plausibility that historians refer to when they say a thesis is "proved."

As a practical test for determining whether you have proved your point, see whether you can give unequivocally affirmative answers to each of these questions: *Have I read and fully under-stood all the primary and secondary sources I was required to use for this problem? Can I concisely state the stages of my argument in a paragraph or two, no matter how long the actual exposition in the final version of the essay? Can I summarize my thesis and conclusion in not more than three precise, unambiguous sen-tences?* Vagueness and ambiguity in historical exposition is a sure indication that something has gone wrong with your thesis and that you have not proved your point. Provided that you have mastered the material and carefully inferred the relationships be-tween facts, the precision and clarity of your words will show that you have created a genuine work of historical truth.

10 / Research Techniques

How to Use the Library

The term research has in recent years assumed magical and mystical connotations. But the research that the historian undertakes can be defined in a simple and practical way. *Historical research means finding and studying books that provide the source material for the historian's work.* Therefore, research techniques for the student of history involve no arcane wizardry. They consist in learning how to make effective use of university and public libraries and also in using effectively the books in the student's own personal library.

At the outset the importance for the serious student of history of owning as many books as he can possibly afford should be emphasized. At every stage of the historian's development, the more books he has at his immediate and personal command, the more his work will be expedited and facilitated. Libraries are of course absolutely necessary, and no one can possibly afford all the books he needs for the subjects that interest him. Nonetheless, when the pressures of research and writing are heavy, there is no gainsaying that working in libraries eats up time and is terribly inefficient if the library is large and the process of finding books, time-consuming (and of course, very small libraries are of little use for any historical research, even for a freshman history paper).

For a freshman student, possibly the best advice is that he should simply buy books that interest him personally, on subjects he finds exciting. In this way, he will rapidly come to recognize the quality of different books and will later on be more expert in his book selections and purchases; of course, it would be good if the freshman also had recourse to advanced reading lists and to upper-division course syllabuses, so that he could be a bit discriminating from the start.

The upper-division history major should concentrate his buying in two categories. He should first acquire as many of the famous "classics" of historiography as possible; presumably he should be familiar with these titles by the time he is well into completion of his history major. The process of buying classics has been greatly facilitated in the modern scholarly age by the "paperback revolution," which has made available many famous historical works, formerly either long out of print or prohibitively priced, in a form anyone can afford. Thus, any student can have in his personal library the works of such major historians as Bloch, Rostovtzeff, Maitland, Tawney, Meinecke, Lefebvre, Panofsky, to name a few. The second area in which an upper-division history major should concentrate his buying is in books relevant to the field in which he thinks he might specialize as a graduate student; for example, if his field will possibly be Tudor and Stuart England, he should start to acquire as many books as possible in that area, to facilitate his later research. This applies both to primary and secondary books.

The graduate student has three basic obligations in filling up his personal library collection. First, he should finish the task of acquiring the most important classics of historiography in the fields related to his major interests. Second, he should complete his purchasing of useful books in his own field of concentration; in particular, graduate students should buy reference books, major dictionaries, and the like. Finally, and most important, graduate students should concentrate on buying as many primary sources in first-class editions as possible, since these are the major tools of their research, both immediately and for the rest of their careers.

To be sure, almost everyone has a financial problem when it comes to buying books. But we would urge every student to try to place as much of his personal resources as possible into the investment of a good library; indeed, the student should make a point of spending just a bit more than he thinks he can really afford. In the long run, the dividends in time and convenience of work and study will more than repay the small sacrifice of not seeing a movie. And in addition to the practical advantages involved, there is the very real personal pleasure of owning books and possessing a growing library—a kind of scholar's delight that is possible for anyone in this wonderful age of relatively inexpensive paperback books.

Whatever the size of your private collection of books, and whatever the level of historical study you are engaged in, sooner or later you will have to make use of the resources of a university research library. The first, and major skill needed by a student in a large research library is to know how to be able to find the books pertinent to his subject. In the first place, this requires a basic knowledge of how to use a catalogue, since even if the library is open-stack, a large collection will make it very hard to locate a book unless the student knows exactly where to look. Basic appreciation of how card catalogues are organized and how book classification schemes work is mandatory for anyone who plans a college career. It is, nevertheless, an amazing truth of American education that serious students can graduate from high school, matriculate in college, and still have no experience with, or knowledge of, the mechanical aspects of the use of a library. If the student is one of these unfortunates, then his first obligation in college, after locating his dormitory room, is to spend a day finding his way around the library and learning how to use it rapidly and with maximum efficiency. Beyond this, reference librarians are always very helpful and willing to advise neophytes in the use of library resources, and the student should not be afraid to ask for help if he needs it.

Beyond this most introductory level, however, what are some of the "tricks" that can mine a wealth of bibliographical information from a card catalogue? Everyone, of course, has his own approach to finding books, and only extensive experience can really teach in this regard; but we can pass along a few techniques of squeezing as much information as possible from a card catalogue.

First, the student should *always use the main card catalogue whenever possible;* "reserve-desk" catalogues are always partial selections, representing only specific books placed on reserve for particular courses by instructors. Thus only the main catalogue can give a full picture of the library's total resources on a given subject. Generally, even when a library is divided into sections or divisions, there will be one central catalogue that will list the entire holdings of the library. For work on any research paper, this is the catalogue to use.

In preparing to find books in the catalogue, the student should come armed with a general knowledge of the various aspects or categories of information that are involved in his subject; in addition, he will probably know the names of one or two books or authors dealing with his topic. Perhaps the best start is to look up the call numbers for those books the student knows he will need; while doing this, the student should carefully note down all of the other books written by the same author. The advantage of this procedure is that most authors tend to write about a particular area of interest, so that several of their books will be on different aspects of the same topic. Thus by looking into other books by authors who have written about his subject, the student is certain to find more material than he knew about to begin with, or to discover new aspects and dimensions of the subject that he was unaware of before. Exactly the same procedure should be followed in looking up the works of primary authors. We might add that one fringe benefit of this procedure for advanced or graduate students is that it builds up their bibliographical background very rapidly and thus facilitates later studying for comprehensive examinations.

In noting down new books by familiar authors discovered through the card catalogue, the student will probably find that he learns of some new subjects and historical personages connected with his topic; these should be added to his list of subject headings or categories of information, to which he will turn next. In looking up subject headings in a card catalogue, the student will have to use his imagination because information is not always entered according to the subject headings that the student has presupposed. L. B. Namier's *The Structure of Politics at the Accession of George III* would not be found in most libraries under the heading of "politics," and sometimes not even under the heading of "Great Britain—politics," since those headings usually contain books on current and theoretical topics rather than historical materials. The most likely subject heading for turning up Namier's work would be "George III" or "Great Britain—History—18th Century." Thus the student is going to have to search extensively to find the proper headings to cover his subject; he cannot expect that the cataloguer was an omniscient being who foresaw every possible use of the contents of every book. One help in finding further subject headings is in the catalogue itself, because at major divisions or large subjects there will be a card with a list of other headings related to the present division. Each of these additional headings should be checked as a possible source of unknown books and pamphlets on the main or related topics of research.

Perhaps just as important as finding the right major subject categories is a thorough investigation of corollary or minor subject categories. The student should not simply confine himself to obvious topical categories in looking for information but should also look under related headings—history of science in the given period or country; history of philosophy, of religion, of art—because all of these diverse categories may contain some books that will have some bearing on the subject being studied. One very important peripheral category is the names of all major people connected with the subject. Even if the subject you are studying is not primarily biographical, valuable information on an institutional or cultural problem might very well be found in biographies. Systematic search of the card catalogue under biographical categories could turn up a book whose title alone might not have seemed relevant to your subject. In short, the *student should do his utmost, by searching various, even remotely related categories,* to use the card catalogue to provide research sources that he might not otherwise have anticipated.

You will avoid tiresome duplication of library work and save time if, as soon as you find a book title relevant to your subject, you *make a permanent bibliographical notation directly from the card catalogue entry.* A bibliographical note—which is most conveniently recorded on an individual file card of useful (usually 3×5) size—should contain the full name of the author, last name first; the full title of the book, the place, publisher, and date of publication; information about how many volumes if the work is a multi-volume set, who the translator is if the work is translated, and which edition is being used; the name of the editor if his contribution to the final contents of the book was significant, and the general name of any major series publication of which the book might be one volume (e.g., Rebenack's edition of Cyprian's *De Opere et Eleemosynis* is in the series of the Catholic University of America, *Patristic Studies,* Vol. XCIV). All of this information will later be needed in any bibliographical entry the student might have to make; and if he obtains this information once and for all at the very beginning of his research, he will not have to be bothered by the trouble of going back and looking up all the card catalogue entries again, or by plowing through stacks and stacks of books in order to make a bibliography. Indeed, even more important than bother or trouble is the factor of immediacy; all too often the student—and the seasoned professional—will find that if he discovers a new reference (not only in a card catalogue, but in reading bibliographies or looking at books on shelves) and does not write it down at once, thinking that he can remember the source and rediscover it later, in many cases the reference will be lost to him forever. He will have a dim memory of the card being somewhere under the heading of "Industrial Revolution" (along with fifty other titles), but even if he has the very rare good fortune of ever finding his reference again, it will only be at the expense of wasted minutes or even hours of hunt-and-peck searching. *Immediate entry of a reference into a permanent bibliographical file system* will prevent such problems once and for all, and then the student will have the reference for the rest of his career, to be used over and over in connection with many different research projects.

This last notion suggests *three practical hints* in connection with preparing permanent bibliography cards. First, if the student knows that he will be spending a great deal of time using one library collection, such as his college library, he can save himself a lot of time by making a notation on his bibliography cards of the call numbers of the books he knows he will want to use a number of times, thereby sparing himself later trips to the card catalogue. Second, cards in a permanent bibliographical file can be used to record more information than simple bibliographical data; the student can note which books have illustrations, or useful indexes, or lists of books on given topics, and so on. In this way his own bibliographical notes will expedite his future research on new subjects. Finally, while it is likely that the student will temporarily keep in one group the bibliography cards related to a paper on which he is immediately working, his permanent bibliographical file should be organized in terms of general topics, with the books entered according to their relationship to general historical problems rather than according to specific topics for papers. By doing this, the file will eventually become a means to organizing and finding materials for *any* research he might pursue. At any stage of his career and studies, the student should do his utmost to take a long-range view, so that the work he does can be part of a cumulative buildup toward later study. Otherwise, he will find that the next year in another course he will be forced to repeat library work that he has already done. Systematic work habits in the first place will make his assignments easier and more successful, and will also lead him directly into advanced and professional work.

The main card catalogue, especially if the library collection is large and rich, is one of the major bibliographical tools available to the student. But there are other sources that must be consulted in order to obtain a list of all the works relevant to a given historical problem or subject. The first place to which most historians would turn in a bibliographical quest is the list of recommended works commonly found at the back of a standard general survey of the period. Thus, for a list of the best books on the Greek city-state, one would turn to the bibliography at the end of M. I. Finley's *The Greeks;* for a bibliography on politics in England in the 1920's the student would consult A. J. P. Taylor, *English History 1914–1945.* When consulting a general work for bibliographical information, you should try to find the most recent one available, so that its recommended list of books is up to date.

Another valuable source of bibliographical information will be found in the reference room of the university library—volumes exclusively devoted to bibliographical listings, usually with explanatory and critical comments. These bibliographical volumes fall into two general categories: *subject* bibliographies and *discipline* bibliographies. The former list books related to a given field of study, for example, Charles Gross, *The Sources and Literature of English History from the Earliest Times to about 1485;* Conyers Read, *Bibliography of British History, Tudor Period, 1485–1603;* and Dahlmann-Waitz, *Quellenkunde der Deutschen Geschichte.* These subject bibliographical volumes are extremely valuable and can save the student hours of exhausting work, but you must be aware of the fact that these bibliographies are only revised every two or three decades, if that often (Gross was published in 1915, and a revised edition is still lacking), and therefore their listings are invariably out of date. You will inevitably have to supplement bibliographical volumes with other sources of information in order to obtain the more recent titles.

The same warning applies to discipline bibliographies. This kind of listing attempts to include all of the titles of major importance related to a particular academic discipline; the disciplines are usually synonymous with university departments. Prominent examples of this kind of reference work would be the *Guide to Historical Literature,* published by the American Historical Association, and the *Cambridge Bibliography of English Literature.*

Some bibliographies are printed once completely, attempting to include all material available up to the time of publication in one general index, while others are printed annually. In the latter case, it will often be necessary to consult each volume of the bibliography for complete information about a given subject, unless the set offers an occasional index covering a number of years.

In general, during the period when the student is first becoming familiar with the library, it would be well worth his while to spend a day or two in the reference room, examining every collection of reference books that might have some bearing on his fields of interest. He should take the time to open and read some of every such reference book, so that when he later has recourse to these sources in doing research work, he will have a general idea of what reference tools are available to him and what kind of information he can expect to find in each.

In this process, the student should be cautioned to pay little attention to general encyclopedias, even very good ones like the eleventh edition of *The Encyclopaedia Britannica.* At best, articles in such encyclopedias can be but a mere introduction to, or quick survey of, a subject and should *never* be given in bibliographical notes in a serious research paper as a reference in their own right.

What is more, the bibliographies in general encyclopedia articles are always woefully incomplete and can never be used as a final bibliographical source without further searching for titles. There is, however, another sort of encyclopedia that has been appearing in recent years, which is rather more helpful; this is the specialized, scholarly encyclopedia of a given academic discipline, such as the *Encyclopedia of the Social Sciences* or the *Encyclopedia of World Art*. In general, the interest in such specialized encyclopedias is not so much in the articles—although these are frequently very good surveys of the scholarship on their subjects and are usually written by leading experts—as in the bibliographical references, which tend to be very thorough and a useful guide to finding source materials.

If encyclopedias at best provide only limited assistance in research at the college level, periodical literature, particularly learned articles published in professional academic journals (such as the *American Historical Review, English Historical Review, Journal of Modern History, Revue Historique, Historische Zeitschrift*), is an immensely important depositary of both secondary and primary material and is therefore indispensable to the advanced college student of history. The problem, however, is to find out which articles in which journals are relevant to one's current subject of research. There are dozens of important journals and many more of peripheral value, but you must know where in the row upon row of bound periodicals in the library stacks you can find the particular journal articles that are absolutely necessary for research on a given problem.

It would be comforting if we could say that all articles in periodicals relevant to historical questions have been programmed into a computer and that all the student has to do is to mark up a computer card in a certain way in order to retrieve the precise bibliographical information he needs. In some fields of the sciences, notably in medicine, this kind of computerized bibliographical information is already available, and some scholars are projecting the same technology for historical bibliography. But until this happy day comes, the student has to face the disquieting fact that there is no single, easily workable way of quickly finding all the periodical literature for his subject. He has to use various bibliographical methods and guides.

Every high school student is familiar with the *Reader's Guide to Periodical Literature,* which is typical of the kind of index that cross-references a large number of periodicals—in this case, mostly magazines of the mass-circulation variety. There are a number of general indexes to periodicals that are particularly valuable to the historical researcher, especially the *International Index to Periodicals* and *Historical Abstracts;* the latter series gives brief summaries of articles as well as bibliographical information. In compiling lists of articles on a particular subject, the student should not overlook indexes in ancillary fields, such as the *Art Index* and the *Music Index,* which often have very useful references for historians.

Beyond these general indexes, individual journals usually have an index—always annually and sometimes compendiously over a long span of years—listing the articles and book reviews that have appeared in the issues of the journal. Often such indexes have subject headings as well as simple alphabetical author listings, and the student should examine the indexes of all journals that might possibly carry articles related to the subject on which he is working. When the student is becoming familiar with the library early in his college career, he should *make a special point of getting to know all of the journals available in his and related fields.* One way of doing this is by making a list of journal titles, finding all of these journals in the library, and leafing through a few volumes or years of each one. In this way the student will come to know the general format of each journal, the approximate editorial policies followed, and the kinds of articles and range of subjects to be found in each, so that later when he is doing research on a given subject, he will know which journals are likely to be useful to him.

Besides indexes to their own articles and book reviews, journals often contain further bibliographical aids. Some journals print not only general lists of books currently published or currently received—even when space does not permit reviews of such books—but also lists of important periodical articles. By reading such lists regularly, students can keep up easily with much of the current scholarship related to the field of the journal. For instance, medieval scholars constantly turn to the rich annual bibliography published by the *Revue d'histoire ecclésiastique*. Such bibliographies can be found in a variety of journals and on an enormous variety of subjects, and they are always very helpful for keeping abreast of the work that has appeared in recent months in a given field.

Finally, journals offer valuable bibliographical assistance when they print "review articles." These are of two kinds; the first sort discusses the past historiography on a given historical topic, giving capsule summaries of the various points of view and kinds of publications that have appeared. The other kind of review article is the retrospective survey of the work of a single historian. Such articles usually give a summarized biography of the historian, a discussion of his most important writings, and then a bibliographical list of his total works. If the student knows that a famous historian has contributed a book or an article to the scholarship on a subject and wishes to know what further work that historian has done, a review article can often prove a convenient source of information.

Surveys of the total work of famous historians can also be found in one bibliographical source too frequently overlooked by students, the *Festschrift*. A *Festschrift*—a German term that has become part of the historian's jargon and is perhaps best translated as "commemorative volume"—is a collection of articles written by friends and students of a famous teacher and published either for presentation to him on a major birthday anniversary or as a memorial to him after his death. Such volumes nearly always begin with a dedicatory essay, frequently platitudinous, but still offering a summary of the biography of the historian being honored, and—what is more important and useful—a complete bibliography of the work of the historian, even including his book reviews. If a *Festschrift* has been published in honor of a given historian, and if a library collection owns the *Festschrift*, it will be listed under the subject entry of his name and should certainly be consulted by the student in search of bibliographical information.

Finally, some bibliographical assistance can be obtained by consulting the printed catalogues of very large libraries and the "union" catalogues that list the holdings of many contributing libraries. Especially important examples of this type of source are the *National Union Catalogue* of American libraries published by the Library of Congress and the catalogues of printed books in the holdings of the Bibliothèque Nationale in Paris and the British Museum in London. These lists can often make the student aware of books that are not available in his own college library.

If in the course of your research, you come across the title of a book that is not in your university library or of an article in a periodical to which your university library does not subscribe, you should ask the reference librarian to obtain the book or periodical for you on interlibrary loan, that is, from another academic library that does have the work in its collection. You can yourself readily find out which libraries in the United States and Canada subscribe to a particular journal by consulting *The Union List of Serials.*

Advanced and graduate students should be aware of one further type of bibliographical catalogue of great value in expediting work and providing information. This is the catalogue of manuscript holdings or of early printed books in a library; such catalogues are published by most of the major libraries of Europe and are usually drawn up by very well-known scholars. Even if the student is not working on a problem that requires direct use of a manuscript or early imprint of his primary source texts, consultation of the appropriate catalogue may often be extremely fruitful. In the brief description of the contents of each manuscript the editor of the catalogue will very frequently include many bibliographical references to important books, articles, and editions, which the student may want to use in his own research.

We have discussed bibliographical tools and techniques at such great length because of the patterns we have observed in the work of students during our years of teaching. It seems to be a common failing on the part of students—even the brightest, most imaginative ones—to be content with a minimum of information, or with bibliographical resources thoughtlessly and carelessly assembled and used. Often these students place too much emphasis on sources of little worth while overlooking some major primary and secondary materials for the subject. If you are serious enough about your work for a course, which should be a miniature model of professional work, you will want to do a first-rate job of investigating every problem you are going to interpret. You must realize that you have a responsibility toward the previous scholarship in your field and toward the primary sources that the past has offered to you.

In order to make sure that you can find and read all the sources for your subject, you must have in your mind, to start with, a clear and quite precise idea of its ultimate limits. The bibliography of history is virtually endless, and unless you set limits to the subject you are researching, you will be overwhelmed by the variety and mass of the material.

Once the student has defined for himself the scope and limits of a problem on which he is working, he should immediately set as a goal for himself the acquisition of all the bibliographical resources for his subject that circumstances and his own level of experience will allow. There is really no adequate excuse for insufficient effort in this direction; even a beginner is able to use a library and should become familiar at once with research techniques, and any student who is trying to make a serious effort to carry on his work maturely can be sure of advice and assistance from his instructor, if he will only seek it. Therefore, the fault for the lack of background or insufficiency of sources in a research paper always lies with the student, not with anyone else.

Of course, the extent to which bibliographical materials can be treated in the paper itself depends on the length and scope of the paper and on the amount of time available for its preparation. Probably in every historical essay, from the beginning student paper to the seasoned professional monograph, only a fraction of the reading done by the scholar will actually appear in any formal sense as a reference. But even so, for any scholar, student or professional, it remains a truism that insofar as he has not read all of the research material available on his subject, to that extent will his work be incomplete.

There is one final aspect of working in a library that might be mentioned, even though at first it might seem rather obvious; this is the matter of *browsing*. Almost every college library has some areas of open shelves—perhaps in the "new-acquisitions" section, in the reserve section, or sometimes even in the main collection—and the student should make a point of spending some of his free time simply wandering around such stacks and looking at the books he finds. In particular, if the stacks for research sources are "open," the student should make a point of looking at the shelves all around the position of the particular book he is seeking, because books are catalogued by subject; and works related to the subject of any given book will be found near that book. By such general browsing, the student will find that he discovers many new sources, and in addition he will give a tremendous boost to his memory of these books if he opens and examines and glances through the contents of the volumes. Thus book-browsing is not merely a form of idle curiosity, but is really a major aspect of the student's, and the scholar's, occupation.

Again a procedural hint and word of caution are needed here. The student should always carry some of his blank bibliography cards with him when he is browsing; and when he discovers a new book or article, he should at once make a full bibliographical notation, including the call number if he will be using that library again. If he does not do this, it is almost certain that the volume will be as lost to him as if he had never seen it. He may remember that the volume was red and was "in the upper left part of the stack on the second floor," but he may never be able to locate the book again, a maddening frustration when he knows that the book once was at his command. All of us, the authors included, have suffered from such temporary laziness, but the student can minimize such experiences if he gets into the habit of making bibliographical notes at the most opportune moment, which is when the source is ready at hand.

Research Note-Taking

Once the student has completed his bibliographical research and has assembled as many sources for his study of a subject as possible, the next step is to comprehend and digest these materials into a form useful for the shaping and writing of the paper. Here, the most important skills needed are an ability to take clear, practical notes and then to collate and organize such notes into permanent note files.

Every scholar has his own individual methods for taking notes and for recalling and referring to what he has read, and it would be futile for us to try to designate every step of a note-taking process as a definitive guide to research techniques. But there are a few points that the student may not have considered before and a few tricks we use in our own note-taking, which we might profitably pass on as suggestions.

The most important statement we could make about taking notes is to urge the student not to take too many notes and not to be more detailed than he needs to be. There is no sight more futile than a student painstakingly transcribing, sometimes almost word for word, the whole contents of a book or article he is reading into a voluminous notebook, and then having to go back later and pick his way through the huge mass of notes, underlining and sorting out what is important. If the sorting-out process had occurred in the first place, in the student's own understanding of the book as he read it, then his note-taking could have involved only a summary plus transcription of the most important passages; and the resultant page or two of notes would have been far more useful than the twenty or thirty pages of close copy of the book so laboriously prepared.

Of course, it is easy to say "do not be more detailed than you need to be," but it is sometimes very hard to know in advance just how detailed that might be. Further research often reveals that a fact or inference which at first one thought was marginal actually has considerable importance for a full study of the topic at hand, and the student will frequently find himself going back to books he has already consulted, in order to clarify or to further elucidate a point. But for the most part, the student can judge the degree of detail needed in note-taking by having a sensitive grasp of the degree of specificity of the topic he is studying, combined with a recognition of the degree of precision and detail in the book he is reading. If the topic is extremely refined and precise, the amount of detail needed in research notes will be much greater than that needed for a more generalized topic treated in a short paper. Likewise, if the source being read is rather generalized in its statements and opinions, it would be rather futile to copy down the text of the source word for word when a quick, summarizing note would express the essential point as well. Again, if the source being read is highly detailed, or is full of factual references, the extent to which the student must take notes on this material depends on its relevance. If the details reported are about some subject central to the student's research topic, then of course he will wish to have very full notes on the report; but if the facts are on a subject rather peripheral to the main lines of the paper, then the student can take a generalized note on the main points revealed by the details, rather than cluttering his note files and his mind— and probably his final paper as well—with hundreds of irrelevant examples.

In short, if the student is as critical and analytical in his note-taking as he is in his reading of his sources, then the process of taking notes will in itself enhance and further the final stages of organization of research material into an argument and a paper. The notes themselves will reveal a focus of ideas and material into subjects of importance and subjects of a more peripheral nature, into generalizations taken for granted and points that require detailed proof and elaboration. While this discussion may perhaps seem to be belaboring an obvious idea, we have given it much emphasis because we have so often seen diligent, serious efforts at research by hard-working students marred by a lack of direction and improper emphasis. At any level, student essay or seasoned scholarly book, the best paper is never one that simply finds out everything that can be discovered about the subject and reports all such discovery without any awareness of significant meaning. Rather the best study is one in which materials are organized into points, points into categories, categories into broad topics, and topics into a unified, all-of-one-piece, writing. If the student ever finds as he writes a paper that he is repeating or copying something from his notes without evaluating its significance, or is including whole batches of facts and information simply because he happens to have found these facts in the course of his research, then he can be sure that he has not really mastered his material sufficiently and that he needs further organization and sifting of his materials before reaching the final draft of his paper.

Finally, we might add a few remarks about some practical aspects of taking notes and of filing them in such a way that they are useful both for immediate and for long-range research purposes. *In note-taking the two chief practical problems are to achieve quick bibliographical reference and to facilitate cross-reference between one source and another.* If the student has followed our earlier suggestion and has made a permanent card file with the complete bibliographical reference material for each book or article that he has observed or consulted, then the bibliographical detail necessary for accurate notes can be kept to a minimum. When taking a note he will just have to record as much of the name of the author and the title as he needs to identify the book in his file of bibliography cards. He should also cite the page reference for each note taken. This, by the way, is quite important and is similar to the point made earlier about taking the full bibliographical information about a book at the moment when the book is in hand. If you find a piece of information that is useful enough to be noted down, *you should make a page reference together with the note,* because otherwise it will be your frequent misfortune never to be able to find again exactly the page to which you want to refer. This kind of trouble can easily be avoided if the student will always keep in mind that the cardinal rule about bibliographical practice is "do it now."

The second aim, useful cross-reference between one source and another, is the most difficult problem of all in building an effective master note file. There are two possible approaches to collecting notes from a number of different sources. Some prefer to group all notes from one book together, and then to have some kind of outline index to the final mass of notes. Others prefer to *establish subject categories in advance* and to put together in the note file under one such subject all the notes from a variety of sources pertaining to that subject. The personal preference of the authors is for the latter method. Digesting an entire source into notes for any possible research topic is a procedure, we feel, that relates more to remembering the source itself as a whole than to remembering the contribution the source makes to the investigation of any given subject. Thus, to make a notation on a source as a whole, we follow the method of preparing a brief précis of the work, as discussed in a previous chapter. In making notes intended for precise reference and immediate use in our research, we find it much more convenient, and much more conducive to our fuller understanding of the problem involved, if we have grouped in *one place* all the various factual information and points of view, drawn from many sources, about a single subject we have turned up in the course of our research.

As you become experienced in research you will develop a system of taking and filing notes that suits your personality and level of intelligence. For a start, you will find the following method, while it may seem elaborate and time-consuming, to be foolproof:

1. Keep bibliographical entries on 3 x 5 cards for each book or article you come across.

2. File these bibliographical cards in a card file box in alphabetical order, by author or editor.

3. From time to time go through your individual bibliographical cards, and on 5 x 8 cards prepare subject bibliographies. File these in a card file box in alphabetical order ("Parliament" before "Peasantry").

4. Notes taken from sources should be written in ink or typed on either 5 x 8 cards or sheets of loose-leaf paper. At the top left of the card or sheet write in the topic of the material in the notes ("Gladstone's Opinion of Disraeli's Foreign Policy," "Carleton Hayes' Definition of Nationalism"). At the top right of the card or sheet put in the precise bibliographical reference, including the page number.

5. If taken on 5 x 8 cards the source material notes should be filed in a manila folder. If taken on sheets, the notes should be kept in a loose-leaf notebook. Either way you will have immediate access to the source notes on the subjects you are currently investigating. You can carry these notes around and consult them when you want.

6. Leave wide margins on the left-hand side of your source notes. Here can be entered cross-references and thoughts that occur to you about the material.

7. Keep a separate idea file in which are listed general themes and conclusions on the subject of your paper and the problem that begins to take shape in your mind. These idea notes will be invaluable when you come to make outlines and to shape and write your paper.

8. Source notes that you ultimately find are superfluous for your paper should be carefully filed away, under subject headings, for possible future use.

9. When you have read enough secondary and primary sources to develop a tentative view of the organization of your paper, sit down and *prepare a working outline.* Go through your source notes again and make notations on the outline, indicating which topics have been fully researched, which seem to be only partly researched, and which remain to be investigated. As your research continues, and the structure of the paper changes in your mind, prepare a new working outline and in the same way indicate the progress of your research. Keep your current outline in a handy and highly visible place, such as on the wall over your desk. This will allow you to see day by day the work that remains to be done. You are very likely to reach a stage in your research when you seem to have come to a dead end and when you feel that you are simply going around in circles. Under no circumstances stop working; if you do, the material will go cold on you, and you will be in far worse trouble. The way out of a research impasse is to look carefully at your current working outline and to research those topics that have not yet been done. As you get into this new material, fresh ideas will occur to you, and you will at last begin to see a glimmer of light at the end of the dark corridor.

10. At regular stages in your bibliographical quest, and your note-taking on sources, *go through the bibliographical and source notes, and relate the material in the notes to the topics in your*

working outline. This can be done in one of two ways. If you do not have many notes and the organization of the paper is a fairly simple one, mark with a pencil at the top of your note card a number which keys your note to the relevant heading and sub-heading in your outline (Ic, IIIb5, etc.). If you have a great many notes and the subject and organization of your paper are highly complex, another procedure is more useful. Designate a single 5 x 8 card or a loose-leaf sheet for every item and subitem in the outline. Then specify on the sheet or card where in your source notes the material can be found that deals with the particular subtopic, and which books and articles in your bibliographical file contain material on the topic. If you follow these methods, you will be in firm command of your material when you come to the stages of final organization and the writing of your first draft.

11. Use one particular kind and size of note card or paper for each kind of file. Otherwise you will have a scrapbook, not a note file. Write on one side of a note card or a sheet only. Material written on the back of note cards is easily forgotten and lost. If you have more material than can fit on one card or sheet, which frequently happens when taking source notes, simply continue on to another card and then staple the cards together. Make sure, however, that you note at the top of the second card the original heading that appeared at the top of the first card. This is a precaution against the staple coming loose and the cards being separated. Never take notes in pencil because pencil markings smear and readily become illegible.

The research techniques outlined in this chapter have been well tested and if conscientiously followed will be enormously helpful to you in your work. Nothing is sadder for a history teacher than to see a student wandering about the library in a daze, trying to do research in a completely disorganized and haphazard fashion. There is no one absolute way to do historical research any more than there is one exclusive method for any human endeavor. As you become an experienced researcher, you will develop all sorts of short-cuts and tricks to facilitate and speed your work. If you have an extraordinary aptitude for historical thinking, you may some day be able to follow the techniques employed by those exceptionally brilliant scholars who turn their minds into historical computers. They somehow manage to take a great many notes mentally and to file these notes in a memory bank ready for instant retrieval. But the novice and apprentice student of history should never attempt this kind of supersonic technique. He should follow the down-to-earth, tried and tested methods we have outlined in this chapter, which will help him become a highly successful historical researcher.

11 / Historical Prose

THE QUALITIES OF STYLE

If history is what historians create, then history only exists in historical writings. The making of a history paper involves several distinct steps in research and critical thinking. Not less important is the actual writing of the paper—the quality of the prose. There are several aspects of writing a paper that have to do with matters of good English and style.

You may feel prompted to say at this point that we are only repeating what you have heard countless times in the English composition courses you have taken and what you can read in any standard composition handbook or style manual, and you are substantially right. But many students that we have encountered in our history courses seem to ignore all matters having to do with grammar and style as soon as they leave the doors of the English classroom. Indeed, they seem to avoid them almost self-consciously. Every college teacher of history who has, quite properly, lowered a student's grade for illiterate writing, has heard the complaint: "This is a course in history, not a course in English." This attitude reveals a total lack of comprehension by the student of what communication of ideas involves. No historical concept, no matter how original, can be properly or adequately communicated by an English-speaking student until it is stated clearly in standard, forceful English. Any criterion less than this is simply not going to produce good or valid history. Apparently this problem is not unique to history; throughout academic circles one hears the complaint that student writing is very poor in quality and that students seem indifferent to the necessity for good English as a first requirement to success in any academic endeavor. A recent study at an eastern college, taking all student writing in all courses into account, turned up the appalling result that by any sort of parameter the best writing in college was done by freshmen, and that the quality of written English decreased yearly until the worst writing was that handed in by seniors! If a student is to have any measure of professional quality in his work, he must learn that good English is not merely the subject of one course taken at the beginning of a college career, but is rather the entire basis for any possible success in communicating his thought on any subject. Just as the student must learn to think like an historian, so too he must learn to write like an historian, which in the first place means learning how to write with precision, organization, and clarity.

The first requirement of a good historical form is that *the paper must have a precise main point.* Putting this same notion another way, we could say that *every paper should simply be a thoughtful and thorough development and proof of one basic thesis or idea.* Clear presence of a main point is fundamental to any sense of cohesion or organization in a paper; without a main point the paper becomes simply a collection of random data, neither very informative nor very pleasant to read.

One matter of definition should be cleared up at once: *a main point is not the same thing as the subject of the paper.* A subject is simply the kind of material or the range of information that the author intends to investigate, without any statement of point of view or conclusion. For instance, a variety of different papers could be written on the subject of "Bismarck's Foreign Policy." A main point, in contrast, is always a *thesis,* i.e., a contention about the subject. Such contentions always involve claims that a particular conclusion is a correct view of the significance of a certain subject, and such claims of correctness must always be proved by proper definition of terms and study of primary and secondary sources. For the subject just given as an example, one possible main point is "Bismarck's foreign policy reveals his deep commitment to the idea of German national superiority in European power politics." Another possible main point on the same subject is "Bismarck's foreign policy reveals a new trend in German ideas of *raison d'état*, away from the older notion of preserving the balance of power and toward a new philosophy of aggrandizement in international politics." Still a third possible main point for the topic is "Bismarck's foreign policy derives from two generally accepted nineteenth-century political and philosophical notions, the idea of progress and the idea of manifest destiny."

In each of these cases, it can be seen that *the main point represents a stand,* a commitment to some explanation of the historical truths to be determined in a study of Bismarck's policy. The student who states only that his paper "intends to study aspects of Bismarck's policy" has failed to give his idea any focus or to make any kind of precise claim that he can prove by critical and analytical examination of the evidence at his disposal. It is a precise contention, a main point, which gives an historical work focus, which makes its claims exciting and interesting, which puts forth the paper as a challenge to historical imagination and to historical insight.

Once the main point has been clearly established, the introduction to a paper or thesis should offer a detailed analysis of the implications of the thesis, together with some sketch of how those implications will be taken up and treated in various parts of the main body of the paper. You should note that we use the concept of "introduction" here in the generic sense. The introduction need not be the first portion of the text of the paper. Indeed, in the impressionistic approach to form, the "introduction" will appear as the final, concluding summary of the entire work. Also, in terms of actually writing the paper, *the introduction will probably be the last part to be written.* You cannot write the introduction until you know what you are introducing and you cannot be sure of the contents and organization of the final version of your study until you have actually written the paper.

Usually, the analysis of the implications of the main point involves an explanation by the writer of the significance of the *critical words of his main point;* i.e., he must make clear to the reader the precise way in which he is using his terms. For instance, in the first of the sample main points given above—"Bismarck's foreign policy reveals his deep commitment to the idea of German national superiority in European power politics"—the writer would be obligated to explain exactly what dimensions of Bismarck's foreign policy will be treated in his work. Is he going to include diplomacy or merely exercise of military power? What is the nature of the "deep commitment" in the eyes of the writer; is he discussing Bismarck's conscious planning only, or also a *"Geist"* (spirit), typical of the age, which he feels Bismarck is implicitly following? What, in the writer's opinion, did Bismarck understand by the concept of "Germany"? And is the "idea" of German superiority a political program only, or a deep spiritual-racial-cultural notion? In this way, the writer will clarify the terms of his discussion, prevent the confusion that results from failure to "define his terms," and by implication, set up the topics for his discussion and arguments, since presumably each of the author's individual definitions of these terms will be arguable and will be discussed in detail later.

The analysis of the critical terms of the thesis, along the lines suggested in the preceding paragraph, should lead directly into the *main body of the paper,* which will be a well-organized critical discussion of the research material pertinent to the subject the student has assembled. When we say well organized, we mean that the entire paper should appear to the reader as a discussion of different aspects of the main point. There should be a clear sense that the material covered derives from the main point and elucidates some particular aspect of it. This method is also the basis for structuring the material discussed into paragraphs and, in a longer work, into sections or chapters. The student must be sure that such a thread of continuity is clearly discernible in his work and that the relationships among all the material he discusses can be clearly sensed by the reader. Nothing should appear as irrelevant, or as "padding." This rule must be followed even when the paper is written in the impressionistic style; indeed, without such a central thread of continuity, the whole possibility of proving a thesis by an impressionistic approach will be lost.

The way to achieve such a thorough-going organization for most writers is to work from a *writing outline,* and a few words might be in order about good and bad practice in the preparation of outlines. Many students are as confused about the nature of outlines as they are about the distinction between subject and main point. *A writing outline is a skeleton guide to the patterns of flow of thought and ideas in a work,* not merely a list of the topics and examples covered in the work. The latter would be of no use at all in providing a scheme of the author's conceptions. Instead, the writing outline must be a series of contentions and themes, a list of the subpoints, topic sentences, and the like that are the *crucial steps in the development of the author's argument.* Only in this way will an outline make apparent the flow of ideas, the steps of the logic in the organization of the paper. Again, if the examples to be discussed are included in the outline, the guide should communicate a sense of exactly what view of the examples is to be taken in order to make them useful as illustrations of the idea with which they are connected. Simply slapping down examples gives no clue concerning the reason why they are validly part of the discussion of the subject.

To illustrate this point, a poor outline on the topic of Bismarck's Foreign Policy might look something like the partial outline that follows. (To the right of the outline we have placed the questions whose answers the outline *fails* to indicate.)

I. Introduction   *[What is the author going to say? What is his main viewpoint?]*

II. Bismarck's policy   *[What is it? What are the terms of discussion?]*

    A. Ems telegram

    B. Siege of Paris   *[Why are these examples given? What*

    C. Letters, 1870–71 *significance do they have for the point?]*

III. German nationalism, *[What will be said?]*
     1860–1914

A good outline might have all of the same categories of discussion, but each heading would be a *precise claim or idea,* so as to make the lines of thought clear and apparent. For example:

  I. Introduction:
    Bismarck's actions reveal a plan of deliberate power politics. The source of his beliefs in earlier German nationalism. Bismarck as essentially Prussian.
 II. Key events in Bismarck's career reveal the deliberate planning behind his policy, with his aim to establish German superiority in power.
    A. His changes in the Ems dispatch calculated to set up a test of power
    B. His insistence on besieging Paris even when French capitulation was a *fait accompli* shows his desire to manifest the clear supremacy of German power.
    C. Details in his letters show his self-conscious commitment to the superiority of German power and its inevitable triumph.

In this infinitely superior second outline, the idea to be discussed in accordance with each topic is clear. It can be seen from even the partial example given that the structure of the thought results from making each category of the outline an aspect of the thesis set forth in the introduction. This kind of outline would be a real asset to a writer trying to organize his thoughts and achieve a sense of coherence in his argument.

Once the writer has entered the course of his discussion, several further aspects of clear thought and style, and coherent organization, become very important. Chief among these aspects is the factor of precision. A writer who is precise will always be extremely careful about the *exact meanings of the words he uses;* he will try to avoid vagueness of meaning so that no possible misunderstanding of his concepts can arise. The necessity for such concern with precision is that no two writers will use several terms all in exactly the same way, and it cannot be expected that there will be common agreement about the meaning of even very routine-seeming terms, unless the particular use of the terms is clearly indicated. This care is especially required when the meaning of a term is critical to an author's argument. The student should be most cautious when he uses key historiographical terms such as "caused," "led to," "was a factor of secondary importance when compared to," and so on. He must also be absolutely clear in his precise meaning when he uses conceptual terms such as feudalism or romanticism. These terms always imply judgment, and judgment is always personal, so a writer who uses these terms should make very clear to his reader the exact sense in which he uses them. In two sample student papers, which are given in the next chapter, one of the chief failings that these students showed was their imprecise use of connotative historical terms, and even of standard English words.

Besides precision, some other criteria of historical form are important. *Consistency* is always a requirement in well-organized writing. It may seem a bit strange to mention that consistency is often overlooked, but we have seen many student papers in which one paragraph explicitly contradicted the conclusions and even the facts of some previous paragraph. Probably the cause of such failure in writing is that the student worked on his paper piecemeal and did not revise it, or else he simply wrote his paper straight through, paragraph by paragraph, taking up one batch of information after another, without bothering to write a second draft. Consistency will always be achieved if the student learns to think of his papers as unitary discussions of a single point, if he tries to relate everything in the body of his paper back to some central thread, and if he gives himself enough time to write two or more drafts.

The criteria of *accuracy* and *thoroughness* must be observed. Accuracy involves faithfulness to the sources of information pertinent to the discussion, especially to the texts of primary sources. At the most fundamental level accuracy means that a writer has a moral responsibility not to distort or change the words of his sources to make them fit his own expectations. Unfortunately, many scholars, even some well-known professionals, are frequently guilty of this. A more subtle kind of inaccuracy or distortion comes from improper emphasis, e.g., trying to make a peripheral or secondary claim in a source appear to be the main theme or emphasis of the source. Many if not most scholarly disputes rage over exactly such matters of emphasis in reading primary sources. Accuracy will be enhanced if the student always sets for himself a goal of complete thoroughness in his work, if he makes an effort to know all of the sources relevant to his subject and to know each source in detail. This kind of thoroughness should prevent any serious distortions in reading the sources and should give the student firm ground for valid and meaningful interpretation.

If every paper the student writes has a clear main point, i.e., a thesis to be proved; if all of the critical terms used by the student are defined carefully; and if the development and discussion of the thesis exhibits precision, consistency, accuracy, and thoroughness; then the quality of the student's writing is certain to be very fine, and the strengths of his historical insight and argument will be communicated with great success and in a manner that will give his readers the pleasurable feeling of encountering a well-written historical essay, one that has the ring of truth.

PROBLEMS IN EXPOSITORY WRITING

In theory every college student has successfully completed a solid course in English style and composition, and every student owns and has constant reference to a good handbook of grammar and style. However, if the papers we receive are any indication, the English course seems to have left a startling number of students unchanged, or at least unabashed, in regard to good writing; and the manuals are, to all appearances, gathering dust on the shelves.

Nothing can mar the good effect of a thoughtful paper more than sloppiness in appearance or in quality of style; and *every history teacher, whether he says so explicitly or not, is affected in his judgment of a student's work by aspects of style and writing.* Thus it would behoove the student to give as much care and attention to the basic expository aspects of his writing as he does to research and the shaping of his material.

Every student should make a point of having grammar and style manuals handy on his reference shelf. In addition to the style and grammar manuals listed in Chapter 1, we recommend *The Modern Researcher* by Jacques Barzun and H. F. Graff, for style and form in research papers. While it may seem a forbidding and tedious task to read a style manual, you will be surprised by the enjoyment and enlightenment you will derive from perusing Fowler's *Modern English Usage,* Evans' *Dictionary of Contemporary American Usage,* and other such style books, and how much specific help you can obtain from these works when you go back later and look up a particular grammatical or stylistic problem.

It is with no intention of replacing or precluding the indispensable reference manuals, that we offer in the remainder of this chapter a short practical guide to historical prose. The aim of the following discussion is to bring to the student's attention those aspects of grammar, style, and footnote and bibliographical form that, from the experience of reading several hundred student papers, we feel give the most trouble to history students in American and Canadian colleges. Simply by reading our practical historical stylist, you are not going to learn to write good expository prose, but we hope our remarks will serve to make you more careful in your writing and conscious of the most common errors and failings.

Paragraphs and Transitions

The structure of a successful paragraph is almost exactly the same as the general structure of a well-organized paper. Somewhere in the paragraph there should be a *topic sentence,* i.e., a sentence that summarizes the basic point of the paragraph and the material discussed in it. This sentence may be placed at the beginning or at the end of the paragraph. As with the paper as a whole, the topic sentence should usually be some sort of thesis or contention, in order to set up the paragraph as a discussion or argument. The rest of the paragraph can then consist of an explanation of the significant terms of the topic sentence and a proof of the contentions of the topic sentence by discussion of related examples. The well-written paragraph that follows by C. N. Cochrane, a brilliant Canadian scholar, illustrates these points:

[a]A second and much more incisive criticism was one which applied, not to any limited class within the community, but to imperial society as a whole and which, so far as it could be substantiated, [b]indicated a failure on the part of the Roman order to make good its essential claim. [c]It had been generally accepted since the time of Vergil, that the Eternal City had realized an ideal of social justice through the establishment and maintenance of a rule of law; and that, in thus discharging her secular mission, *Romanitas* had found justification in the eyes of the world. [d]But, as Ammianus points out, the subject, to whom this priceless book was offered, accepted it only to find himself enmeshed in one of the most elaborate legal systems ever devised, and hence a potential victim to the machinations of lawyers by whose sinister activities the ideal of justice was systematically warped and perverted. [e]This danger had become increasingly

[a]*The paragraph begins by stating a general frame of reference.*

[b]*The thesis is presented.*

[c]*The frame of reference is restated in more precise detail, which explains the meaning of the earlier general terms.*

[d]*The thesis is restated in more precise detail as the topic sentence.*

[e]*Further precision and detail offers further refinement of meaning of the thesis.*

great with the evolution of bureaucracy and socialism during the fourth century; for, under these conditions, imperial society had become more than ever before a society of lawyers. [f]Lawyers crowded the ranks of the civil hierarchy, importing into it their characteristic point of view. . . . [g]To Ammianus, as a simple and rugged soldier, lawyers are a violent and rapacious crew. . . . Once in their clutches the victim is sucked to the marrow without a hope of getting away. (Amm. xxx.4.8. foll).[1]

[f]*Restatement for emphasis and detail.*

[g]*In giving the example, the author explains the significance or background of his source, to make the validity and point of view of the source clear. He gives precise reference to the portion of the source text he is using.*

One of the most pleasing aspects of the paragraph just quoted is the way in which each sentence seems to build in progressive fashion from the preceding one. The author's style is thus smooth, and his organization and flow of thought are readily apparent.

Some common failings in poorly written paragraphs are lack of a topic sentence, so that the entire paragraph seems to lack focus or to have a point; creation of a paragraph that is nothing but a collection of examples, without explanation or analysis; failure to explain examples so that topic sentence and examples do not appear related; and use of vague references or undocumented examples.

Constructing grammatical sentences and coherent paragraphs is not sufficient. Each sentence must relate to the preceding sentence, and each paragraph to the preceding paragraph. This technique of expository prose, which is called *transition,* is perhaps the most important method of creating coherent flow in expository writing; and *transitions are the aspect of writing style most often mishandled by even the best writers.* The notion of transition is easy to understand. It is absolutely necessary to create a connec-

---

[1] C. N. Cochrane, *Christianity and Classical Culture* (New York: Oxford University Press, 1944; Oxford paperback, 1964, pp. 315–16.) Reprinted by permission.

tion between one sentence and another, or between one paragraph and another, in such a way as to make clear the exact progression of thought or logic, and in order to create a style that flows smoothly throughout the course of the narrative. The achievement of good transitions in practice requires considerable experience in writing and also great sensitivity to the meaning of words.

Transitions are created at two levels: by words of transition and by sentences of transition. The former group, words of transition, involves words so commonly used that not enough thought is given to them. Words of transition have a powerful role in defining the exact nature of the logic used by a writer, and he should be very much aware of the difference in shade of meaning between one transition word and another. If the student will pause for a moment to reflect that the words "but" and "however" have quite different connotations, he will learn not to exhibit the sloppy stylistic failing of using them interchangeably. It would be a very advisable exercise for any student seriously interested in improving his writing style to try to list all the words or expressions of transition he can think of and to then dwell on the shade of meaning or the nuance of logic that each connotes. Proper use of these words of transition will aid the student a great deal in improving the precision of his writing.

Sentences of transition are rather a different matter. Like all transitions, they help to link one section, e.g., a paragraph, to another and to show the direction of the flow of thought. Generally, *the last sentence of one paragraph and the first sentence of the next paragraph are the ones involved in this linkage.* In the course of these two sentences there should be some summary of the preceding discussion and some indication of how the next section will relate to the preceding one. The relation can be shown in one of several ways, by discussing more fully some aspect of the preceding point, by taking up a new point altogether, or by providing a second or third section of a continuing discussion of some larger point. In addition, transition sentences have one function crucial to the success of the overall organization of the entire paper. They must reveal how the particular point being discussed is related to the general main thesis, which is the *raison d'être* that unifies the whole discussion. All of this shows that transition sentences must be written thoughtfully and with considerable care, because they bear most of the responsibility for manifesting the overall organization of the paper.

Again some examples of good transitions may demonstrate our meaning more fully. The first example shows how the final sentence of one paragraph summarizes the point of the preceding discussion, while the first sentence of the next paragraph indicates that the following discussion will introduce a subject which, while new in the course of the narrative, still will relate to and be an elaboration of the previous point:

By so doing, he aptly illustrates, if not the nature of the Trinity, at any rate the triumph of pagan over Christian ways of thought. And in thus bearing witness to a victory for the old way of thought over the new, he associates himself, in effect, with what still survived of the sentiments and aspirations consecrated in the secular system of Rome.

In these circumstances it becomes instructive to consider the estimate which contemporary secularism placed upon the position and prospects of the Empire.[2]

Another transition shows that the preceding paragraph ended simply, for rhetorical effect, with a precise example; therefore, the first sentence of the succeeding paragraph had to summarize the preceding point as well as demonstrate that the coming paragraph would develop one detail of that point:

Accordingly, among their retainers, the crooner has replaced the philosopher, the teacher of histrionics that of oratory; they seal their libraries like tombs, but construct for themselves hydraulic organs. (Amm. xiv.6.18)

[2] *Ibid.*, pp. 313–14.

By thus resigning themselves to the cult of futility, the Roman aristocrats no doubt exposed themselves to criticism such as has always been levelled against the idle rich.[3]

Another kind of transition is one in which the preceding paragraph has outlined several topics that will subsequently be discussed; the transition sentence then announces that one such topic is being taken up:

The first [class] consisted of pagans who, though they had manifested little or no enthusiasm for the reactionary programme of Julian, nevertheless rejected the alternative proposed by Christianity. The second was composed of an increasing number who, while professing adherence to the new faith, saw it in reality through pagan eyes.

Of the former, Ammianus Marcellinus may be taken as representative.[4]

If a transition indicates a continuation of a preceding discussion, one of the best techniques for making this clear is to *repeat in the transition sentence a key word of the summarizing sentence:*

As the prototype in history of "the Christian Prince," he was profoundly concerned to work out the logic of his position; and it is this fact, more than anything else, which determined the scope and character of his effort to bring about a radical readjustment of existing relationships between the temporal and the spiritual powers.

Indications of such a readjustment were, indeed, already apparent. . . .[5]

These examples should demonstrate that an important part of the grace and style sensed in the writing of an author results from the skill with which he handles the moments of transition in his narrative.

In the case of rather long papers (15 pages or longer) the burden of sustaining transitions can be made easier by *dividing the paper into three or four sections.* Each section, designated by a Roman numeral, represents a major aspect of the theme. The beginning of a new section will immediately reveal to the reader

---

[3] *Ibid.*, p. 315.   [4] *Ibid.*, p. 311.   [5] *Ibid.*, p. 324.

that a turning point in the argument has been reached, and the writer will find it less difficult to make a transition between these half-stops in the flow of his essay.

Footnotes and Bibliography

There seems to be a double myth current about footnotes; students believe that they are merely pedantic encumbrances, which stand in the way of the typing of a paper; while pedants feel that footnotes are an end in themselves, to be treated with the formal respect due a venerable relic, which tradition demands must have a certain format. Actually, footnotes are an important technique of reference used in any research paper; they are not a form in themselves, but are rather an abbreviation for a reference to available source material. A prime use of footnotes, or of footnotes and bibliography in combination, since the two are part of the same structure of reference, is to keep the course of the main narrative flow of the text free and uncluttered from confusing side issues or references.

Developing skill and subtlety in the use of footnotes is an art that requires some practice. In general footnotes have three chief uses:

1. Footnotes provide precise reference to sources relevant to a particular discussion, especially reference to passages in primary sources that support the points the author is discussing:

> Koser, *Geschichte Friedrichs des Grossen*, 4th & 5th ed., I, 159.[6]
>
> *Refutation, Oeuvres*, 8, 208, f.[7]

2. When a fuller discussion of some point or background that the author does not intend to deal with at length exists in

[6] Friedrich Meinecke, *Machiavellianism*, tr. Douglas Scott [New Haven, Conn.: Yale University Press, 1957; Frederick A. Praeger, Inc. (paperback), 1965], p. 276, n. 1. Reprinted by permission of Yale University Press and Routledge & Kegan Paul Ltd.

[7] *Ibid.*, p. 278, n. 1.

other works, he can refer the reader to such discussions by footnote reference and thereby expand the context of his discussion
without cluttering up his text:

> See my analysis of the origins and aims of this work in the *Hist.
> Zeitschr.*, 117.[8]
> Regarding the rationalist element in Frederick's politics, cf. also
> Küntzel, *Zum Gedächtnis Friedrichs d. Gr.*, *Marine-Rundschau*, 1912,
> 206 ff.; and his presentation of Frederick in the *Meister der Politik*,
> published by Marcks and v. Müller.[9]

The opposite side of this coin is that the footnote can be used to
disagree with the discussion of a point by another writer:

> This was clumsily misunderstood by Lavisse, *Le Grand Frédéric
> avant l'avènement*, when on p. 169 he makes the judgment: *Non, il
> n'était pas bon.*[10]

3. Footnotes can be used for discussion of subsidiary points
that would confuse the fundamental flow of logic of the main
body of the text, or for subsidiary material of various kinds, e.g.,
for explanation of the choice of sources:

> The Title *Réfutation du prince de Machiavel* was chosen by Preuss
> (on the basis of a description given by Frederick himself—to Voltaire on
> the 6th Nov. 1739) when for the first time he published in its entirety
> this purely Frederickan form of the book, in the *Oeuvres*, 8. Cf. v.
> Sommerfeld, *Die äussere Entstehungsgeschichte des Antimachiavell
> Friedrichs d. Gr.*, Forsch. zur brand.u.preuss.Gesch., 29, 460. He dem-
> onstrates that even the text of the *Réfutation* does not represent Fred-
> erick's very first plan of 1739, and that the changes in the edition of the
> *Antimachiavell* worked on by Voltaire go back, partly, to yet another
> version sent to Voltaire by Frederick himself. For the sake of brevity,
> we refer to the book here by the title of *Antimachiavell* which has be-
> come traditional, but for obvious reasons we are using the text of the
> *Réfutation*. Madsack, *Der Antimachiavell* (1920), pp. 62 ff., has over-
> looked the important investigation by Sommerfeld.[11]

[8] *Ibid.*, p. 276, n. 4.   [9] *Ibid.*, p. 284, n. 1.   [10] *Ibid.*, p. 282, n. 1.
[11] *Ibid.*, p. 278, n. 5.

or for bringing in further examples, so as not to obscure the lines of the main text with too many examples:

> Cf. For instance the instructions to Major v. Borcke in 1751, regarding the education of Prince Frederick William, *Oeuvres* 9, 39, and the satirical poem of 1770 on the rulers of his time, *Oeuvres* 13, 41 ff.[12]
> It may be recalled that Spinoza, too, in his *Tractatus politicus* Ch. 6 P. 14 and Ch. 7 P. 23 recommends general rules for rendering some of the princes of the royal blood harmless.[13]

or to continue the discussion of a point already made in the main body of the text; this may involve either further detail on the same point:

> He was certainly able to conceal this basic motive from his contemporaries, and to justify the maintenance of the "barbaric" agrarian system by a regard for the agreements between landowners and peasants and for the interests of agriculture based as they were on these. *Essai sur les formes de gouvernement,* 1777, *Oeuvres,* 9, 205 f.[14]

or to allow the insertion of cautions and hedges on a point which for rhetorical reasons and for the sake of the argument is clearly and definitively stated in the main text:

> [The main text states:] But the future ruler in him was developed earlier than the philosopher.
> [The footnote given for that sentence states:] One may say this, although the first stirrings of a philosophical interest showed themselves much earlier—as early as 1728 he called himself *Frédéric le philosophe.*[15]

These principles, illustrated by footnotes from a book by Friedrich Meinecke, the dean of twentieth-century German historians, make it clear that footnotes are not only pedants' appendages to research or ways of avoiding accusations of plagiarism; rather, they are powerful tools in the scholar's expository vocabulary, permitting thorough support and documentation of

---

[12] *Ibid.,* p. 278, n. 5.   [13] *Ibid.,* p. 278, n. 4.   [14] *Ibid.,* p. 284, n. 2.
[15] *Ibid.,* p. 275, and n. 2.

points, careful elaboration or reference to elaboration of details, and yet at the same time contributing to clarity of thought in the main body of the text.

Students are forever asking about the form of footnotes. A reasonable answer to this problem is that *form in footnotes does not exist as an end in itself,* but rather serves the end of making the note useful. Insofar as a footnote is a bibliographical reference, its aim is to permit the reader to find exactly the page in the precise book to which the note refers. No more complicated form is necessary than the minimum needed to provide this information.

What information is required? For a bibliographical entry, whether it appears in a final bibliography or in the note itself, one wants to know the name of the author, the full title of the book, how many volumes, which edition is being used, who the editor and/or translator are, if applicable, and finally the date of publication (*not* of printing) of the edition, the publisher, and the place of publication. In addition, for the footnote reference, one needs to know which volume is being used and what page or pages were consulted. The usual form is simple to follow; for a footnote it is:

> Karl Vossler, *Mediaeval Culture,* tr. W. C. Lawton, 2 vols. (New York: F. Ungar, 1958; a reprint of the original 1929 American ed.), Vol. I, pp. 19–20 [no edition is cited, as this is a first ed.].

For a bibliography entry, the form is only slightly different:

> Vossler, Karl, *Mediaeval Culture,* tr. W. C. Lawton, 2 vols. (New York: F. Ungar, 1958; a reprint of the original 1929 American edition).

Entries in a bibliography are alphabetical by author or editor, and the common practice of indenting the second line of each entry allows the reader to see the authors cited at a glance. A bibliography should contain two separate lists—one for primary sources and one for secondary sources.

There is one convention we have suggested in our examples which is not mentioned in any handbook we know of, and yet seems to us to be of extreme importance. In this wonderful age of the reprinting in hardcover and paperback of many old important scholarly works, it is going to be more and more true that students will be referring to many books in recently published copies. To refer only to the recent date of publication would be to give a most misleading conception of the literature of the subject; it would seem as though all books used were written after 1960. Thus it is our opinion that while scholars must, of course, carefully cite exactly the edition they are using because of the possibility of changes in pagination and the like, in the reference the proper original date of the work should be pointed out, so that the reader will understand that, as in our example, the historiography and scholarship of Vossler belongs to the era of 1930, not to that of 1960.

If a bibliography is appended to the paper, as it should be, you do not have to give full bibliographical information on a work each time you cite it in a footnote. *Give the full bibliographical reference the first time you cite the work in a footnote; thereafter a simplified short-title form will suffice:*

Vossler, *Mediaeval Culture,* Vol. I, pp. 19–20.

Indeed if only one work by a given author is cited in the paper, his name alone can be used as the short style reference:

Vossler, Vol. I, pp. 19–20.

If the work is a minor title within a major title, as a single article from a journal or a single essay from a collection, the minor title is placed within quotation marks and the major title is italicized. In the bibliography entry the total span of pages of the article should be shown:

Bergin, Thomas G., "Dante's Provençal Gallery," *Speculum* XL, 1 (Jan. 1965), pp. 15–30.

Rupp, E. G., "Luther and the German Reformation to 1529," *The New Cambridge Modern History, Vol. II: The Reformation,* ed. G. R. Elton (New York: Cambridge University Press, 1962), pp. 70–95.

Generally, footnotes are placed at the bottom of the page on which they are cited, but they can also be grouped together at the end of the paper. Concerning such technical details, the undergraduate should simply follow the wishes of his teacher. A graduate student writing for publication can follow the style sheet of the journal or publisher to whom he intends to submit his article.

As for the mass of Latin words and latinisms customarily sprinkled in footnotes, such as *op. cit.* (the work cited) or *loc. cit.* (the place cited), these vestiges of the genteel tradition in scholarship are nowadays passing out of fashion since they are cumbersome and occasionally ambiguous and generally more trouble than they are worth. Most historians now use short titles after an initial citation of the full bibliographical entry rather than Latin references. One Latin term that is convenient and is still commonly employed but frequently misused is *Ibid.* (the same). *Ibid.* is always italicized, always has a period after it because it is an abbreviation, and always refers only to the work cited in the *previous footnote*, not to any earlier citation. There is one other Latin abbreviation that is still commonly used by scholars and will be found to be convenient—*cf.* for "compare." ("But *cf.* Godechot's view of the Atlantic Revolution.")

Clean Typescripts and Careful Proofreading

In the great majority of American colleges, most papers submitted by students have to be in typescript; and for graduate courses and professional publication no other standard is admissible from the point of view of convenience, time spent on reading, and clarity. Papers marred and disfigured by sloppy preparation and hasty assembling, or papers obviously too hastily typed and handed in with dozens of errors that escaped proofreading are simply not acceptable. All such errors are the result of laziness and carelessness on the part of the student, and they will undoubtedly annoy the teacher. Sloppiness of this kind always prejudices the teacher against the paper he is reading, and *students should recognize that one part of the responsibility they assume as writers is to submit a neat manuscript.* Of course, occasional corrections here and there are inevitable, as no typist is perfect; but even such corrections should be neat and not inserted in messy scribbles. And as for proofreading, the student should simply take it as a rule that there is no such thing as a "typographical error"; there are only proofreader's oversights.

Errors of Grammar and Style Frequently Encountered

Besides the larger aspects of style already discussed—developing a main point, defining terms, constructing coherent paragraphs and meaningful transitions, and supporting all points by examples and documentation derived from adequate research—there are a number of details of grammar and form that are frequently sources of error in undergraduate papers. If you make these kinds of mistakes, you should at once learn to correct them, because such errors can turn an otherwise good paper into one that is unpleasant to read and will therefore be viewed very critically.

Some of the most common errors of which students are guilty are as follows:

1. AWKWARD SENTENCES. There is a variety of causes of awkwardness in sentences. Among them are the conflation of clauses:

Franz Joseph who was Emperor of Austria's plan. . . .

and the piling up of phrases within phrases:

Wilhelm, who was attacking, when he was ready, ...

One very common cause of awkwardness in sentences is failure on the writer's part to recognize the necessity of parallel construction in good English style:

> The picture won the prize because its color was striking and for the way it speaks to the heart.

In the preceding example there are two cases of lack of parallelism; the two phrases should begin with "because" for proper balance, and the verbs should be in the same tense.

   2. INEXACT METAPHORS AND FIGURES, AND COLLOQUIALISMS. It is expected that the usage of a paper will be consistent. Since most expository writing, and all historical writing, involves formal, precise usage, lapsing into "cute" images or figures generally is more offensive than witty:

> This was made more difficult by the freewheeling medieval philology . . . part "Bad Boys' Book of Beasts" (we are sternly warned off this approach by the editor), the *Book of Beasts* is, in any case, a pleasure to read.

This example exhibits a number of errors. Apart from the cute phrase, there are also several inexact terms: what does "freewheeling" mean, and what value judgment is involved in the vague term "pleasure"? The diction should, therefore, be more precise. Besides this, the sentence structure is made awkward by the piling up of phrases, by the lack of parallel construction, and by the imprecise and awkward punctuation.

   Vagueness in diction, which is demonstrated by "pleasure" in the last example, is perhaps the commonest fault in poor writing, and is the constant enemy of precision. This penchant for vague, banal, insignificant remarks, as again in the following sentence—

> Bismarck was a very interesting man.

—is not only bad style, but reflects underlying ignorance and intellectual poverty.

3. ERRORS IN GRAMMAR. The variety of errors in grammar that teachers of history encounter is simply legion. Among them are errors in agreement, both of subject and verb, and of pronoun and antecedent:

Neither one of them were very successful.
Each should have attended to their own problems.

And run-on sentences, with or without a comma splice:

The tyranny of Peisistratus was overthrown, democracy was restored.

Poor spelling:

Edward the Confessor was always preying.
The Renaissance continued the study of Scriptural exejesus.[16]

Error in apostrophe:

Each side had its' own point of view.

Incorrect diction, i.e., faulty choice of words:

To prove that Dreyfus was innocent, Zola attacked the credulity of the officers' testimony.

And errors in reference, including ambiguous or missing antecedent for pronoun:

Cromwell told Henry that he could earn money from dissolving the monasteries.

The preceding sentence has additional errors; the wrong preposition is used—"from" should be replaced by "by"—and "dissolve" is vague diction in this context.

Another error in reference is the use of "this" without an antecedent, or of "the" when either "a" or a general case should be used:

Napoleon III decided on a war policy. This was very foolish. [*What was very foolish?*]

---

[16] These spelling errors are taken from actual student papers in a freshman survey course at a west coast university.

This is the personality always associated with the artist. (*Change to "artists" and omit "the"*)

Finally, there is poor punctuation, which has so many forms that we could not possibly exemplify them all. The simplest guide to correct punctuation is to *read the finished paper out loud, giving exactly the inflections indicated by the punctuation as written.* If the student reads well and has a sensitive ear, this procedure will readily turn up most major punctuation errors.

Cheating or Defrauding

There are two common forms of fraud or cheating in papers, plagiarism and padding of bibliography. For the student who deliberately carries on these practices, we can say nothing, because his error is self-conscious. If one wishes to hand in a literal transcription of someone else's work, there is really little that can be done, since to tell the truth, most of the time this practice will not be discovered, although discovery will result in instant expulsion. One wonders, however, why such a student is wasting his time with college work in the first place, since if he took the same attitude in the business world he would be really making a profit— until he went to jail.

There are, however, forms of plagiarism and padding that are not willful, but that result rather from confusion about procedure. A paraphrase of a source one has read without any reference to the fact that one is paraphrasing is a form of plagiarism. At the very best, such work will be marked very low because of its lack of originality. The simplest way to avoid such difficulty is to be absolutely sure that *when you have depended on a source, primary or secondary, for any information or opinion that appears in the text of the paper, a footnote reference is given to the source.* This will not only overcome any problem of an accusation of copying, but will also give you some measure of the originality of your own work.

The same judgment applies to padding of bibliographies. Usually, when this is done deliberately as a means of creating the appearance of extensive reading, the result is simply pitiful, because if the text of a paper shows lack of reading and poor information and study, no amount of titles listed in the bibliography will deceive an experienced reader, such as an instructor. But again, there is sometimes an unconscious error by students in this regard. Frequently students will list in a bibliography every book they encountered, thinking that the book should be mentioned because it exists, or because they "looked at it." This is a false notion of the function of a bibliography. *The bibliography should reveal the dimensions of the range of thought and information in the paper itself;* and if only three books that were read pertained to a given subject, only three books should appear as references. The student can be certain of avoiding this difficulty if he *lists in his bibliography only those works actually referred to in the text or footnotes of the paper.* Again, this procedure will benefit the student by revealing the actual dimensions of his research.

In conclusion, you must understand that full mastery of historical prose is not quickly gained unless you are already skilled in expository writing. Your development of an effective style will come only through constant care and self-criticism, the experience of writing several papers, and a sure sensitivity to the wonderful nuances of the English language. If you do not now enjoy this kind of sensitivity to the qualities of good writing, you should set yourself a special reading program. Every week read slowly and carefully at least twenty pages of first-class expository historical prose, and examine each sentence and paragraph and the quality of diction for the subtle methods used by the author. To start off your reading program of historical prose, we recommend the works listed below. Note that the books are arranged in four categories. In the first three lists the presentation follows a chronological sequence in accordance with either the time of writing or the subject matter.

HISTORICAL CLASSICS OF THE EIGHTEENTH AND NINETEENTH CENTURIES
Edward Gibbon, *The Decline and Fall of the Roman Empire*
Edmund Burke, *Reflections on the French Revolution*
Thomas Babington Macaulay, *History of England from the Accession of James II*
Thomas Carlyle, *History of the French Revolution*
F. Pollock and F. W. Maitland, *History of Engtish Law before the Time of Edward I*
Henry Adams, *History of the United States During the Administrations of Jefferson and Madison*

TWENTIETH-CENTURY WORKS ON EUROPEAN AND ENGLISH HISTORY
C. M. Bowra, *The Greek Experience*
R. W. Southern, *The Making of the Middle Ages*
M. D. Knowles, *The Monastic Order in England*
Garrett Mattingly, *The Armada*
R. H. Tawney, *Religion and the Rise of Capitalism*
G. R. Elton, *England under the Tudors*
G. M. Trevelyan, *The English Revolution* (1688)
John Carswell, *The Old Cause* (eighteenth-century Whiggery)
W. H. Lewis, *The Splendid Century* (France under Louis XIV)
Lord David Cecil, *Melbourne*
Cecil Woodham-Smith, *The Reason Why* (the charge of the Light Brigade)
G. M. Young, *Victorian England: Portrait of an Age*
W. L. Burn, *The Age of Equipoise* (Victorian England)
Jacques Barzun, *Berlioz and the Romantic Century*
A. J. P. Taylor, *English History 1914–1945*
Winston S. Churchill, *The Gathering Storm* (the 1930's)
Geoffrey Barraclough, *Introduction to Contemporary History*

AMERICAN HISTORY
Vernon L. Parrington, *Main Currents in American Thought*
Perry Miller, *The New England Mind*
Arthur M. Schlesinger, Jr., *The Age of Jackson*
Allan Nevins, *The Ordeal of the Union* (the Civil War)
Edmund Wilson, *Patriotic Gore* (the Civil War)
Richard Hofstadter, *The Age of Reform*
Eric Goldman, *Rendezvous with Destiny* (twentieth century)

CANADIAN HISTORY
Donald Creighton, *Dominion of the North*
A. R. M. Lower, *From Colony to Nation*

12 / Two Student Papers Critically Examined

To make clear the many techniques and rules you must observe in writing historical prose, you are now asked to study two student papers with detailed corrective comments.

The papers chosen are book reviews submitted by students in a freshman Western civilization survey. The required exercise was a two-page critical review of two interpretive works on ancient history: Sabatino Moscati's *The Face of the Ancient Orient* and W. F. Albright's *From Stone Age to Christianity*. The students were told that their reviews must have an historiographical approach, that is, must deal with the author's assumptions and values, and that their paper had to have one main point developed in its 500–750 word length.

In the book reviews that follow, the instructor's markings and comments are also included (in handwriting) to give you an idea of how instructors react to certain kinds of writing. You may be surprised by the forthrightness of the instructor's remarks. Teachers cannot afford to be respecters of persons; frank criticism is the most effective kind. We have numbered only those sentences referred to in the detailed comment following the paper.

The papers chosen are representative of strong and weak efforts at historical writing. One paper is almost, but not quite, extremely good; the other is almost, but not quite, very bad. We have intentionally avoided choosing an absolutely first class and an absolutely failing paper because the most extreme examples would not have been typical of students' work, nor illustrative of the surprisingly narrow margin of refinement that exists between a very good piece of work and a rather poor one.

Here is the good paper, which received a grade of B+ :

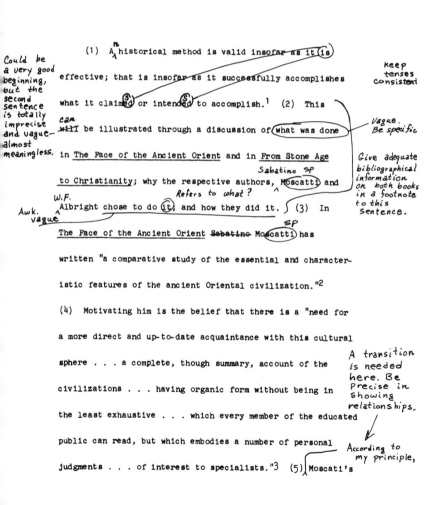

method will be valid only if it provides the means to this,

his desired end. The method ~~that~~ [wordy] he employs is one of

outlines, skeletal structures, genres, types: a

formulalike simplicity. (6) It is a method of "schematic

treatments" and "subjective interpretations."[4]

This is a very good characterization, but illustrate it with examples.

(7) In making judgments (one) must admit the limitation

of ignorance. (8) As a (layman) (we) cannot determine the

up-to-dateness nor the value to specialists of <u>The Face</u>

<u>of the Ancient Orient</u>. (9) Nonetheless it can be said

that the book is ✗direct,✗ it is a ✗summary,✗ and it is

readable. (10) This far then, the method accomplishes

what was intended and is therefore valid. (11) How success-

fully the entire ~~goal~~ [purpose] was realized must remain a matter of

degree. (12) There is some doubt in (our) [ref?] mind as to how

"complete" a "summary" can be and whether the "organic form"

is meaningless in its simplicity. (13) Our feeling toward

Moscati is similar to that of Albright toward (Hegal) [sp]:

Unnecessary to say this. No one thinks you are a specialist.

Agreement: Make all 3 singular or all plural.

An awkward "nonsense" sentence. It says, "The degree of success... is a matter of degree." Recast— or omit.

You ask very good questions of your analysis, but you avoided asking the fundamental questions: What are Moscati's historiographical values? Are these values valid?

        . . . he was able without difficulty to classify

        practically all phenomena . . . which gives his

        philosophy a strangely artificial appearance,

        at the same time that it imposes itself by its

        simplicity and harmony.[5]

Indeed, is any form at all discernible in his descriptions of civilization?

(14) ~~W. H.~~ Albright's <u>From Stone Age to Christianity</u>
—Vague
(treats) the development of monotheism in the Near East. The

subject is chosen to illustrate that "human life moves in

patterns and configurations whether we consider the life

of an individual or the life of a nation, whether we

describe the movement of a culture or the development of

a thought."⁶ His method of accomplishing this end is the

subject of nearly a third of the book. (15) ~~It is his~~
  Albright believes
~~feeling~~ that in historiography "as in all other fields of

scholarship and science the two most important essentials

for success are precision and critical judgment."⁷ Through

the accumulation of "critically sifted data"⁸ and a "long

occupation with these facts," the historian will be able

to reach "certain conclusions to the pattern which they

form and the picture which they fit. . . . "⁹ (16) Although

we agree that the devotion to data "may sometimes have
  sp
made it (diffucult) for the reader to follow the unfolding

scroll of history,"¹⁰ we cannot deny the overall effectiveness

Again
good, of Albright's method. (17) By this very devotion to
and much
more   inductive reasoning, to analysis and synthesis of data, he
aware of   i.e. convincingly
values   (Be precise.)
than above. has successfully demonstrated the wavering but upward curve

of human evolution and the rising, climatic, and falling

Transition—
tell why you
suddenly
begin this
new subject.

——— wordy

curve of individual historical patterns.[11]

As can now be seen, the validity of a historical method

depends not on what the method is, but rather on how well

Good; but Crude, undeveloped.

it functions. *In relation to a given problem. (Be precise, specific)* Notes

Why is this a valid source for your purpose?

[1] Definition of "valid" from Webster's New International

of the English Language

Dictionary (2nd ed., unabridged) (Springfield, Mass.: G. & C.

Publishers

Merriam Co., 1960), p. 2813.

[2] Moscatti, Sabatino, The Face of the Ancient Orient

(Garden City, New York: Anchor Books, Doubleday & Company,

Inc., 1962), p. xv.

[3] Ibid., p. xv-xvii.

[4] Ibid.

[5] Albright, William Foxwell From Stone Age to Christianity,

2nd ed. (Garden City, New York: Anchor Books, Doubleday

& Company, Inc., 1957), p. 86

[6] Ibid., p. 82.

[7] Ibid., p. 48.

[8] Ibid., p. 26.

[9] Ibid., p. 82.

[10] Ibid., p. 400.

[11] Ibid., p. 401.

A superior paper, yet you can do better. Try to be even more concise and to the point.

B+

Far too many errors in typing and usage.

From the outset of this paper (1) we gain the impression that this student has some organization and a specific goal in his writing: he gives what should be the start of a general main point, expressed as an argument. Unfortunately, the next sentence (2) does not follow up the lead; this sentence should have clarified the ideas of the first sentence and made a start at defining the critical terms. Instead, the student simply gives some meaningless generalizations, using extremely vague words ("what was done") and pronouns with ambiguous antecedents ("it"). Fortunately, such lapses are quite rare in this paper; there is only one other example of vague diction (14-"treats"). One unnecessary and jarring note in this introduction was that the student tried to support the truth of *his* definition of "valid" by reference to a dictionary; this was really misleading, because the exact meaning of a term central to the student's thesis will emerge from the student's own analysis of the problem, not from any a priori definition.

Once the introduction is completed, the student begins his body, or major discussion, by giving a profile of a book, and then evaluating that profile in terms of the values implied in the main point of the paper. He then presents a similar discussion of the second book. This procedure is very successful for a number of reasons. One very important result of the student's organization is that it permitted him to fulfill the requirements—giving a critique of two books—while still allowing his paper to be the development of only one main point. His paper was tied together into a whole by the way in which the judgments ultimately related back to the main point, and the student was careful to point out this relationship (5, 10). Indeed, the instructor suggested that by inserting a transitional phrase the student might have been even more explicit about this kind of relationship (5).

In giving the profile of the two books, the student has generally had an historiographical approach, i.e., he has not simply summarized the two books but has tried to identify the salient features of the methods and the value judgments of the books. In almost all cases (cf. 6) the student has substantiated his claims by reference to precise facts, in this case, precise passages in the books (3, 4, 6, 15).

It is pleasing to the reader that, using the values he has established, the student is not afraid to make firm judgments and to reach conclusions, never, however, trying to go beyond his evidence and always trying to support his claims with references to his sources (9–12, 16–17). In general, it can be seen in this paper that description is used to lead up to conclusions, which is just as it should be.

The writing is by and large quite pleasing. Not only is the student refined and literary in his choice of words and well-organized in his construction of paragraphs, but his narrative has a smooth flow enhanced by his good use of transitions between sentences to show the course of his thought (9, 10, 16, 17). Occasionally, there is faulty transition or lack of transition when starting a new paragraph (14). Other serious faults, which mar the good impression of the writing, are critical misspellings, including the gross misspelling of the name of one of the authors studied (2, 3, and n. 2), some typographical errors, and errors of agreement and of reference (8). But in general, most readers would gain the impression that the author's discussion has been coherent and thorough enough, that he is justified in his conclusion, which is—properly—a restatement of his main thesis with new detail and preciseness of claim.

The second student paper, which received a grade of C−, offers a complete contrast to the first; yet the whole failure of the second paper is a matter of degree, of not following the various requirements involved in good writing with any precision or care.

What, specifically, is your one main point?

In what terms? Speak in terms of values.

(1) In this paper, I hope to (contrast) Sabatino Moscati's

The Face of the Ancient Orient and W. F. Albright's From

Stone Age to Christianity. (2) These books seemed to me

Don't be vague; be precise.

to be (very different,) and I will show this in terms of

method, organization, and content.

Poor transition Do not just repeat yourself.

(3) ~~As I have said, the methods with which these two men write history are entirely different.~~ (4) While Moscati,

as he himself states, describes ancient Oriental history (in

Explain and describe such terms.

terms of) "historical (outlines)"[1] for all phases of life,

Avoid overuse of phrase, "in terms of."

Albright puts stress on the evolution of religion:

". . . Religion is an essential part of human

cultural evolution—and much more important . . .

than some phases which have been given factitious

You simply repeat yourself. Very poor style.

significance in our own day."[2]

(5) While Moscati believes in giving a general outline,

Albright contends that religion is the root of a culture.

Vague. what kind of group?

(6) Moscati also organizes (each group) in terms of (their)

Vague wording; be specific, precise.

its

agreement

(function in history) (i.e., "Components" are Sumeria, Babylonia

Give specific page citations for all such references.

and Assyria, and Egypt). Albright starts out with a discussion

of the evolution of religion and culture of the earliest

Sabatino

[1] S. Moscati, The Face of the Ancient Orient (Garden City,

N.Y.: Doubleday & Company, Inc., Anchor Books, 1962), p. xv.

William Foxwell

[2] (W. F.) Albright, From Stone Age to Christianity (Garden City,

N.Y.: Doubleday & Company, Inc., Anchor Books, 1957), p. 85.

times, then seems to class all further information (in terms of) its influence on Israel and the Hebrews. (7) Moscati's

SP

view is (bread,) and he relates the cultural aspects of

transition →   *thus*

society to the "spirit of the age," he belongs to the

Naming is not explaining.

(history-of-ideas) school of historiography. Albright

Don't just list; explain the contrasts you are making here.

considers history in the light of changes in, and influences

on, the religion of certain peoples. In this, he reflects

his training as a Biblical scholar.

Define

(8) Some differences can be explained by the (levels) of

ref?

writing that each man used. Moscati, as he (mentions,) says

the interest in the book was generated by a series of

lectures he had given. (9) He wrote the book in the way

he gave the lectures, (in) more of an over-all picture of

Poor usage; try a verbal form here.

the cultures and their contributions to the whole. Albright

writes more in defense of his position, maintaining the

SP

"prima(ry) of archeology in the broad sense,"3 / and (religion

of

in a narrower sense of archeology. (10) He seems to write

more for those familiar with (the basics) of ancient history,

Diction ——————————————————————— *usage*

than for readers who are just (starting.) His scholarly

language and references are a basic part of his argument,

but they often disrupt the thought. Moscati's approach

for

is simpler and easier of the layman to understand.

3Ibid., p. 2.

You are just taking up one point after another. Relate everything to one central theme.

Another reason for difference may be found in the dates of the books. Albright's book was the first published, and only minor changes have been made in the second edition. Moscati's book was first conceived fifteen years after, and published twenty years after Albright's. Since new discoveries are always being made (or so both authors implied), Moscati's might have more, or at least newer, material on which to base his judgments.

Awkward writing. Be precise and succinct

Then, too, there are the limitations set by the authors *awkward* as to the scope of the books. Albright begins his study with the Early Paleolithic Age, about 100,000 B.C., whereas Moscati starts with the early Sumerians of the third millenium B.C. Albright ends with the era of Christ; Moscati ends with the era of the Persians. (11) And Moscati *awkward* covers only ten peoples, while Albright converses on a large number of contemporary peoples.

Poor usage

(12) As a reader of these books, I found that Moscati *sp* was much clearer to me, but its obvious that he doesn't go *tone* too deeply in his analysis. Albright was mor scholarly,

But you fail to discuss values or judgments. Answer why — not just what.

Irrelevant. Your conclusion should be expressed within the frame of reference of your paper.

but also mor confusing. (13) I found both interesting and I recognize that no two historians see history in the same way, as was brought out in lecture.

C−

Your writing shows promise but lacks form. Begin with one, specific main point; develop it paragraph by paragraph; end by recapitulating the main idea and considering its larger implications.

From the outset, we are confused about the subject and aims of this paper, because the author has given no precise point or thesis as the basis for argument. Instead he uses vague terms (2-"very different") and never explains his own critical values (1-how will he "contrast" the books?). An examination of the rest of the paper shows that this vagueness is a consistent trait and that no precise ideas will emerge from this paper (6, 7, 8, 9, 10, 13). Indeed, even when making reference to the terms used by the authors being studied, the writer fails to be precise in his identifications (4). This problem is not helped by the lack of specific reference to his sources, to support his observations about them (6, 7, 9).

For the most part, the student fails to make judgments of his own; his paper is mostly a list of observations about the sources, general rather than precise and critical, without any attempt to reach conclusions. Even when a conclusion is drawn, it is vague and is the result of assigning categories rather than analyzing values (7). The student has generally failed to carry out a serious historiographical assessment: he has not made clear the author's assumptions and values.

Similarly, the organization of the paper suffers in a variety of ways. There is a distinct lack of transition, a failing that breaks the paper up into small unrelated units; indeed, when the student tries to make a transition, it usually appears as simply a crude repetition, which is a very immature way to organize thought (3, 5). This fragmentation is also created by the way in which the student simply takes up one topic after another, making no attempt to create a flow of ideas or to relate his topics to some central scheme of organization.

Finally, the style is quite poor. His choice of words is often awkward and inaccurate. And as is often the case with students who have not thought enough about what they are writing, he falls back on hackneyed expressions that say little and sound dull (10, 11, 12). One cannot find any drive toward a conclusion at the end, and finally the reader is left with the helpless feeling that this paper has reflected a lot of "busy-ness" that had no direction and no outcome.

The detailed critiques of the two student papers clearly establish that in the successful paper there was attention to detail, to evidence in support of points, to clarity of style, and to organization—so that the paper became a proof of a point. In the poor paper all of these essential matters were lacking or insufficient. The lesson to be learned from studying these two papers and the critical evaluations of them is one you cannot afford to neglect or forget. *You must take great pains with your writing. Reading history is not enough. The historian's craft is a form of communication of knowledge and ideas.* If history is what an historian does, then in the most fundamental sense history is what an historian writes. Writing is the goal of all your work as a student of history, and only through your development of skill as a writer will you be able to manifest your talent as an historian.

13 / Historiography and the Philosophy of History

HISTORIOGRAPHY AS A FORMAL SUBJECT

Through your history courses, and the experience you gain as a practicing historian in the researching and writing of papers, you will rapidly develop a critical insight and sophisticated perception. You will develop a taste for what is good history and what is not, and you will achieve a sensitivity that will enable you to respond almost subconsciously to a lecture or book in a favorable or unfavorable way. You will have reached an important level of expertise in the historian's craft when after reading a few pages of a book or listening to the first few minutes of a lecture you can pretty well see the assumptions and values that are determining the historian's structuring of the material; the test of whether you have reached this level is the ability to anticipate quite accurately the general shape of the whole book or lecture from the assumptions and values indicated in the opening remarks.

You must not be impatient about reaching this level of historical craftsmanship. If you conscientiously do the work required of you, it will come sooner or later. There are, however, two kinds of formal study that will sharpen your insights and speed up the process of mastering the variety of assumptions and values that underlie creative historical thinking. The first of these is formal work in historiography and the second is the philosophy of history.

We have used the term historiography in this book to mean the determining of the assumptions and values upon which the historian draws to infer the relationship between facts and to create an ordered and synthetic view of the past. Historiographical judgments can be made by any student through careful and critical reading of the works of modern historians and by paying some attention to the biography and social and intellectual milieu of the author of the book he is, reading. The author's life and background will indicate his experiences and the ideas upon which he will draw in his relating of facts and making of inferences.

Historiography can, however, be studied in a more formal manner as a distinct historical field, and the term is nowadays often used in this way. This meaning of historiography implies a systematic study of all the important historians, particularly those of the last 100 years. Systematic historiographical study is therefore equivalent to the history of historical writing and should be very useful for the college student because it will allow him to see the whole sweep of historical literature and the changing assumptions and values that govern historical judgment in the modern world. Conscientious reading, research, and writing should in any case over a three- or four-year period give the student this broad knowledge of major historiographical trends, but a formal course on the history of history will undoubtedly expedite the gaining of this insight and understanding.

You must be on your guard, however, against faulty work in formal historiography. If you take a course on the subject, *you must read for yourself substantial and representative selections of the major modern historians.* You must not take on faith the summary opinions of your instructor on the characteristics of the historians whose work is being considered in the course. If you do not attempt to examine the historians for yourself, you will simply be accepting someone else's assumptions; you will be placing historians in intellectual pigeonholes, and you will gain no real understanding of the values and qualities of the influential historical thinkers whose work is the subject of the course. It is because formal work in historiography often descends to foisting upon the students the preconceived notions of the lecturer that many eminent and wise scholars are opposed to offering such a course in the curriculum of their departments. Historiography courses are best given as small seminars in which the students can read each week a large section of the work of an important historian and can discuss this work in class. A lecture course in historiography will do you far more harm than good unless the instructor is known to be extremely learned and judicious, and places a heavy obligation upon the students to read and evaluate the historical literature for themselves.

It is unfortunate that no work exists in English offering a general introduction to the history of history that we can recommend with confidence. By far the best book on the subject is the work of the English philosopher and historian R. G. Collingwood, *The Idea of History*, which was written in the early 1930's. Many sections of the book exhibit extraordinary insight and sensitivity, but the work is written with a heavy commitment in favor of one school of history; and the book is now somewhat out of date because there have been some fundamental shifts in historiographical trends in the last three decades.

As your historiographical knowledge increases, you will see that each historian is not an island unto himself. Rather his approach and values and methods correspond quite closely, although perhaps never entirely, with several other writers in the same generation. Therefore *it is legitimate to group historians into distinct schools* provided that you remember that such grouping does not free you from the obligation also to examine critically each historian's work in and for itself, with reference to the historian's mastery and use of the primary sources of the subject.

An historian may have belonged to a school whose assumptions now seem limited and outdated, but this does not mean that the scholar's work should automatically be assigned to the rubbish heap. Historians inevitably draw a great many or even most of their assumptions and values from contemporary political and social thought. The world moves on, intellectual fashions change, and concepts that were truisms to one generation become absurdities to the next. This is why no work of history, however careful, learned, and perceptive, can endure unquestioned as a definitive study for more than thirty years. A new generation coming along is bound to see the world a little differently, and the operative assumptions of a great historian from the previous generation are in time going to look a little awkward and naive and sometimes outrageously wrongheaded. That is still no reason, however, for you to dismiss a master historian of the previous generation with a sneering label. You may find a book at first sight pathetically devoted to a principle that now has been shown to be illusory. But as you read on, you may be amazed to discover how much information of great value can still be gained from an older work.

You may also be surprised to find that however outmoded and unfashionable some of an author's assumptions and values now seem, a powerful mind and a great personality has triumphed over the intellectual limitations of his own era. The compelling force of an author's humanity may have enabled him to make judgments about human conduct and observations on the tragedies and glories of human life that seem as true today as when the scholar published his work 30 or 50 or 100 or even 2,000 years ago. There is still no better account of the corrupting effects of greed and power on men of great ability and good will than Thucydides' *History of the Peloponnesian War*, written in the fifth century B.C. One of the most brilliant of all accounts of a once-vital institution slowly lapsing into ossification and decay is to be found in the biography of an English Benedictine abbot written by one of his monks, Jocelyn of Brakelond, around the year 1180. We have come a long way from the ideas of the Enlightenment, but no historian has yet surpassed Edward Gibbon's ability to depict the aspirations, conflicts, and accidents that worked together to decide the fate of a whole society. The history of medieval English law written in the later years of Queen Victoria by F. W. Maitland shows the functioning of political and judicial institutions, within a cultural and social context, in a subtle and interrelated way that has not been equalled by the work of any twentieth-century sociologist.

In surveying the development of historical writing since 1850, we find it is possible to group historians into seven distinct schools: organic, scientific-nominalist, dialectical-intellectual, dialectical-materialist, personal-social-intuitive, functional-institutional, and sociological-behavioral.

The Organic School

This approach to history was almost universal in the Western world between 1850 and about 1890. The historian sought to identify in the past institutions, cultural eras, and civilizations that had the integrated unity and birth-maturation-death cycle found in living organisms. Historians at all times make heavy use of metaphor in order to communicate general interpretations, but this school's distinguishing of basic organic patterns, which originated and grew in the manner of biological entities, was an historical doctrine, not just a manner of expression.

The organic school found three levels of growth and function in history. The first level was that of political and legal institutions, including the largest institution of the national state itself. It was this kind of organic historian—of whom one of the best was the English scholar William Stubbs—who discovered that the great oak of the English parliament or the American town meeting developed out of the microcosmic acorn of the early medieval

meetings of warriors in the German forests. This widely held conception was severely challenged by illiberal German behavior in
the twentieth century and by the radically different concepts of
the functional-institutional school. The second level of organic
interpretation was that of the *"Zeitgeist,"* of the integrated and
pervasive cultural pattern that was supposed to provide the "Spirit
of the Age." Its most brilliant exponent was the German-Swiss
historian of the Renaissance, Jacob Burckhardt. This concept is
still used by many intellectual and cultural historians, although in
a rather modulated and cautious way. The third level of organic
historical interpretation is the view of a whole civilization (the
West, Ancient World, etc.) as a biological entity that follows the
life cycle. The organic view of civilization still has many adherents
—such as Arnold Toynbee—and it is very hard to speak of the
development of a distinctive civilization without using biological
metaphors.

The Scientific-Nominalist School

Nineteenth-century historians used these grandiose organic
concepts to interpret whole eras in the past to a very large educated public. After 1900, history became much less a branch of
literature and much more an academic subject. The new breed of
academic historians disdained the vulnerable organic concepts of
their predecessors and tried to model their work on the precise
methodology of the natural and mathematical sciences. They developed professional techniques for advanced historical research
and acquired a vast amount of new data by use of these thoroughly disciplined and so-called "scientific" methods.

Unfortunately the scientific historians threw out the baby
with the bath. In their heyday in the early decades of the twentieth century, "scientific" academic historians disdained to speak to
a wide public and, like medieval nominalist philosophers, refused
to believe in the reality of general concepts in history. In French

and English universities particularly, they were hostile to any general and meaningful interpretation, organic or otherwise. Under the leadership of the scientific-nominalist school, what history gained in the way of erudition it at the same time lost as an educational force in modern society. The damp smell of the laboratory-type seminar inhibited the historian from communicating with educated society; and since many historians were no longer interested in relating their knowledge to the problems of the contemporary world, they could not make their books either significant or enjoyable. The inhuman rigors of doctoral training gave the historian effective tools for tackling the archives but clouded over his imagination and destroyed his sensitivity to the joys and tragedies of the human experience. History was in danger of losing its primary function of understanding human life and of becoming an exclusively academic department cut off from educated society. History as a public dialogue and entertainment was avoided by scholars who had the discipline and knowledge for serious contributions and was left to so-called popular historians who devoted themselves to the elaboration of vulgar myths.

The Dialectical-Intellectual School

During the first three decades of the twentieth century an extremely influential group of superb scholars was at work in German universities, seeking to combine the erudition of scientific-nominalist methodology with significant interpretation. This school found its forerunner in the early nineteenth-century philosopher Hegel and its immediate inspiration in the writings of the late nineteenth-century thinker Wilhelm Dilthey. It was this school that for the first time gave to the history of ideas a central and determining role in the making of the past and present. The German school drew a sharp distinction between movements of thought in European history and emphasized the profound impact on subsequent development of certain critical eras when these dialectically conflicting ideas confronted one another. The methods and assumptions of the German dialectical-intellectual school were carried to America in the 1930's as a result of the Nazi dispersion of the best minds in German universities. The German adherents of this school of *Geistesgeschichte* produced some historians of overwhelming learning and insight, such as the medievalist Carl Erdmann and the historian of modern Europe, Friedrich Meinecke.

The Dialectical-Materialist School

The efflorescence of the dialectical-intellectual school was paralleled by the emergence to considerable prominence after about 1910, particularly during the 1930's, of a group of academic historians in England, France, and the United States (as well as, of course, in Russia) who followed the historical theories of Karl Marx. Marx had taken the dialectical-historical structure of his teacher Hegel and replaced ideas as a causal force in history by the means of production (or in other words, economics). While the dialectical-materialist school produced a lot of nonsense, from its ranks there also came a number of very great historians such as R. H. Tawney, the authority on sixteenth- and seventeenth-century England, and Albert Mathiez, one of the most brilliant of all historians of the French Revolution. The dialectical-materialist, or Marxist, school was the first group of historians to examine systematically the development of the peasant and proletarian classes, and it therefore provided new insights into the course of economic and social change.

The Personal-Social-Intuitive School

Particularly in England and the United States during the first half of the twentieth century there was a group of historians who had in common great skill in literary exposition, an interest in portraying personality (without application of any particular psychological theory), and a desire to describe the more dramatic side of social and political change in a straightforward narrative way. Relying on their sharp intuition and common sense, this group—among whom stand out G. M. Trevelyan and the medievalist David Knowles in England, and Allan Nevins in the United States—brought back to history the popular audience and public influence that the scientific-nominalist school had cast aside.

The Functional-Institutional School

Although the personal-social-intuitive group was widely esteemed, its attitude seemed too belletristic and its methods too intuitive and uncritical for many of the more serious minds in the historical profession. Inspired by the pioneering work of the great English legal historian F. W. Maitland at the very beginning of the century, a transatlantic school of historians emerged in the twenties, thirties, and forties that aimed to examine the working of political and social institutions in a realistic, functional way, free from the now-discredited assumptions of the organic school. What the functional-institutional school tried to achieve was an understanding of the forms of conduct and values that emerge in a particular era in response to man's struggle for power, wealth, status, and freedom. Among the scholars who had the greatest success in evoking the complexity of social and political organization and the forces for change were the French historian of the feudal world, Marc Bloch, and the American historian of the eighteenth-century Atlantic world, R. R. Palmer.

The Sociological-Behavioral School and the Problem of Causality

In the 1950's, particularly in England and France, a new generation of historians emerged unprecedented (since the end of the nineteenth century) for its vitality and originality. It is often said that there are more scientists now at work than in the whole previous history of mankind. It should also be noted that among historians in their late thirties and forties there are probably more scholars with imagination and insight to deal with the fundamental problems of historical change than during the previous three generations. The new generation of historians has the advantage of the enormous erudition thrown up by a half century of scientific history. They have also markedly reverted to the attitudes of nineteenth-century historians in trying to use this erudition to communicate their understanding of historical change to the ever-increasing educated public. In explaining and categorizing the past, the new generation of historians has shown a fondness for the concepts of the sociological, behavioral, and psychological sciences. While this tendency has been unpalatable to many senior members of the historical profession, it is really in accordance with the tradition of historical writing in the past hundred years. History does not have a separate language of its own; it uses the language of common sense, the terms and concepts in use among educated people. Therefore if younger historians today use terms borrowed from psychology, sociology, and anthropology, they are actually only speaking in the context of the language of higher culture in their society. If an historian in the 1960's tries to explain an historical problem in terms of "alienation" or the "communications network," he is following the traditions of nineteenth-century historians who depended so much on the ideas of the "nation" or the "origins of institutions"; and he is probably doing a little better than the scholars of the 1930's with their fixation on social "classes."

The sociological-behavioral school follows very closely the interests and assumptions of the functional-institutional group but with greater attention to the methods and concepts of the social sciences. Among these methods is the use of "models" or "paradigms"—generalized patterns or structures extrapolated from individual instances of such recurring social phenomena as "industrial societies" or "scientific revolutions." Nowadays, in study-

ing a particular society (or movement or institution) historians
try to determine the general pattern or model to which the society belongs. Then they establish the peculiarities of the society
under study and analyze the ways in which it departs from the
general paradigm. These differences are of great importance to
the historian because they allow him to identify how and why a
particular society, movement, or institution, in a specific place
and at a specific time, developed distinctive qualities. Thus, many
societies have experienced an industrial revolution, and these all
exhibit certain common qualities that pertain to the model of an
industrial revolution; but no two industrial revolutions in the past
have developed in precisely the same way and have induced
exactly the same consequences.

This method of building and applying models enables historians to deal with the rather complex and controversial question
of causality in history. In the 1930's and 1940's, partly in reaction
to the tendency of many earlier historians to emphasize one particular factor, such as the class struggle, as the constantly recurring cause of social change, some scholars were calling for the
abandoning of the search for causes in history in favor of a purely
descriptive "acausal" kind of historiography. But causation seems
to be a fundamental category of human thought which the historian can only neglect at the price of greatly reducing the significance and value of historical study. Whenever some great
event occurs in our personal lives, we want to know its causes;
similarly we want to know how and why change occurred in the
history of human society. Through the method of model-building,
the historian has a systematic and valid way of explaining causation in history. *When we speak of the causes of change in history,
what we are really doing is trying to show how and why a particular society, movement, or institution developed in the distinctive way that it did, given the context of the paradigm to which
it belongs.* Thus, we can say that in 1750 the governments of both
France and Prussia fall under the paradigm of absolute monarchy,

which is characterized by the subtle interaction and balancing of royal autocracy, oligarchical bureaucracy, and aggressive aristocracy. Yet over the next half-century the political history of France and Prussia follows fundamentally different directions. When the historian asks for the causes of the difference in the political development of France and Prussia in the second half of the eighteenth century, he is really asking how and why each state departed from the absolute monarchy paradigm of 1750.

MAIN TRENDS AND PROBLEMS IN THE PHILOSOPHY OF HISTORY

Philosophy is having second thoughts. It is thinking about the nature of some form of human thought and the implications of some body of human knowledge in the most ultimate and far-reaching ways. There are three main branches of philosophy—metaphysics, epistemology, and ethics. Metaphysics ponders the question of what is the ultimate reality that human thought perceives. Epistemology is the theory of knowledge; it considers the question of whether and how the human mind has the power to know the ultimate reality of things. Ethics is the theory of moral values: given the ultimate reality of the universe and considering whether and in what ways we know this reality, what should be the criteria of human conduct?

It is obvious that this kind of refined second thinking is extremely abstract, difficult, and tenuous. Some people have a taste and aptitude for it; most educated people, even highly intelligent and creative experts in their own fields of knowledge, have neither the inclination nor the ability for reflecting on philosophical problems. They find philosophy to be airy, imprecise, and impractical speculation, largely playing with words and inventing insoluble paradoxes.

The majority of practicing historians take a hostile or indifferent attitude toward the philosophy of history, which is thinking about the ultimate nature of historical reality, the process of gaining historical knowledge, and the moral assumptions underlying historical judgments. *By no means do you have to be a good philosopher of history to be a good historian* any more than you have to be a philosopher of science to do important and original work in physics or biology. On the contrary, the beginning student of history and even a graduate student should be cautioned against too great involvement with metaphysics, epistemology, and ethical philosophy. A passionate interest in the problems of the philosophy of history can actually inhibit the historian's craft by making him so painfully self-conscious about the theoretical nature of his work that he is unable to write a line of historical prose. If you are so entranced by philosophical problems that you lose interest in reading primary and secondary sources, then you may be on your way to becoming an important philosopher of history (although this is highly unlikely, since first-class philosophers in any generation are as rare as violinists of the quality of Heifetz and Oistrakh), but you have stopped being an historian.

With these reservations in mind, we think that the historical craftsman, including the college student of history, will be helped in his work by having an introductory knowledge of the main trends in the modern philosophy of history. This is so for three reasons:

1. A critical, restrained awareness of the problems raised by the philosophy of history in connection with reality, epistemology, and values should make you a better historian because you will become conscious of all the theoretical implications of your work. This will make you less naive and simpleminded in your assumptions and more judicious, careful, and self-critical in your thinking and writing.

2. It is becoming evident that the younger, rising generation of historians are far more interested in the philosophy of history than their teachers were. If some of the more original minds in the historical profession are going to write books in which allusions

are made to theories and theorists of the philosophy of history, you will have to have some acquaintance with the field in order to understand fully what this younger generation of historians is saying.

3. The problems raised by the philosophy of history, as is the case with any branch of philosophy, may not indeed be soluble. Once he understands the special terminology and learns what the theorists are saying, the student will possibly feel that on every issue that the philosophers of history debate, a plausible argument can be made for either side. But even then, this kind of mental gymnastics is a lot of fun, and it freshens and toughens the mind for historical research and writing.

As was the case with most other forms of thought, the great turning point in the philosophy of history came at the end of the nineteenth century. Until that time philosophers had always been concerned with the nature of the historical process. They presented various doctrines to account for the *inner reality of history,* the inner force that caused the development of the historical process. *History was regarded as an objective thing existing outside the historian's mind.* The only problem was to identify the cause that moved this historical process. Process was regarded as intrinsic in history, and no attention was paid to the historian himself, who was simply held to recognize and describe the inner reality that produced historical change. The Greek and Roman writers believed that history moved in ever-recurring cyclic patterns and that a process of growth and decay was the ultimate historical reality. From the fourth to the eighteenth century it was widely believed that divine providence moved history.

The early nineteenth-century German thinker, G. W. F. Hegel, certainly the most influential philosopher of history of the past two hundred years, found an objective causal reality inside the process of history itself, a "spirit" that moved inexorably forward to the present in the dialectical pattern of thesis, antithesis, and synthesis. We have previously noticed that Karl Marx combined Hegel's dialectical reality with economic determinism to arrive at the conclusion that the thrust of the inevitable class struggle was the reality within the historical process.

Thus well into the latter part of the nineteenth century, philosophy assumed the *real* nature of an objectified history, and philosophers of history concerned themselves largely with creating an historical metaphysics. They portrayed in various ways the historical reality that was assumed to exist outside the mind of the historical observer and beneath the surface of facts and to impel history forward to a goal of glory or damnation.

At the end of the nineteenth century a new doubt set in as to the ability of the human mind to get outside of itself and to focus upon a final and causal reality that stood over and against individual human minds. This relativism shattered the central place metaphysics had held for a century in philosophical thinking and directed philosophers to concern themselves with epistemological problems, with whether and how the human mind can know anything outside itself. This general shift in Western thought had a profound effect upon the philosophy of history. Process and causation could no longer be regarded as implicit in an objectified history itself. Rather, they were part of the historian's own thinking, part of the decision-making that led him to make judgments about history. *Historical process was not an objectified reality: it was the act of thinking and writing itself. Historians did not discover history: they created it.* Far from standing at the climactic point of history from which he could loftily look downward to survey and explain what was happening outside of himself, the historian now found himself alone, recognizing that it was the synthetic power of his own mind that created an integrated and meaningful historical process out of the endless confusion of the past. The historian's own values were seen to be the measure of truth that he used in making judgments on the past.

In the older attitude philosophers of history could take the existence of facts for granted. For Hegel and Marx, history witnessed the operation of real tangible facts. They had no doubt that the historian could discover the reality of the historical process. Twentieth-century relativism, however, believes that each historian selects and criticizes according to his personal values. Therefore the modern philosophy of history has had to cope with the new and unfamiliar question "What is a fact?" Epistemology, rather than metaphysics, has been the central focus of the philosophy of history since 1900.

These fundamental changes in both the focus and doctrine of the philosophy of history were effected by late nineteenth- and early twentieth-century philosophers of the "neo-Hegelian" school. It is true that the eighteenth-century Italian philosopher Vico had already claimed that historical knowledge was heavily dependent on the historian's imaginative invention. But Vico's original theories went unheralded until Hegel's more radical followers noticed a basic paradox and tension in Hegelian theory and by examining it closely set the modern philosophy of history on the road to epistemological relativism. Hegel observed that "the Owl of Minerva takes flight when the shadows of night are falling" and that history is "the progress of consciousness of Freedom," that is, the historical process is an intellectual structure, a refined idea of the past, giving it meaning and unity. Hegel had assumed that in constructing this historical image, the individual historian's or philosopher's mind was reflecting an absolute intelligence in the universe. But if this last assumption is held to be doubtful or untenable, we are left not with an historical process controlled by an objective, "real," universal idea, but a process created by the insights of individual human minds.

This relativist theory allowed the German philosopher Wilhelm Dilthey to stress the importance of the historian's own "experience" for understanding the experience of people in the past. It led the Italian thinker Benedetto Croce to claim that the past is part of an "eternal present"—history exists in the present thoughts of the historian and not in some already-existing objectified past. It allowed the English philosopher and historian R. G. Collingwood to view history as the product of the historian's "imaginative construction." And it led the German philosopher (who sought refuge from Hitler in America) Ernst Cassirer to stress the way in which our understanding of the past is shaped by connotative "myths" or "symbolic forms."[1] Dilthey did his important work in the 1880's, Croce and Collingwood in the second and third decades of the twentieth century, and Cassirer in the period between 1930 and 1945.

By the 1930's the trend to epistemological relativism had reached extreme proportions. The distinguished American historians Carl Becker and Charles Beard were so impressed by the theories of the neo-Hegelian school that they proclaimed, respectively, that every man was his own historian and that writing history was simply an act of faith. Since the late 1930's, there has, however, been a withdrawal from the extreme view that history is simply a bunch of private myths and has nothing whatever to do with an objective or universal truth. The terrible consequences of the historical fantasies propounded by Nazi and Communist propaganda have made Western philosophers carefully reconsider whether the historian does not after all follow some general rules of rational thinking, parallel to the kind of universal reasoning used in the natural sciences. The American philosophers Carl Hempel and Ernest Nagel find a middle ground between old-fashioned belief in the absolute truth of history and the recent extreme relativism. They believe that historical analysis does follow "probabilistic" rules about human conduct (for example, the

[1] Wilhelm Dilthey, "The Understanding of Other Persons and Their Life Expressions," in Patrick Gardiner, ed., *Theories of History* (New York: Free Press of Glencoe, Inc., 1959), p. 213; Benedetto Croce, *History, Its Theory and Practice* (New York: Harcourt, Brace & Company, 1921; New York: Russell and Russell, 1960), p. 61; R. G. Collingwood, *The Idea of History* (New York: Oxford University Press, 1936), p. 14; Ernst Cassirer, *The Logic of the Humanities* (New Haven, Conn.: Yale University Press, 1961) pp. 159–63.

assumption that people who have jobs do not like to lose them) and that the historian employs a reasonable process of explanation and logic. Consequently, the philosopher is able to place historical thinking in the category of empirical science.[2] Some professional historians would subscribe to a middle-ground view similar to the Hempel-Nagel epistemology. They would point out that:

Granted that historians examining the same era of the past may have profound differences in interpretation, may see some very different patterns of cause and effect in the events they examine, they will still agree on many things. And as history has developed as a science in the past century, historians have arrived at many common conclusions on the interpretation of the past, while still disagreeing on others. There *is*, therefore, a universe of discourse among historians, a hard substratum of commonly agreed-on truth about the past as well as a continuing debate on other aspects of the past upon which agreement may and probably will be reached eventually.[3]

This current middle-ground belief in a universe of historical discourse does not preclude the tremendous impact of neo-Hegelian relativism, not only on the modern philosophy of history but also on the actual work of historians. Causation is no longer seen as a fixed objective thing outside the historian's mind. Causation is now widely regarded as the *explanation* of the relationship between the data obtained from a study of primary sources. Nowadays historians seldom ask of a major interpretation: "Is it true?" Rather they ask whether a particular statement of causation is "significant" and "valid." Because of the impact of epistemological relativism, historical truth is now seen to be probabilistic rather than absolute.

[2] Carl G. Hempel, "The Function of General Laws in History," in Gardiner, *Theories of History*, pp. 345–53 [originally in *Journal of Philosophy*, vol. 39 (1942), pp. 35–48]. Ernest Nagel, "Some Issues in the Logic of Historical Analysis," in Gardiner, pp. 376–82 [originally in *Scientific Monthly*, vol. 74 (1952), pp. 162–69].

[3] Norman F. Cantor, *Medieval History* (New York: The Macmillan Company, 1963), p. 3.

The precipitous twentieth-century decline of belief in an objective historical reality raised disturbing and fundamental questions on the ethical side of the philosophy of history. *Whether it is valid to exercise a moral judgment on the conduct of men in the past* has probably been a more difficult and pressing issue for the practicing historian than the paradoxes of epistemological relativism. The moral problem can be stated simply: the historian, it is held, does not *discover* an external reality but in a sense *creates* one by the synthetic power of his mind. By what right can he then make moral judgments about people in the past that he is describing? *If the historian does not discover an objectified reality, how can he presume to judge past ages by an objective standard of moral value?*

These are not easy questions to answer, and the rise of epistemological relativism at the beginning of the twentieth century encouraged the extreme moral relativism of German historians in the 1920's and 1930's. Their doctrine of *historismus* (historicism) excluded the historian from making any ethical judgments about individual or collective human conduct. Since at the same time Marxist historians claimed that traditional moral values were merely "bourgeois ideologies," and the scientific-nominalist school denounced moral judgments as expression of unscientific "bias," there was a widespread tendency by 1930 to deny to the historian the possibility of using *any* kind of universal ethical values in making judgments about the past.

The reaction against moral relativism in the writing of history during the past three decades began with an emotional recoil against Nazi atrocities. The effect has been the predication of a kind of law-of-nature doctrine of moral judgment in history. If past conduct transgresses universal feelings that certain acts, such as mass murder and the ruthless and selfish exploitation of laboring people, are reprehensible, then the historian has a right and a duty to discriminate between ethical light and darkness.

Many historians are not satisfied with such limited parameters of moral judgment. *They believe that if the historian creates the past, he has to create a world in which righteousness and evil are present. It would be a limited and impoverished imaginative reconstruction of an historical era which has no right or wrong in it.* The defect of nineteenth-century historians was in their so-called "Whig" or middle-class liberal Protestant scale of values, but not in their intention to distinguish those people and forces who had contributed to, and those who had opposed, the advance of civilization. At least among the younger generation of historians today are many who feel that if the past is indeed an eternal present, the most important criterion for establishing its structure and significance is the moral one. The broad education and heterogeneous experience of historians today is likely to prevent them from judging men and movements in the past by a naive, narrow, one-dimensional scale of values. They are worldly-wise people with a sense of the tragedies, frustrations, and absurdities of human existence. They are likely to be informed, sound, and fair in their judgments. They are willing, moreover, to risk error in moral judgment and the superseding sooner or later of some of their criteria of values in order—as Lord Acton said—not to debase the moral currency, by withdrawing from the historian's primary obligation to favor the forces of justice in the course of history.

If these introductory remarks on historiography and the philosophy of history have made you eager to embark on *advanced and abstract historical thinking,* you will find the following works illuminating and exciting. In order to avoid a bad case of intellectual indigestion, do not try to read them all at once; but a slow and careful reading, at a pace of a few pages a day, from these books will be of great value in shaping your historical insights.

HISTORICAL METAPHYSICS AND EPISTEMOLOGY

Ernst Cassirer, *The Logic of the Humanities*
R. G. Collingwood, *The Idea of History*
Benedetto Croce, *History, Its Theory and Practice*
Mircea Eliade, *Cosmos and History*

Patrick Gardiner (ed.), *Theories of History* (particularly the essays in this volume by Wilhelm Dilthey, William Dray, Carl G. Hempel, and Ernest Nagel)

G. W. F. Hegel, *The Philosophy of History*

Karl Löwith, *Meaning in History*

Stephen Toulmin and June Goodfield, *The Discovery of Time*

VALUES IN HISTORY

Marc Bloch, *The Historian's Craft*

Herbert Butterfield, *Christianity and History*

Herbert Butterfield, *The Whig Interpretation of History*

E. H. Carr, *What is History?*

J. H. Hexter, *Reappraisals in History*

Friedrich Meinecke, *Die Enstehung des Historismus* (no English translation is available)

Index